ASIAN DESIGN DESTINATIONS

ACKNOWLEDGEMENTS

Arne A. Klett: For Sandra.
Karen Ballmann: For Marcus and Finn.

We would like to thank all the agencies and architects involved for all
their information, support and interaction. We would like to thank the
following individuals in particular: Steven Buttlar, Aya Chigusa, Stacey
Dean, Andrew Dixon, Isabel Eglseder, Bettina Faust, Akiyo Fujii, Carolin
Grove, Adam Helmer, Bernice Henderson, Tina Hsiao, Sheladina Joseph,
Chris Lee, Warren Lucas, Fa Kanjanajongkon, Martand Khosla, Simone
Krist, Stefanie Lehnart, Matilda Pereira, Madhura Prematilleke, Simone
Roemheld, Markus Schlichenmaier, Svenja Schulkinis, Inga Schwer,
Lilly Streng, Rebecca Taylor, Nicola Theumer, and at the publisher,
Lars Pietzschmann and Dania D'Eramo.
Thank you for all your commitment and trust.

© 2010 Tandem Verlag GmbH
h.f.ullmann is an imprint of Tandem Verlag GmbH

Texts: Karen Ballmann, Arne A. Klett
Editors: Annette Galinski, Petra Ahke
Layout: Arne A. Klett

Produced by Arne Klett – Graphik

Project coordination for h.f.ullmann:
Lars Pietzschmann, Dania D'Eramo

Coordination of the translations:
Textcase, Utrecht
Translation into English:
Trahern Gemmell for Textcase
Translation into French:
Aurélie Blain for Textcase
Translation into Dutch:
Jos Rijnders for Textcase

Coverdesign: Arne A. Klett

Overall responsibility for production:
h.f.ullmann publishing, Potsdam, Germany

Printed in China

ISBN: 978-3-8331-5625-0

10 9 8 7 6 5 4 3 2 1
X IX VIII VII VI V IV III II I

If you would like to be informed about forthcoming h.f.ullmann
titles, you can request our newsletter by visiting our website
(www.ullmann-publishing.com) or by emailing us at:
newsletter@ullmann-publishing.com.
h.f.ullmann, Birkenstraße 10, 14469 Potsdam, Germany

ARNE A. KLETT · KAREN BALLMANN

ASIAN DESIGN DESTINATIONS

From the Middle East to the Far East

h.f.ullmann

TRADITION MEETS MODERNITY
FASCINATING ARCHITECTURE, INSPIRING FORMS AND PERFECT DESIGN

[ENG] ASIAN DESIGN DESTINATIONS is a collection of places that stand out for their unconventional design or captivating architecture: hotels, restaurants, spas, shops, cultural centers, and iconic landmarks in Southeast Asia and the Middle East. It is a book on architcture that tells of innovation and ingenuity, of creations that defy belief, of the interaction between forms, colors, and materials, as well as trends, currents, and fashions, of things destined to remain, and those already forgotten. What they all have in common is creativity, a love of detail, a bold sense of engagement and commitment. Linked by a willingness to experiment, the highest precision, and a unique spirit, they are the work of tireless pioneers forever engaged in new and increasingly audacious exploits.

They all share a strong connection to the culture and traditions of their respective countries. And the ambition to create ever more beautiful, ever more exciting things, yet in perfect harmony with man and nature.

The viewer will encounter mystical sites, firmly rooted in centuries of ritual and ceremony, palaces straight out of the *Arabian Nights*, skyscrapers so high they challenge photographers to capture them in full. It is about luxury accommodations in paradisiacal landscapes, man-made islands, and underwater restaurants; about contemporary art, and great sums of money, about preserving the environment, and the use of natural resources; about city planning, and joining urban areas, about change, both in politics and in the mind; about the needs of the individual and those of the masses.

Are they passing fads? Or defining movements in design and architecture that are here to stay? Only time will tell. In the meantime, ASIAN DESIGN DESTINATIONS is a selection that hopes to delight and inspire the reader on his or her journey to the most remarkable destinations in Asia and the Middle East.

TRADITION TRIFFT AUF MODERNE
FASZINIERENDE ARCHITEKTUR, INSPIRIERENDE FORMEN UND VOLLENDETES DESIGN

DEU ASIAN DESIGN DESTINATIONS ist eine Sammlung von Plätzen, die aufgrund ihres ungewöhnlichen Designs oder faszinierender Architektur auffallen: Hotels, Restaurants, Spas, Shops, kulturelle Einrichtungen oder Landmarks in Asien und Nahost. Es ist ein Architekturband, das von Erfindungsreichtum, Innovationsfreude, von unmöglich Geglaubtem erzählt, von einem Spiel mit Formen, Farben und Materialien, aber auch von Tendenzen, von Trends und Moden, von Dingen, die bleiben werden und solchen, die in Vergessenheit geraten. Gemeinsam ist allen Kreativität, Liebe zum Detail, großes Engagement und Hingabe. Experimentierfreude, höchste Präzision und ein besonderer Geist verbinden sie – der Geist der unermüdlichen Forscher, die sich immerzu einlassen auf Neues, noch Wagemutigeres.

Für alle gilt die starke Bindung an die Tradition, die Kultur des jeweiligen Landes – der Ehrgeiz, immer Schöneres, Aufregenderes zu schaffen, aber in Harmonie mit der Natur und den Menschen.

Es begegnen dem Betrachter mystische Orte, fest verwurzelt in jahrhundertealten Riten, Paläste aus 1001 Nacht, Wolkenkratzer so hoch, dass man sich mühen muss, sie an einem Stück zu fotografieren. Es geht um Luxus-Herbergen in paradiesischen Landschaften, um künstliche Inseln und Restaurants unter Wasser. Um moderne zeitgenössische Kunst, um viel Geld, den Erhalt der Umwelt und die Nutzung natürlicher Ressourcen. Um Stadtentwicklung, die Zusammenführung von Stadtteilen, um politischen Wandel und den Wandel im Kopf, um die Bedürfnisse einzelner und die sehr vieler Menschen.

Ob es sich am Ende um Moden oder bleibende wegweisende Richtungen in Design und Architektur handelt, wird die Zeit zeigen. So lange ist ASIAN DESIGN DESTINATIONS eine Auswahl, die den Betrachter auf seiner Reise an die faszinierendsten Ziele in Asien und Nahost inspirieren und erfreuen mag.

LORSQUE LA TRADITION RENCONTRE LA MODERNITÉ

UNE ARCHITECTURE FASCINANTE, DES FORMES EXALTANTES ET UN DESIGN PARFAIT

FR ASIAN DESIGN DESTINATIONS rassemble tous ces lieux qui se détachent par un design hors du commun ou une architecture étonnante : hôtels, restaurants, spas, boutiques, centres culturels et structures devenues symboliques d'Asie du Sud-est et du Proche-Orient. Cet livre d'architecture raconte l'inventivité et la joie d'innover, les créations relevant le défi de l'impossible, l'interaction merveilleuse des formes, les couleurs et les matériaux, mais aussi les tendances, les courants et les modes, les choses supposées marquer leur époque et celles déjà oubliées. Le point commun de ces œuvres, c'est la créativité, l'amour du détail ou un sens audacieux de l'engagement. Toutes liées par la volonté d'expérimenter, par une précision infime et par un esprit unique, elles ont été réalisées par des pionniers insatiables engagés à jamais dans des exploits toujours nouveaux.

Ces lieux sont tous fortement liés à la culture et aux traditions de leur pays respectif. Ils ont l'ambition de faire toujours plus beau, toujours plus excitant, tout en préservant une harmonie parfaite entre l'homme et la nature.

Le lecteur découvrira des sites mystiques, enracinés dans des siècles de rituels et de cérémonies, des palais tout droit sortis des Mille et une nuits ou des gratte-ciels si hauts qu'ils défient les photographes de les prendre en entier. Il ne s'agit ici que d'endroits luxueux situés dans un cadre paradisiaque, d'îles artificielles et de restaurants sous-marins. Il s'agit aussi d'art contemporain et de grosses sommes d'argent, de la préservation de l'environnement et de l'utilisation intelligente des ressources naturelles. Il s'agit encore de développement urbain, de lien entre les quartiers, de changement à la fois politique et personnel, des besoins de l'individu et de ceux du groupe.

Ne sont-ils que le fruit des modes ou bien celui de tendances déterminantes en matière de design et d'architecture ? Seul le temps le dira. En attendant, la sélection d'ASIAN DESIGN DESTINATIONS espère régaler et inspirer ses lecteurs dans leur voyage vers les destinations les plus remarquables d'Asie et du Moyen-Orient.

TRADITIE ONTMOET MODERNE TIJD

FASCINERENDE ARCHITECTUUR, INSPIRERENDE VORMEN EN ONOVERTROFFEN DESIGN

NED ASIAN DESIGN DESTINATIONS is een verzameling van plaatsen, die opvallen door hun ongewone ontwerp of fascinerende architectuur: hotels, restaurants, kuuroorden, winkels, culturele instellingen of oriëntatiepunten in Zuidoost-Azië en het Nabije Oosten. Het is een architectuurboek, dat vertelt van vindingrijkheid, plezier in het vernieuwen, van wat voor onmogelijk werd gehouden, van een spel met vormen, kleuren en materialen, maar ook van tendensen, van trends en modes, van dingen die zullen blijven en die in vergetelheid raken. Gemeenschappelijk hebben ze creativiteit, liefde voor het detail, grote betrokkenheid en overgave. Plezier in het experimenteren, uiterste precisie en een bijzondere geest verbindt ze. Die van de onvermoeibare onderzoekers, die zich altijd weer op iets nieuws, iets nog gedurfders storten.

Al deze plaatsen hebben een sterke binding met de traditie, de cultuur van het betreffende land. De ambitie steeds iets mooiers, opwindenders te maken, maar in harmonie met de natuur en de mens.

De toeschouwer treft mythische plaatsen aan, diep geworteld in eeuwenoude riten, paleizen uit 1001 nacht, wolkenkrabbers zo hoog, dat het moeite kost om ze in hun geheel te fotograferen. Het gaat om luxeherbergen in paradijselijke landschappen, om kunstmatige eilanden en restaurants onder water. Om moderne eigentijdse kunst, om veel geld, het behoud van het milieu en het gebruik van natuurlijke hupbronnen. Om stadsontwikkeling, het bij elkaar brengen van stadswijken, om politieke verandering en verandering in het hoofd, om de behoeften van enkelingen en die van heel veel mensen.

Of het uiteindelijk om modeverschijnselen of blijvende baanbrekende richtingen in design en architectuur gaat, zal de tijd uitwijzen. Zolang is ASIAN DESIGN DESTINATIONS een selectie, die de toeschouwer hopelijk inspireert en verheugt op zijn reis naar uiterst bezienswaardige doelen in Azië en het Midden-Oosten.

HOTELS
LUXURY LODGINGS AND RESORTS

BANYAN TREE DESERT SPA & RESORT, AL AREEN

KINGDOM OF BAHRAIN | JUFFAIR | HOTELS

ENG The luxurious BANYAN TREE DESERT SPA & RESORT is situated in the middle of the desert. It is part of the ambitious Al-Areen Development Initiative. The architecture marries traditional Arabian with contemporary Asiatic elements. The spa comprises 1,000 square meters (10,764 square feet), not counting 78 villas of 400 to 740 square meters (4305 to 7965 square feet), equipped with a swimming pool, steam bath, and infinity pool. The Saffron luxury restaurant, one of the resort's six restaurants, floats in the middle of a lake. The design of the gardens was modeled after Arabian royal palaces. The Bahrain International Circuit is only five minutes away—the resort, like a fata morgana, is in the middle of nowhere and yet so close to it all.

DEU Mitten in der Wüste liegt das luxuriöse BANYAN TREE DESERT SPA & RESORT. Es ist Teil der ambitionierten Al-Areen-Development-Initiative. Die Architektur ist ein Zusammenspiel aus traditionellen arabischen und zeitgenössischen asiatischen Elementen. 1 000 Quadratmeter umfasst der Spa, dazu 78 Villen mit 400 bis 740 Quadratmetern, ausgestattet mit Pool, Dampfbad und Infinity-Badewanne. Das Luxusrestaurant Saffron, eines von sechs Restaurants, schwimmt inmitten eines Sees. Die Gestaltung der Gärten orientierte sich an dem Vorbild arabischer Königspaläste. Zum Bahrain International Circuit sind es gerade einmal fünf Minuten – wie eine Fata Morgana liegt das Resort im Nirgendwo und doch so nah an der Welt.

FR Le luxueux BANYAN TREE DESERT SPA & RESORT se trouve en plein désert. Il est né de l'ambitieux programme Al-Areen Development Initiative, et son architecture allie la tradition arabe à des éléments asiatiques contemporains. Le spa s'étend sur 1000 mètres carrés, sans compter les 78 villas de 400 à 740 mètres carrés, toutes dotées d'une piscine et d'un sauna. Le Saffron, l'un des six restaurants gastronomiques du complexe, flotte au centre d'un lac, et ses jardins s'inspirent des palais royaux d'Arabie. Il ne faut pas plus de cinq minutes pour accéder au circuit international de Bahreïn. Tel un mirage, le complexe qui s'élève au milieu de nulle part est pourtant proche de tout.

NED Midden in de woestijn ligt het luxueuze BANYAN TREE DESERT SPA & RESORT. Het maakt deel uit van het ambitieuze Al-Areen-Development-Initiative. De architectuur is een samenspel van traditionele Arabische en eigentijdse Aziatische elementen. Het kuuroord beslaat 1000 vierkante meter, met daarbij 78 villa's van 400 tot 740 vierkante meter, uitgerust met zwembad, stoombad en infinity-ligbad. Het luxueuze restaurant Saffron, een van de zes restaurants, drijft midden in een meer. De vormgeving van de tuin is gebaseerd op die van koninklijke Arabische paleizen. Naar het Bahrain International Circuit is het slechts vijf minuten – als een fata morgana ligt het resort in het niets en toch zo dicht bij de wereld.

AMANKORA

KINGDOM OF BHUTAN | JAKAR | HOTELS

ENG "Kora" means "circular pilgrimage" in Dzongkha, the national language of Bhutan. The AMANKORA BUMTHANG is the last in a total of five exclusive mountain lodges offering pilgrims the soothing benefits of rest and contemplation on their journey through five breathtaking mountain valleys. It is a luxurious sanctuary in the very midst of the mystical Himalayas, with fascinating views of villages and monasteries in the surrounding area. The décor is stark, modern, yet traditional. It strictly adheres to environmental guidelines and the principle of harmony between man and nature.

DEU Im Dzongkha, der Landessprache Bhutans, bedeutet „Kora" „wiederkehrende Pilgerreise". Das AMANKORA BUMTHANG ist die letzte von insgesamt fünf exklusiven Berglodges, die dem Pilger auf seiner Reise durch fünf wunderschöne Bergtäler wohltuende Rast und Kontemplation verheißen. Ein Luxusrefugium im Innersten der mystischen Bergwelt des Himalaya mit faszinierenden Aussichten auf Dörfer und Klöster der Umgebung. Modern, schlicht, aber traditionell ist die Einrichtung. Streng folgt sie ökologischen Grundsätzen und dem Prinzip des Einklangs von Mensch und Natur.

FR « Kora » signifie « pèlerinage circulaire » en langue dzongkha, la langue nationale du Bhoutan. L'AMANKORA BUMTHANG est le dernier né d'une suite de cinq hôtels offrant aux pèlerins un véritable havre de paix et de contemplation pour ponctuer leur voyage à travers cinq vallées montagneuses à couper le souffle. Ce luxueux sanctuaire côtoie les cimes mystiques de l'Himalaya et offre une vue fascinante sur les villages et monastères des environs. Son décor austère et moderne n'en est pas moins traditionnel : suivant à la lettre les recommandations en matière d'environnement, il respecte un principe millénaire visant l'harmonie entre l'homme et la nature.

NED In het Dzongkha, de landstaal van Bhutan, betekent 'kora' 'terugkerende pelgrimstocht'. Het AMANKORA BUMTHANG is de laatste van in totaal vijf exclusieve berglodges, die de pelgrim op zijn reis door vijf wondermooie bergdalen weldadige rust en contemplatie beloven. Een luxueus toevluchtsoord diep in de mystieke bergwereld van de Himalaya met fascinerende vergezichten op dorpen en kloosters in de omgeving. Modern, eenvoudig maar traditioneel is de inrichting, die volgens strenge ecologische grondslagen en het principe van harmonie tussen mens en natuur is vormgegeven.

21

TAJ TASHI
KINGDOM OF BHUTAN | THIMPHU | HOTELS

ENG There's something special about Bhutan, a deeply religious country in the Himalaya Mountains. Its people live in close connection with nature, liberated from the hustle and bustle of civilization, yet without abstaining from its comforts. The TAJ TASHI luxury hotel, situated in Bhutan's capital of Thimpu, also subscribes to this principle. Both the exterior and interior design reflect the essence of Bhutan's rich artistic and architectural traditions, offering lavish contemprary luxury. This could very well be the last Shangri-La.

DEU Es ist etwas Besonderes um Bhutan, dieses tief religiöse Land in den Gebirgen des Himalaya. Seine Menschen leben in enger Verbundenheit mit der Natur, abgekehrt von der Hast der Zivilisation, ohne aber auf ihre Annehmlichkeiten zu verzichten. Diesem Prinzip verschrieben hat sich auch das Luxushotel TAJ TASHI, das im Zentrum von Thimphu, der Hauptstadt Bhutans liegt. Die Außen- und Innengestaltung bildet die Essenz aus der traditionsreichen bhutanischen Kunst und Architektur, eingebettet in den großzügigen Luxus unserer Zeit. Das letzte Shangri-La – mag sein, dass es genau das ist.

FR Le Bhoutan, pays profondément religieux niché au cœur de la chaîne himalayenne, a vraiment quelque chose de spécial. Vivant en relation étroite avec la nature, libérés du bouillonnement de la civilisation, ses habitants ne renoncent pas pour autant aux agréments qu'il offre. L'hôtel de luxe TAJ TASHI, situé dans la capitale bhoutanaise Thimpu, répond lui aussi à ces critères. Son aspect tant intérieur qu'extérieur fait écho aux foisonnantes traditions artistiques et architecturales du Bhoutan, tout en témoignant d'un luxe très contemporain. Cet hôtel pourrait être le Shangri-La dont parlait James Hilton.

NED Iets heel bijzonders heeft Bhutan, dit zeer religieuze land in de bergen van de Himalaya. De mensen leven nauw verbonden met de natuur, afgekeerd van de haast van de beschaving, maar zonder afstand te doen van de gemakken. Dit principe huldigt ook het luxehotel TAJ TASHI, dat in het centrum van Thimphu, de hoofdstad van Bhutan ligt. De essentie van het binnen- en buitenontwerp wordt gevormd door de traditionele Bhutaanse kunst en architectuur, ingebed in de royale luxe van onze tijd. Het laatste Shangri-La – misschien is dat nou net wat het is.

AMANSARA
CAMBODIA | SIEM REAP | HOTELS

ᴱᴺᴳ The modern traveler can easily believe he's the guest of a king at the AMANSARA luxury hotel. Servants and a chauffeur, luxury suites with their own pool—this 1960s architectural jewel, built by Laurent Mondet for none less than King Sihanouk, is lacking in nothing. The monarch's guesthouse, which Amansara has restored true to the original, continues to be a place of rest and contemplation, inviting the traveler to deeply immerse himself in the legacy of 500 years of Khmer civilization, the ruins and temples of Angkor Wat.

ᴰᴱᵁ Zu Gast bei einem König wähnt sich der heutige Reisende im Luxushotel AMANSARA. Diener und Chauffeur, Luxussuiten mit eigenem Pool – es fehlt an nichts in diesem architektonischen Kleinod aus den 1960er-Jahren, erbaut von Laurent Mondet im Auftrag keines Geringeren als König Sihanouk. Das von Amansara originalgetreu restaurierte Gästehaus des Monarchen ist früher wie heute ein Ort der Ruhe und Besinnlichkeit, der dem Reisenden ermöglichen möchte, das Vermächtnis von 500 Jahren Khmer-Zivilisation, die Ruinen und Tempel von Angkor Wat, tief in sich aufzunehmen.

ᶠᴿ Rien de plus facile pour le voyageur moderne que de se croire l'invité d'un roi, en séjournant à l'hôtel AMANSARA. Domestiques et chauffeur, suites luxueuses avec leur piscine privée – ce bijou architectural des années 1960, édifié par Laurent Mondet pour le roi Sihanouk, est absolument parfait. La maison d'hôtes du monarque, restaurée selon les plans d'origine pour créer l'Amansara, est encore aujourd'hui un lieu de repos et de contemplation. Elle invite le voyageur à s'immerger profondément dans cinq siècles de civilisation khmère, près des ruines et des temples d'Angkor Wat.

ᴺᴱᴰ De huidige reiziger waant zich te gast bij een koning in het luxehotel AMANSARA. Bedienden en chauffeurs, luxesuites met eigen zwembad – er ontbreekt niets in dit architectonische juweel uit de jaren 1960, gebouwd door Laurent Mondet in opdracht van niemand minder dan koning Sihanouk. Het door Amansara getrouw naar het origineel gerestaureerde gastenverblijf van de vorst is nog steeds een oord van rust en ingetogenheid, dat de reiziger in staat wil stellen de nalatenschap van 500 jaar Khmer-beschaving, de ruïnes en tempels van Angkor Wat, diep in zich op te nemen.

AMAN AT SUMMER PALACE BEIJING

CHINA | BEIJING | HOTEL

ENG To escape the summer heat of the Forbidden City, the imperial family retreated to their nearby Summer Palace on Kunming Lake and its extensive gardens. Historic pavilions, some over 100 years old, are just a few steps away. These served to shorten the time that guests had to wait for an audience with the Emperor. Today this unique location houses THE AMAN. The restoration process closely followed the historical design. The interiors of the 42 rooms and suites pay homage to the style of the original palace: four-poster beds, floors made from Peking Jin clay tiles, wooden screens, and bamboo sun blinds create the ambience of a bygone era.

DEU Um der Sommerhitze in der Verbotenen Stadt zu entfliehen, zog sich die kaiserliche Familie in den nahe gelegenen Sommerpalast am Kunming-See mit seinen weitläufigen Gärten zurück. Nur wenige Schritte entfernt stehen historische Pavillons, von denen einige über 100 Jahre alt sind. Sie dienten den Palastgästen, um Wartezeiten auf Audienzen zu verkürzen. Heute residiert hier THE AMAN. Der Restaurierungsprozess orientierte sich eng am historischen Vorbild. Das Interieur der 42 Zimmer und Suiten ist eine Hommage an den Stil des ursprünglichen Palastes: Himmelbetten, Böden aus Pekinger Jin-Tonkacheln, hölzerne Wandschirme und Bambusmarkisen verleihen der Anlage das Ambiente einer vergangenen Epoche.

FR Pour échapper à la chaleur estivale de la Cité interdite, la famille impériale se retirait dans sa résidence d'été de Kunming Lake et ses gigantesques jardins. Non loin de là se trouvent des pavillons, dont certains ont été édifiés il y a plus d'un siècle. Ils avaient pour fonction d'accueillir les invités et de leur permettre de patienter avant leur audience avec l'empereur. Aujourd'hui, c'est sur ce site unique que se dresse l'AMAN. Le processus de restauration a fidèlement conservé l'aspect des bâtiments. À l'intérieur, 42 chambres et suites rendent un vibrant hommage au style originel du palais : lits à baldaquins, sols carrelés de céramique de Pékin, panneaux de bois et persiennes de bambou donnent au lieu une ambiance surannée.

NED Om de zomerhitte in de Verboden Stad te ontvluchten trok de keizerlijke familie zich terug in het nabijgelegen zomerpaleis aan het Kunming-meer met zijn uitgestrekte tuinen. Op slechts enkele passen ervandaan staan historische paviljoens, waarvan er enkele ruim 100 jaar oud zijn. Ze dienden om het wachten van paleisgasten op audiënties te bekorten. Tegenwoordig zetelt hier THE AMAN. Het restauratieproces was nauw afgestemd op het historische voorbeeld. Het interieur van de 42 kamers en suites is een eerbetoon aan de stijl van het oorspronkelijke paleis: hemelbedden, vloeren van gebakken Pekinese kleitegels, houten kamerschermen en baboemarkiezen verlenen het complex de ambiance van een voorbij tijdperk.

THE EMPEROR
CHINA | BEIJING | HOTELS

^{ENG} THE EMPEROR is situated on the eastern side of the Forbidden City, the quiet side where the Emperors' royal bedrooms are also located. This 55-room boutique hotel has embraced its design in the most impressive way. There is a reason for everything here, nothing is mere coincidence. The hotel successfully combines its cultural heritage with modern design. Guests are welcomed by a drawing of the Emperor on the room door. The interior is straightforward and minimalist. The individual room elements are visually linked by an invisible band, conveying peace and harmony.

^{DEU} An der Ostseite der Verbotenen Stadt, auf der ruhigen Seite der kaiserlichen Gemächer, liegt THE EMPEROR. Dieses Boutique-Hotel mit 55 Zimmern hat sich dem Design eindrucksvoll verschrieben. Alles hat hier seinen Grund, nichts ist dem Zufall überlassen. Gelungen ist die Verbindung aus kulturellem Erbe und modernem Design. Eine Zeichnung des Kaisers an der Zimmertür heißt den Gast willkommen. Das Interieur ist minimalistisch und geradlinig. Ein unsichtbares Band verknüpft die einzelnen Raumelemente optisch miteinander, vermittelt Ruhe und Harmonie.

^{FR} THE EMPEROR se trouve dans la partie est de la Cité interdite, une aile tranquille qui accueillait autrefois les chambres de l'empereur. Cet hôtel-boutique de 55 chambres en a totalement épousé les formes. Ici, chaque élément à sa raison d'être : les coïncidences n'ont pas leur place dans ce lieu ayant su merveilleusement allier son héritage culturel à un design moderne. Une illustration de style impérial orne chaque porte pour accueillir les hôtes. L'intérieur joue l'élégance et le minimalisme : les différents éléments des chambres sont connectés entre eux grâce à une ligne invisible, permettant de créer un sentiment de paix et d'harmonie.

^{NED} Aan de oostzijde van de Verboden Stad, aan de rustige kant van de keizerlijke vertrekken, ligt THE EMPEROR. Dit boetiekhotel met 55 kamers is op indrukwekkende wijze gewijd aan het ontwerp. Alles heeft hier een reden, niets is aan het toeval overgelaten. Zeer geslaagd is de verbinding van cultureel erfgoed en modern design. De gast wordt verwelkomd door een tekening van de keizer op de kamerdeur. Het interieur is minimalistisch en rechtlijnig. Een onzichtbare band verbindt de afzonderlijke kamerelementen optisch met elkaar, brengt rust en harmonie tot stand.

W HONG KONG

ENG The W HONG KONG is located in bustling Kowloon, amid skyscrapers, modern glitz, oriental markets, and colonial splendor. Yasumichi Morita and Nicholas Graham were the architects behind its exclusive design treasures and unique features. The materials they used correspond to the five elements in Chinese philosophy: wood, stone, water, fire, and metal. They designed the levels of the hotel to alternate between tree-trunk-like columns and enormous murals. Other highlights include the wet rooftop pool with a view of the entire peninsula, and the wall mosaic with storybook butterflies by Australian designer Fabio Ongarato.

DEU Im quirligen Kowloon, inmitten von Wolkenkratzern, im Zentrum von modernem Glanz, orientalischen Märkten und kolonialer Pracht liegt das W HONG KONG. Exklusive Designkostbarkeiten und Unikate wurden von Yasumichi Morita und Nicholas Graham entworfen. Die verwendeten Materialien entsprechen den fünf Elementen der chinesischen Philosophie: Holz, Stein, Wasser, Feuer und Metall. Abwechselnd gestalteten die Architekten die Stockwerke mit baumstammähnlichen Säulen und riesigen Wandbildern. Weitere Highlights sind der Wet-Rooftop-Pool mit Blick über die ganze Halbinsel und das Wandmosaik mit märchenhaften Schmetterlingen vom australischen Designer Fabio Ongarato.

FR Le W HONG KONG se trouve dans le quartier très animé de Kowloon, entre les gratte-ciels, fastes de la modernité, les marchés orientaux et les vestiges coloniaux. Les architectes Yasumichi Morita et Nicholas Graham sont à l'origine de ce design exceptionnel. Les matériaux font écho aux cinq éléments de la philosophie chinoise : le bois, la pierre, l'eau, le feu et le métal. Les étages de l'hôtel alternent des colonnes semblables à des arbres et de gigantesques parois. Fleuron de cet hôtel, le toit s'est paré d'une piscine offrant une vue sur l'ensemble de la péninsule ainsi que d'une fresque murale en mosaïques représentant des papillons fabuleux, créée par l'australien Fabio Ongarato.

NED In het beweeglijke Kowloon, te midden van wolkenkrabbers, in het centrum van moderne luister, oosterse markten en koloniale pracht ligt het W HONG KONG. Exclusieve designkostbaarheden en unicaten werden door Yasumichi Morita en Nicholas Graham ontworpen. De toegepaste materialen stemmen overeen met de vijf elementen van de Chinese filosofie: hout, steen, water, vuur en metaal. Afwisselend hebben de architecten de verdiepingen vormgegeven met boomstamachtige pilaren en reusachtige muurschilderingen. Verdere hoogtepunten zijn de Wet-Rooftop-Pool met uitzicht op het hele schiereiland en het wandmozaïek met sprookjesachtige vlinders van de Australische ontwerper Fabio Ongarato.

COMMUNE BY THE GREAT WALL KEMPINSKI BEIJING

CHINA | BADALING HIGHWAY | HOTELS

ENG THE GREAT WALL, Exit # 20 at Shuiguan Badalin: the address of the COMMUNE BY THE GREAT WALL KEMPINSKI. A most unusual hotel due to its immediate proximity to the Great Wall, the eight-square-kilometer (three-square-mile) extent of its grounds, and its construction—a cross-section of contemporary architecture, designed by twelve Asian architects and built in two sections. It comprises 42 villas, each with four to six bedrooms. Twelve interpretations that create a harmonious whole. An impressive testament to contemporary Asian architecture.

DEU The Great Wall, Exit No. 20 bei Shuiguan Badaling: die Adresse des COMMUNE BY THE GREAT WALL KEMPINSKI. Ein ganz außergewöhnliches Hotel aufgrund seiner unmittelbaren Nähe zur Chinesischen Mauer, seiner Flächenausdehnung auf acht Quadratkilometern und seiner Bauweise, einem Querschnitt zeitgenössischer Architektur, entworfen von zwölf asiatischen Architekten, erbaut in zwei Bauabschnitten. Es umfasst 42 Villen mit vier bis sechs Schlafzimmern. Zwölf Auffassungen und trotzdem ein harmonisches Ganzes. Ein beeindruckendes Zeugnis zeitgenössischer asiatischer Architektur.

FR La grande muraille, sortie N° 20 à Shuiguan Badalin : voici l'adresse de l'hôtel COMMUNE BY THE GREAT WALL KEMPINSKI. Cet hôtel est hors norme par sa proximité immédiate avec la Grande Muraille de Chine, ses huit kilomètres carrés d'extension au sol et son design unique – un mélange d'architectures contemporaines, pensé par douze architectes asiatiques et construit en deux parties. L'hôtel comprend 42 villas, composée chacune de quatre à six chambres. Ces douze conceptions architecturales réussissent à former un ensemble harmonieux. Un témoignage impressionnant de l'architecture asiatique contemporaine !

NED THE GREAT WALL, Exit No. 20 bij Shuiguan Badalin: het adres van de COMMUNE BY THE GREAT WALL KEMPINSKI. Een heel bijzonder hotel doordat het vlakbij de Chinese muur ligt en zich uitspreidt over acht vierkante kilometer, en vanwege de bouwwijze: een dwarsdoorsnede van eigentijdse architectuur, ontworpen door twaalf Aziatische architecten, gebouwd in twee bouwfasen. Het omvat 42 villa's met vier tot zes slaapkamers. Twaalf opvattingen en toch een harmonisch geheel. Een indrukwekkende getuigenis van eigentijdse Aziatische bouwkunst.

THE LALU

ENG Australian architect Kerry Hill created a totally unique style for the LALU's architecture. His goal was to simplify the Zen style down to its very essence using wood, stone, and metal. The result is sparse and no-frills, and modern and timeless at the same time. The resort, which has won multiple awards, is harmoniously incorporated into its setting on the Lalu Peninsula at Sun Moon Lake, fulfilling Hill's ultimate architectural and design dreams.

DEU Der australische Architekt Kerry Hill schuf für die Architektur des LALU einen ganz eigenen Stil. Sein Ziel war eine auf die Spitze getriebene Vereinfachung des Zen-Stils unter der Verwendung von Holz, Stein und Metall. Das Ergebnis ist schlicht und schnörkellos, modern und zeitlos zugleich. Das mehrfach ausgezeichnete Resort fügt sich harmonisch in die Umgebung, die Halbinsel Lalu am Sun Moon Lake, ein und erfüllt damit Hills ultimative Anforderung an Design und Architektur.

FR L'architecte australien Kerry Hill a donné à LALU un style absolument unique. Son objectif était de réduire le style zen à sa forme la plus pure à l'aide du bois, de la pierre et du métal. Le résultat est épuré et sans fioritures, à la fois moderne et intemporel. Sur la péninsule de Lalu près du lac Sun Moon, ce complexe, plusieurs fois récompensé, s'intègre harmonieusement à son environnement et répond ainsi aux critères que s'était imposés l'architecte.

NED De Australische architect Kerry Hill schiep voor de architectuur van het LALU een geheel eigen stijl. Zijn doel was een op de spits gedreven vereenvoudiging van de zen-stijl, met gebruikmaking van hout, steen en metaal. Het resultaat is eenvoudig en strak, modern en tijdloos tegelijk. Het meermaals onderscheiden resort past harmonisch in de omgeving, het schiereiland Lalu aan het Sun Moon Lake, en vervult daarmee Hills nadrukkelijke eisen aan design en architectuur.

TANGULA LUXURY TRAINS
CHINA | HOTELS

ENG The TANGULA LUXURY TRAINS travel a northern route between Beijing and Lhasa, passing through the Tibetan Plateau, and a southern route between Beijing and Lijiang in Yunnan Province. The clear, contemporary interior of these hotel trains is accented by Chinese influences and the use of natural materials. Finely graded colors and textures, soft leather, fine silks, and exotic woods create a special atmosphere. And add to this the view through the giant panorama windows, which act as elegant frames for the stunning landscapes passing by outside.

DEU Die TANGULA LUXURY TRAINS verkehren auf einer nördlichen Route von Peking über die Tibetische Hochebene nach Lhasa und einer südlichen zwischen Peking und Lijiang in der Provinz Yunnan. Das klare zeitgenössische Interieur der Hotel-züge wird durch chinesische Einflüsse und die Verwendung natürlicher Werkstoffe akzentuiert. Feine Farbabstufungen und Texturen, weiche Leder, edle Seiden und exotische Hölzer schaffen eine besondere Atmosphäre. Dazu der Blick durch riesige Panoramafenster, die wie edle Rahmen für die besonders eindrucksvollen vorbeiziehenden Landschaften fungieren.

FR Les TANGULA LUXURY TRAINS font route vers le nord de la Chine, entre Pékin et Lhassa, à travers les reliefs tibétains ou vers le sud du pays, entre Pékin et Lijiang, dans la province du Yunnan. L'utilisation de matériaux naturels et d'influences chinoises souligne la décoration intérieure claire et contemporaine de ces trains-hôtel. D'élégants camaïeux de couleurs et de textures, cuir souple, soie fine et bois exotiques, créent une atmosphère bien spéciale. Depuis les fenêtres panoramiques, dont les lignes encadrent avec élégance des paysages étonnants, la vue est tout simplement unique.

NED De TANGULA LUXURY TRAINS rijden op een noordelijke route van Beijing over de Tibetaanse hoogvlakte naar Lhasa en een zuidelijke route tussen Beijing en Lijiang in de provincie Yunnan. Het heldere eigentijdse interieur van de hoteltreinen wordt geaccentueerd door Chinese invloeden en het gebruik van natuurlijke materialen. Fijne kleurschakeringen en texturen, zacht leer, edele zijde en exotisch hout scheppen een speciale sfeer. Met daarbij nog het uitzicht door enorme panoramavensters, die als sierlijke omlijstingen fungeren voor de bijzonder indrukwekkende voorbijtrekkende landschappen.

MAHUA KOTHI BANDHAVGARH JUNGLE SAFARI LODGE

ENG "Kurtiyas" is the name for the little houses in the Indian jungle. These were the inspiration for the MAHUA KOTHI LODGE's twelve suites, located in the middle of Bandhavgarh National Park. The combination of the traditional Central Indian building style, characterized by earth tones, wood, bamboo, and earthen floors, with the conveniences of modern life is what gives these unusual luxury accommodations their special appeal. An unconventional blend of simplicity, textures, colors, and luxury. And all that in the middle of a virtually untouched natural area filled with a variety of interesting sights—including tigers.

DEU „Kurtiyas" nennen sie die kleinen Häuser im Dschungel Indiens. Ihnen nachempfunden sind die zwölf Suiten der MAHUA KOTHI LODGE, inmitten des Bandhavgarh Nationalparks. Die Kombination aus der traditionellen Bauweise Zentralindiens, gekennzeichnet durch Erdtöne, Holz, Bambus sowie Lehmböden, und den Annehmlichkeiten des modernen Lebens macht den Reiz dieser ungewöhnlichen Luxusherberge aus. Eine eigenwillige Mischung aus Schlichtheit, Texturen, Farben und Luxus. All das inmitten einer fast unberührten Natur, die viel Sehenswertes bereithält: auch Tiger.

FR Les « Kurtiyas » sont de petites cabanes construites dans la jungle indienne. Ces dernières ont inspiré les douze suites du MAHUA KOTHI LODGE, situé en plein cœur du parc national de Bandhavgarh. Le style architectural traditionnel du centre de l'Inde, caractérisé par des tons minéraux, le bois, le bambou et des sols de terre battue, y est délicatement adapté au confort moderne. C'est cette alliance magique qui produit un attrait immédiat pour le lieu. Ce mélange non conventionnel de simplicité, de textures, de couleurs et de luxe s'élève au beau milieu d'une nature presque intacte, riche en curiosités, parmi lesquelles figurent les tigres.

NED 'Kurtiya's' noemen ze de huisjes in de jungle van India. De twaalf suites van de MAHUA KOTHI LODGE zijn er een nabootsing van, midden in het Nationaal Park Bandhavgarth. De combinatie van de traditionele bouwwijze van Centraal-India, gekenmerkt door aardkleuren, hout, bamboe alsmede leemvloeren, en de gemakken van het moderne leven vormen de aantrekkingskracht van deze ongewone luxeherberg. Een eigenzinnige mengeling van eenvoud, texturen, kleuren en luxe. Dit alles te midden van een bijna ongerepte natuur, die veel bezienswaardigs bevat: ook tijgers.

THE LEELA KEMPINSKI KOVALAM BEACH

INDIA | KOVALAM | HOTELS

ENG THE LEELA KEMPINSKI KOVALAM is situated on a cliff nestled between two beaches with a gorgeous view of the famous Kovalam coastline. The spacious park grounds are home to approximately 5,000 coconut palms. The resort was designed by renowned Indian architect Charles Corea. He has created a stylish ensemble, modern and contemporary yet refined with India's cultural treasures, taking into account even the smallest of details.

DEU THE LEELA KEMPINSKI KOVALAM liegt auf einem Felsen, eingebettet zwischen zwei Stränden mit einer wunderschönen Aussicht auf die berühmte Kovalam Coastline. Die weiträumige Parkanlage umfasst etwa 5 000 Kokospalmen. Der Entwurf für das Resort stammt vom renommierten indischen Architekten Charles Corea. Er kreierte ein stilvolles Ensemble, zeitgenössisch modern, verfeinert mit Kostbarkeiten der indischen Kultur, durchdacht bis in jedes noch so kleine Detail.

FR THE LEELA KEMPINSKI KOVALAM se trouve au sommet d'une falaise. Entouré de deux plages, il offre une vue sensationnelle sur la fameuse côte de Kovalam. Environ 5 000 cocotiers ponctuent le vaste parc de l'établissement, sorti tout droit de l'imagination du célèbre architecte indien Charles Corea. Ce dernier a su créer un ensemble élégant, moderne et contemporain, intégrant le raffinement de la culture indienne, et pensé jusque dans ses moindres détails.

NED THE LEELA KEMPINSKI KOVALAM ligt op een rots, ingebed tussen twee stranden met een wondermooi uitzicht op de beroemde Kovalam-kust. Het uitgebreide parkcomplex omvat ongeveer 5000 kokospalmen. Het ontwerp voor het resort is afkomstig van de gerenommeerde Indiase architect Charles Corea. Hij creëerde een stijlvol ensemble, eigentijds modern, verfijnd met kostbaarheden uit de Indiase cultuur, doordacht tot in het allerkleinste detail.

THE PARK

ENG Chic, lively, young, loud, trendy, ultra-modern, stylish—this boutique hotel unites a wealth of contrasts. The architecture follows the Hindu philosophy of the five elements, which has the aim of constructing buildings dominated by a harmony between man and nature. And all of this is linked with modern art and top-notch design. THE PARK doesn't just harmonize man and nature, but also the old India and the new, the majestic splendor of the past and the sparse simplicity of today. A fireworks of curves created by star designers Prakash Mankar and Sir Terence Conran.

DEU Chic, lebhaft, jung, laut, trendy, ultramodern, stylish – das Boutique-Hotel vereint viele Gegensätze. Die Architektur folgt der Hindu-Philosophie der fünf Elemente, die das Ziel hat, Gebäude zu bauen, in denen Harmonie zwischen Mensch und Natur herrscht. All das ist hier an moderne Kunst und Top-Design geknüpft. Im THE PARK sind nicht nur Mensch und Natur im Einklang, sondern auch das alte und das heutige Indien, das Majestätisch-Prachtvolle der Vergangenheit und die einfache Schlichtheit von heute. Ein Feuerwerk aus Kurven, entworfen von den Stardesignern Prakash Mankar und Sir Terence Conran.

FR À la fois chic, animé, jeune, tendance, ultramoderne ou élégant, cet hôtel-boutique est une somme de contrastes. Son architecture, guidée par les principes de la philosophie hindoue, respecte la présence des cinq éléments et favorise ainsi l'harmonie entre l'homme et la nature. L'ensemble de ces principes philosophiques est unifié par un design moderne de premier ordre. THE PARK ne lie pas seulement l'homme à la nature, mais il associe également l'Inde d'autrefois à l'Inde actuelle, la splendeur majestueuse du passé à la simplicité minimaliste de notre époque. Ce feu d'artifice de courbes est l'œuvre des designers Prakash Mankar et Sir Terence Conran.

NED Chic, levendig, jong, luid, trendy, ultramodern, stijlvol – het boetiekhotel heeft vele tegenstellingen in zich verenigd. De architectuur volgt de hindoefilosofie van de vijf elementen, die tot doel heeft gebouwen te vervaardigen waarin harmonie tussen mens en natuur heerst. Dit alles is hier verbonden met moderne kunst en topdesign. In THE PARK zijn niet alleen mens en natuur in harmonie, maar ook het oude en het huidige India, de majestueuze pracht van het verleden en de eenvoudige ongekunsteldheid van nu. Een vuurwerk van rondingen ontworpen door sterdesigners Prakash Mankar en Sir Terence Conran.

65

TAJ LAKE PALACE

INDIA | UDAIPUR | HOTELS

ENG It's like being the guest of the Maharaja at his Summer Palace. The TAJ LAKE PALACE is distinguished by its synthesis of extravagant splendor from the days of yore and the luxury of modern life. This palatial luxury hotel with its snow-white marble seems like something from a fairy tale. Many will wonder whether their eyes deceive them when they view this white giant, so unreal as it appears to float like a fata morgana on top of Lake Pichola.

DEU Es ist, als wäre man zu Gast im Sommerpalast des Maharadscha. Die Synthese aus verschwenderischer Pracht längst vergangener Tage und dem Luxus des modernen Lebens zeichnet das TAJ LAKE PALACE aus. Wie einem Märchen entstiegen scheint dieses prunkvolle Luxushotel aus schneeweißem Marmor. Manch einer wird sich fragen, ob er gerade einer Täuschung erliegt im Angesicht des weißen Riesen, der so unwirklich wie eine Fata Morgana im Picholasee zu schwimmen scheint.

FR On a l'impression d'être invité au palais d'été du Maharaja. Le TAJ LAKE PALACE est remarquable car il synthétise la splendeur extravagante d'antan et le luxe de la vie moderne. Le marbre d'un blanc immaculé de ce luxueux palais semble tout droit sorti d'un conte des *Mille et une nuits*. Face à ce géant aux courbes oniriques flottant, comme par magie, sur le Lake Pichola, nombreux sont ceux qui croient voir un mirage.

NED Het is alsof men te gast is in het zomerpaleis van de maharadja. De synthese van kwistige pracht uit lang vervlogen tijden en de luxe van het moderne leven kenmerkt het TAJ LAKE PALACE. Dit luisterrijke luxehotel van sneeuwwit marmer lijkt wel afkomstig uit een sprookje. Menigeen zal zich de ogen uitwrijven als hij tegenover de witte reus komt te staan, die zo onwerkelijk als een fata morgana in het Pichola-meer lijkt te drijven.

ALILA VILLAS ULUWATU

INDONESIA | BALI | HOTELS

ENG The personal butler, the heavenly view and the interior design in perfect harmony with the building, the design "flowing" from interior to exterior. That's one part of it. The other part: a master plan that goes beyond architecture and design because what it's all about is sustainability, protecting and maintaining the environment. The architects at WOHA are responsible for that. The result is a beautiful luxury resort, registered with Green Globe certification and the highest level of ESD certification, an initiative against electrostatic discharge in living areas—and the very first Balinese hotel to do so.

DEU Der persönliche Butler, der traumhafte Blick und eine Innenarchitektur, die mit dem Gebäude eins ist, denn das Design „fließt" von innen nach außen. Das ist die eine Seite. Die andere: Eine Gesamtkonzeption, die über Architektur und Design hinausgeht, da es ihr um Nachhaltigkeit, den Schutz und Erhalt der Umwelt geht. Verantwortlich dafür sind die Architekten von WOHA. Das Ergebnis ist ein wunderschönes Luxusresort, eine Registrierung für die Green-Globe-Zertifizierung und der höchste Level der ESD-Zertifizierung, einer Initiative gegen elektrostatische Entladungen in der Wohnumgebung – und das als erstes balinesisches Hotel.

FR Un maître d'hôtel attitré, une vue paradisiaque, une architecture intérieure en harmonie avec l'aspect extérieur du bâtiment... ne sont qu'un début. Voilà la suite : une conception qui dépasse la notion d'architecture et de design parce qu'elle n'est que développement durable, protection et maintien de l'environnement. Les architectes de chez WOHA sont à l'initiative de ce magnifique et luxueux complexe, pouvant s'enorgueillir du label Green Globe. C'est le premier hôtel de Bali à être doté de la plus haute certification ESD, une initiative luttant contre les décharges électrostatiques dans les lieux de vie.

NED De persoonlijke butler, de sprookjesachtige aanblik en een inrichting die één met het gebouw is; het design 'stroomt' van binnen naar buiten. Dat is de ene kant. De andere: een totaalconcept dat uitstijgt boven architectuur en design, omdat het gaat om duurzaamheid, de bescherming en het behoud van het milieu. Verantwoordelijk hiervoor zijn de architecten van WOHA. Het resultaat is een wondermooi luxeresort, registratie van de Green Globe-certificering en de hoogste niveau ESD-certificering, een initiatief tegen elektrostatische ontladingen in de woonomgeving – en dat als eerste Balinese hotel.

BULGARI HOTELS & RESORTS

INDONESIA | BALI | HOTELS

ENG The architects: Antonio Citterio and Made Wjiaya. The basic concept: reduced Italian, sophisticated ingredients, and a dash of Balinese architecture and landscape design. There is a characteristic material and color: Bangkiray, mahogany from Java, dark, stained nearly black. The roofs are thatched with alang-alang grass. Two centers: a quiet, private one and a glamorous, public one arranged around a man-made lake with open-air bars. Plus couches on the cliff, a restaurant on the cape, and breathtaking views of the island's most beautiful beach.

DEU Die Architekten: Antonio Citterio und Made Wjiaya. Das Grundkonzept: italienisch reduziert, erlesene Zutaten und ein Schuss balinesische Architektur und Landschaftsgestaltung. Charakteristisch ist ein Material und eine Farbe: Bangkiray, Mahagoni aus Java, dunkel, fast schwarz gebeizt. Die Dächer sind bedeckt mit Alang-Alang-Gras. Zwei Zentren: ein privates ruhiges und ein glamouröses öffentliches, angeordnet um einen künstlichen See mit Open-Air-Bars. Dazu Sofas auf dem Kliff, ein Restaurant auf dem Kap, und das mit atemberaubendem Blick auf den schönsten Strand der Insel.

FR Les architectes : Antonio Citterio et Made Wjiaya. Le concept : une pointe d'éléments italiens sophistiqués et une goutte d'architecture et de paysagisme balinais. Les matériaux et couleurs caractéristiques : le Bangkiray, un acajou de Java, sombre, presque noir, des toits recouverts d'alang-alang naturelle. Deux espaces : un premier, calme et privé, et le second, glamour et public, entourant un lac artificiel et des bars à ciel ouvert. Ajoutez également des banquettes au sommet de la falaise, un restaurant sur le cap et une vue imprenable sur la plus belle plage de l'île.

NED De architecten: Antonio Citterio en Made Wjiaya. Het basisconcept: Italiaans beperkt, uitgelezen franje en een dosis Balinese architectuur en landschapsvorming. Karakteristiek is het gebruik van één materiaal en één kleur: bangkirai, mahonie uit Java, donker, bijna zwart gebeitst. De daken zijn bedekt met alang-alang gras. Twee centra: één privé en rustig en een ander openbaar en glamoureus geplaatst rond een kunstmatig meer met openluchtbars. Daarbij sofa's op het klif, een restaurant op de kaap en dat alles met een adembenemende blik op het mooiste strand van het eiland.

COMO SHAMBHALA ESTATE

INDONESIA | BALI | HOTELS

ENG "Holy place of bliss" is what the native Balinese call this divinely beautiful valley of primeval forest. This is the home of the COMO SHAMBHALA ESTATE, one of the world's first 5-star, full-service health retreats. Here you will find a balance between understatement, individual design, and quiet luxury. The architecture and interior design are emphatically purist and make use of indigenous materials. The aim is to enable complete concentration on body, mind, and soul.

DEU Als „heiligen Ort der Glückseligkeit" bezeichnen die Einheimischen dieses außergewöhnlich schöne Urwaldtal. Es ist die Heimat des COMO SHAMBHALA ESTATE, einem der weltweit ersten 5-Sterne-Full-Service-Health-Retreats. Hier befinden sich Understatement, individuelles Design und unaufdringlicher Luxus in Balance. Architektur und Inneneinrichtung sind betont puristisch und bedienen sich der heimischen Materialien. Ziel ist es, dem Gast die vollkommene Konzentration auf Körper, Geist und Seele zu ermöglichen.

FR Les Balinais appellent cette vallée à la beauté divine et sa forêt primaire le « Lieu saint du bonheur absolu ». Le COMO SHAMBHALA ESTATE s'y est installé : c'est l'un des premiers 5 étoiles au monde à proposer des cures complètes. On fait ici l'expérience d'un équilibre entre simplicité, design personnalisé et luxe discret. L'architecture et le design intérieur sont d'une pureté l'extrême, et emploient des matériaux locaux. L'objectif ultime du lieu est d'atteindre une concentration totale du corps, de l'esprit et de l'âme.

NED Als 'heilig oord van gelukzaligheid' beschrijven de inheemsen dit buitengewoon mooie oerwouddal. Het is de geboorte-grond van het COMO SHAMBHALA ESTATE, een van de eerste vijfsterren-full-service-health-retreats ter wereld. Hier zijn understatement, individueel ontwerp en bescheiden luxe in balans. Architectuur en inrichting zijn bijzonder puristisch en maken gebruik van inheemse materialen. Doel is de gast in staat te stellen zich volledig op lichaam, geest en ziel te concentreren.

SPACE AT BALI VILLAS
INDONESIA | BALI | HOTELS

ENG Three well-traveled top managers are the creative minds behind the innovative concept of SPACE AT BALI VILLAS. The private area is what's unique about it. This exclusive location is made up of just six luxury villas with lush tropical gardens and large private pools, where you can sleep in four-poster beds and swim under bright blue skies or sparkling stars. Whether on your own, in the company of neighbors, or in the public area with other guests, you can live however you please here.

DEU Drei vielgereiste Top-Manager sind die kreativen Köpfe hinter dem neuartigen Konzept des SPACE AT BALI VILLAS. Das Besondere sind hier die privaten Bereiche: Zu dieser exklusiven Anlage gehören nur sechs Luxusvillen mit üppigen tropischen Gärten und großen privaten Pools. Schlafen im Himmelbett und Baden unter blauem Himmel oder leuchtenden Sternen; für sich allein sein, mit Verbindung zum Nachbarn oder im öffentlichen Bereich in Gesellschaft der anderen Gäste: Leben kann man hier ganz wie man möchte.

FR Le concept innovant des SPACE AT BALI VILLAS est le fruit de la réflexion de trois cadres au passé de grand voyageur. Les zones privées sont ici très particulières : cet établissement exceptionnel ne compte que six villas de luxe, entourées de jardins tropicaux luxuriants et de grandes piscines privées. Ici, dormir dans un lit à baldaquin et nager à ciel ouvert ou au clair de lune est possible. Tout comme vivre selon ses envies : seul, en compagnie de ses voisins ou dans le salon, en présence des autres hôtes.

NED Drie veelbereisde topmanagers zijn de creatieve koppen achter het futuristische ontwerp van de SPACE AT BALI VILLAS. Bijzonder is het privédomein. Tot dit exclusieve complex behoren slechts zes luxevilla's met weelderige tropische tuinen, grote privézwembaden, waar je kunt slapen in hemelbed en baden onder de blauwe hemel of stralende sterren. Voor zich alleen, met contact met de buren of in het openbare domein in gezelschap van de andere gasten, men heeft het hier voor het uitkiezen.

ST. REGIS BALI RESORT AND SPA
INDONESIA | BALI | HOTELS

ENG This elegant resort is located on Bali's southern tip, on the long white sand beach of Nusa Dua. Bensley Design Studios was responsible for the unconventional landscape architecture, the traditional Balinese design, and the harmony with the location's stunning natural environment. The interior was the work of interior designer Manny Samson. Sumptuous imported fabrics, local materials, and artisan craftsmanship, a reflection of the island's rich cultural heritage, are skillfully combined. Plus the finest basic amenities.

DEU An der Südspitze Balis, am langen Sandstrand von Nusa Dua, liegt dieses noble Strandresort. Bensley Design Studios stehen für die ungewöhnliche Landschaftsarchitektur, die traditionelles balinesisches Design und die ungewöhnlich schöne natürliche Umgebung in Einklang bringen. Das Interieur ist ein Werk der Innenarchitekten von Manny Samson. Erlesene importierte Stoffe, lokale Materialien und Kunsthandwerk, Spiegelbild des reichen kulturellen Erbes der Insel, sind gekonnt miteinander kombiniert. Dazu eine Basisausstattung vom Feinsten.

FR Cet élégant complexe se trouve sur la pointe est de Bali, le long de l'interminable plage de sable blanc de Nusa Dua. Bensley Design Studios s'est chargé d'élaborer une architecture qui sort de l'ordinaire en harmonisant la tradition balinaise et l'environnement naturel d'une beauté exceptionnelle. L'intérieur est l'œuvre du designer Manny Samson, qui a judicieusement combiné les étoffes somptueuses importées à l'artisanat et aux matériaux locaux, reflets du riche héritage culturel de l'île. Une création des plus raffinées !

NED Op de zuidpunt van Bali, aan het lange strand van Nusa Dua, ligt dit voorname strandresort. Bensley Design Studio's zijn verantwoordelijk voor de bijzondere landschapsarchitectuur, en brengen traditioneel Balinees design en de buitengewoon fraaie natuurlijke omgeving met elkaar in harmonie. Het interieur is het werk van de binnenhuisarchitecten van Manny Samson. Uitgelezen geïmporteerde stoffen, plaatselijke materialen en kunstnijverheid, afspiegeling van het rijke culturele erfgoed van het eiland, zijn kundig met elkaar gecombineerd. De basisuitrusting is buitengewoon elegant.

ᴱᴺᴳ Borobudor, the largest Buddhist temple in the world, was the source of inspiration for the architects of the AMANJIWO luxury resort. Situated in the middle of a natural amphitheater at the foot of the Menoreh Mountains in central Java, it offers a direct view of this Unesco World Heritage Site, a place recognized as one of the most impressive cultural monuments in all of Southeast Asia. Radiating outwards from the main building in crescent-shaped rays, 36 suites are spread out across the extensive grounds. The design by architect Edward Tuttle, reminiscent of a temple compound, creates a locale both old-fashioned and refined, casual and modern.

ᴰᴱᵁ Borobudor, das größte buddhistische Heiligtum, war die Quelle der Inspiration für die Architekten des AMANJIWO-Luxusresorts. Inmitten eines natürlichen Amphitheaters am Fuße des Menoreh-Gebirges in Zentral-Java gelegen, bietet es einen direkten Blick auf das Unesco-Weltkulturerbe. Ein Ort, der anerkanntermaßen zu den eindrucksvollsten Kulturdenkmälern Südostasiens gehört. Vom Hauptgebäude des Hotels aus verteilen sich in halbmondförmigen Strahlen 36 Suiten über das weitläufige Gelände. Architekt Edward Tuttles Design mit der Anmutung einer Tempelanlage schafft eine Szenerie, die beides ist: archaisch und edel, leger und modern.

ᶠᴿ C'est Borobudur, le plus important temple bouddhiste au monde, qui a inspiré les architectes du luxueux resort AMANJIWO. Situé au cœur d'un amphithéâtre naturel, au pied des monts Menoreh dans le centre de Java, il offre une vue imprenable sur ce site classé au patrimoine mondial par l'Unesco. En effet, ce dernier abrite l'un des monuments les plus impressionnants d'Asie du sud-est. Les 36 suites du resort sont réparties en demi-cercle sur le vaste terrain. Le projet de l'architecte Edward Tuttle rappelle la disposition d'un temple en créant un lieu à la fois archaïque et raffiné, décontracté et moderne.

ᴺᴱᴰ Borobudur, het grootste boeddhistische heiligdom, was de inspiratiebron voor de architecten van het AMANJIWO-luxeresort. Gelegen midden in een natuurlijk amfitheater aan de voet van het Menoreh-gebergte in Centraal-Java biedt het een rechtstreekse blik op het Unesco-werelderfgoed. Een plaats die onomstreden tot de meest indrukwekkende cultuurmonumenten van Zuidoost-Azië behoort. Vanuit het hoofdgebouw verspreiden zich in halvemaanvormige stralen 36 suites over het uitgestrekte terrein. Het ontwerp van architect Edward Tuttle dat als een tempelcomplex aanvoelt, schept een landschap dat zowel archaïsch en voornaam als ongedwongen en modern is.

NIKOI ISLAND
INDONESIA | KAWAL | HOTELS

ENG A place where artisan craftsmanship, good food, and personal service meet in a spectacular landscape. No ceremony, conveniences, or textbook pleasantries. The only concessions to modern life are an iPod dock, electric light, and a fan. Architect Peter Timmer has developed a style that combines native building techniques with traditional materials and modern simplicity. Thanks to this, the island has remained more or less as it was when once encountered long ago: barefoot luxury only 50 miles from Singapore.

DEU Ein Ort, an dem Handwerkskunst, gutes Essen und persönlicher Service auf eine spektakuläre Landschaft treffen. Keine Etikette, kein Service und keine Freundlichkeit aus dem Lehrbuch. Die einzigen Konzessionen an das moderne Leben sind ein iPod-Dock, elektrisches Licht und ein Ventilator. Architekt Peter Timmer entwickelte einen Stil, der die heimische Baukunst mit ebensolchen Baustoffen und moderner Schlichtheit verbindet. So ist die Insel mehr oder minder so geblieben, wie die Macher sie einmal vorgefunden haben: Barfuß-Luxus, und das 50 Meilen vor Singapur.

FR Voici un lieu où se rencontrent, dans un cadre naturel somptueux, artisanat, nourriture divine et services personnalisés. Le protocole, le confort et les fioritures habituelles n'ont pas leur place ici : les seules concessions faites à la modernité sont une station pour iPod, l'électricité et un ventilateur. Le style adopté par l'architecte Peter Timmer combine les techniques de construction locales à base de matériaux traditionnels et la simplicité offerte par l'ère moderne. Grâce à cette alchimie, l'île est restée relativement identique à ce qu'elle a toujours été : une oasis de luxe au naturel, à 80 kilomètres de Singapour.

NED Een plek waar kunstnijverheid, goed eten en persoonlijke service een spectaculair landschap ontmoeten. Geen etiquette, geen service en geen vriendelijkheid uit het leerboek. De enige concessies aan het moderne leven zijn een iPod-dock, elektrisch licht en een ventilator. Architect Peter Timmer ontwikkelde een stijl waarin de inheemse bouwkunst met dito materialen en moderne eenvoud met elkaar zijn verbonden. Zo is het eiland min of meer gebleven zoals de makers het ooit hebben aangetroffen: blootsvoetse luxe en dat op 80 kilometer van Singapore.

LEONARDO BOUTIQUE HOTEL TEL AVIV

ISRAEL | TEL AVIV | HOTELS

ENG A lot of black, along with frescoes and pop art, baroque mirrors, and glass pools. The influences on the interior design range from Renaissance to modern, a design mix at once stylish, fanciful, and sober, and therefore a reflection, both in its variety and its contradictions, of the character and diversity of the metropolis and capital of Tel Aviv. We're talking about the LEONARDO BOUTIQUE HOTEL TEL AVIV, opened in July 2009, with interiors by Israeli designers Moshe Kastiel and Lior Ofer.

DEU Viel Schwarz, dazu Fresken und Pop-Art, barocke Spiegel und Bäder aus Glas. Die Einflüsse auf das Interior Design reichen von der Renaissance bis zur Moderne, ein Design-Mix – stylish, verspielt, nüchtern und damit in seiner Vielfalt, aber auch in seinen Gegensätzen ein Spiegel der Ausstrahlung und Vielgestaltigkeit der Metropole und Hauptstadt Tel Aviv. Die Rede ist von dem im Juli 2009 eröffneten LEONARDO BOUTIQUE HOTEL TEL AVIV, ausgestattet von den israelischen Designern Moshe Kastiel und Liora Ofer.

FR L'architecture intérieure de ce lieu est parcourue d'influences allant de la Renaissance à l'ère moderne : c'est un mélange d'élégance, de bling-bling et de sobriété, mais aussi une réflexion sur la variété et les contradictions de la métropole et capitale qu'est Tel-Aviv. La couleur noire y domine et accompagne les nombreuses fresques, les oeuvres pop art, des miroirs baroques et des piscines de verre. Il est ici question du LEONARDO BOUTIQUE HOTEL TEL AVIV, inauguré en juillet 2009, dont l'intérieur est signé des designers israéliens Moshe Kastiel et Lior Ofer.

NED Veel zwart, met fresco's en popart, barokke spiegels en baden van glas. De invloeden op de binnenhuisarchitectuur reiken van de renaissance tot de moderne kunst. Een designmix die stijlvol, speels, nuchter is en daarmee in zijn verscheidenheid, maar ook in zijn tegenstellingen, een afspiegelingis van de uitstraling en veelzijdigheid van de metropool en hoofdstad Tel Aviv. Het gaat over het in juli 2009 geopende LEONARDO BOUTIQUE HOTEL TEL AVIV, ingericht door de Israëlische ontwerpers Moshe Kastile en Liora Ofer.

THE SCREEN HOTEL
JAPAN | KYOTO | HOTELS

ENG Stylish and very Japanese, small, intimate and keen on detail: THE SCREEN is a colorful and imaginative blend of a ryokan, or traditional Japanese inn, a designer boutique hotel, and more. It's a design melting pot: 13 rooms, created by 13 designers, each with their own individual, unmistakable signature—and each with a very different result. There is one thing, however, that all the designers kept in mind: for it to all fit together in the end.

DEU Stylish und sehr japanisch, klein, intim und detailverliebt: THE SCREEN ist eine farbenfrohe und phantasievolle Mischung aus den traditionellen Ryokans, einem Design-Boutique-Hotel und mehr. Es ist ein Designfeuerwerk: 13 Zimmer, gestaltet von 13 Designern mit je einer individuellen, ganz unverwechselbaren Handschrift. Das Ergebnis ist sehr unterschiedlich ausgefallen. Geachtet haben alle Designer aber auf eines: dass am Ende alles zusammenpasst.

FR THE SCREEN est élégant et résolument japonais, car il est petit, intime et soucieux du détail. Cet endroit est un mélange, coloré et inspiré, entre un ryokan, l'auberge traditionnelle japonaise, un hôtel-boutique de designer et plus encore. C'est un véritable feu d'artifice créatif composé de 13 chambres, pensées par 13 designers différents, chacune possédant sa propre personnalité et une signature reconnaissable. Même si ces associations créent une infinité de styles, tous les designers ont gardé à l'esprit la seule chose importante : l'harmonie de l'ensemble.

NED Stijlvol en heel Japans, klein, intiem en verzot op details: THE SCREEN is een kleurrijke en fantasievolle mengeling van de traditionele ryokans, een design-boetiekhotel en meer. Het is een designvuurwerk: dertien kamers, vormgegeven door dertien ontwerpers met elk een individueel, geheel onverwisselbaar handschrift. Het resultaat is heel divers geworden. Alle ontwerpers hebben echter wel op één ding gelet: dat op het eind alles bij elkaar past.

KANAYA HOTEL ORANGE SUITE

JAPAN | NIKKO | HOTELS

ENG The ORANGE SUITE—produced by Kundo Koyama, the Oscar-winning screenwriter. Where? In the KANAYA HOTEL in Nikko, one of the oldest western-style hotels in Japan, founded in 1873. The concept is a "vitamin hotel". The goal: a hotel inside a hotel where you can go to recharge. Vitamin pills and the color orange are used for this purpose, and everything is orange: the soap, the shampoo, the pillows, the note pads, and much more.

DEU Die ORANGE SUITE – produziert von Kundo Koyama, dem Drehbuchautor mit Oscar. Wo? Im KANAYA HOTEL in Nikko, einem der ältesten Western-Style-Hotels Japans, gegründet bereits 1873. Das Konzept heißt „Vitamin Hotel". Das Ziel: ein Hotel im Hotel zum Energietanken. Vitamintabletten und die Farbe Orange dienen der Zielerreichung – alles ist orange: die Seife, das Shampoo, die Kissen, die Notepads und noch vieles mehr.

FR L'ORANGE SUITE est l'œuvre du scénariste oscarisé Kundo Koyama. Où le trouver ? Dans le KANAYA HOTEL à Nikko, l'un des plus anciens hôtels de style occidental du Japon, inauguré en 1873. Sur le papier, il prend le nom de « vitamin hotel » car son objectif est d'être un hôtel dans l'hôtel, où l'on vient recharger ses batteries. Les vitamines et la couleur orange sont employées un peu partout à cet effet, du savon au shampoing en passant par les oreillers, les blocs-notes et bien plus encore.

NED De ORANGE SUITE – geproduceerd door Kundo Koyama, de draaiboekschrijver met Oscar. Waar? In het KANAYA HOTEL in Nikko, een van de oudste hotels in westerse stijl van Japan, al in 1873 opgericht. Het concept heet 'Vitamine Hotel'. Het doel: een hotel in het hotel om energie bij te tanken. Vitaminetabletten en de kleur oranje dienen om het doel te bereiken – alles is oranje: de zeep, shampoo, kussens, schrijfblokken en nog veel meer.

KEMPINSKI HOTEL ISHTAR DEAD SEA

JORDAN | AMMAN | HOTELS

ENG A region filled with mystery and ancient tales of Cleopatra, Marc Anthony, and the Queen of Sheba, this is where you will find the KEMPINSKI HOTEL ISHTAR. Three luxurious enclaves, arranged around gardens, lagoons, little rivers, waterfalls, and private pools, not to mention a wonderful view of the Dead Sea. The Hanging Gardens of Babylon were the inspiration behind the design. 345 rooms and suites, built from native stone. A monumental building in which clear, simple lines are transformed into Arabian shapes and motifs. And for fans of contemporary design there are the Ishtar Villas, the accompanying boutique resort.

DEU An diesem Ort voller Geheimnisse und Geschichten von Kleopatra, Marc Anton und der Königin von Saba findet sich das KEMPINSKI HOTEL ISHTAR. Drei luxuriöse Enklaven, umgeben von Gärten, Lagunen, kleinen Flüssen, Wasserfällen und privaten Pools, dazu ein wunderbarer Blick auf das Tote Meer. Inspirationsquelle für das Design waren die Hängenden Gärten der Semiramis. 345 Zimmer und Suiten, gebaut aus heimischem Stein. Ein monumentales Gebäude, in dem klare einfache Linien in arabische Themen und Formen gewandelt sind. Und für die Liebhaber zeitgenössischen Designs: Ishtar Villas, das dazugehörige Boutique-Resort.

FR C'est dans une région résonnant encore des mystères et récits historiques de Cléopâtre, Marc-Antoine et de la Reine de Saba, que se trouve le KEMPINSKI HOTEL ISHTAR. Ses trois luxueuses enclaves sont entourées de jardins, lagons, cours et chutes d'eau ou piscines privées, sans oublier une vue splendide sur la mer Morte. Son créateur s'est directement inspiré des jardins suspendus de Babylone pour cet hôtel de 345 chambres et suites, édifié en pierres locales. C'est un véritable monument où des lignes épurées se transforment doucement en courbes et arabesques. Les Ishtar Villas, le complexe boutique qui complète l'hôtel, combleront les adeptes de design contemporain.

NED Op deze plaats vol geheimen en verhalen van Cleopatra, Marcus Antonius en de koningin van Saba bevindt zich het KEMPINSKI HOTEL ISHTAR. Drie luxueuze enclaves, omringd door tuinen, baaien, kleine rivieren, watervallen en privézwembaden, en met ook nog een prachtig uitzicht op de Dode Zee. Inspiratiebron voor het ontwerp waren de Hangende Tuinen van Semiramis. 345 kamers en suites, gebouwd van inheems steen. Een monumentaal gebouw, waarin heldere eenvoudige lijnen in Arabische thema's en vormen zijn omgezet. En voor de liefhebber van eigentijds design: Ishtar Villas, het bijbehorende boetiekresort.

113

3 NAGAS BY ALILA

LAOS | LUANG PRABANG | HOTELS

ENG Laos, the "kingdom of a million elephants", is a country of both indescribable beauty and rich cultural heritage. The 3 NAGAS BY ALILA is located in the heart of Luang Prabang, the former capital. It encompasses three Unesco World Heritage Sites over a century old, which were painstakingly restored in 2003. The site impressively combines the past with the present, and contemporary style with the building's original architecture. Simplicity, refined with elegance and meticulous attention to the smallest of details—that's what makes this boutique hotel so special.

DEU Laos, das „Königreich von einer Million Elefanten", ein Land von unbeschreiblicher Schönheit, ist zugleich reich an kulturellem Erbe. Im Herzen Luang Prabangs, der früheren Hauptstadt, liegt das 3 NAGAS BY ALILA. Luang Prabangs umfasst drei Unesco-Weltkulturerbe-Stätten, die mehr als ein Jahrhundert alt sind und 2003 behutsam restauriert wurden. Dieser Ort verbindet eindrucksvoll die Vergangenheit mit der Gegenwart, zeitgenössischen Stil mit der Originalarchitektur des Gebäudes. Einfachheit, verfeinert mit Eleganz und das akribische Beachten noch so kleiner Details – das macht dieses Boutique-Hotel besonders.

FR Le Laos, « royaume au million d'éléphants », est un pays à la beauté indescriptible et à l'héritage culturel riche. Le 3 NAGAS BY ALILA se situe au cœur de Luang Prabang, l'ancienne capitale dans laquelle s'érigent encore trois sites pluriséculaires classés au patrimoine mondial par l'Unesco et minutieusement restaurés en 2003. Le site combine de manière impressionnante le style contemporain à l'architecture originelle du bâtiment et relie ainsi harmonieusement le passé au présent. La simplicité revisitée par l'élégance et une attention méticuleuse aux détails les plus insignifiants sont ce qui confère à cet hôtel-boutique toute sa spécificité.

NED Laos, het 'koninkrijk van een miljoen olifanten', is een land van onbeschrijflijke schoonheid dat tevens rijk is aan cultureel erfgoed. In het hart van Luang Prabang, de vroegere hoofdstad, ligt het 3 NAGAS BY ALILA. Het omvat drie Unesco-werelderfgoed-locaties, die meer dan honderd jaar oud zijn, en in 2003 nauwkeurig zijn gerestaureerd. In deze plaats is op indrukwekkende wijze het verleden met het heden verbonden, eigentijdse stijl met de oorspronkelijke architectuur van het gebouw. Eenvoud, verfijnd met elegantie en de uiterst precieze uitvoering van de allerkleinste details – dat is wat dit boetiekhotel zo bijzonder maakt.

LE GRAY

LEBANON | BEIRUT | HOTELS

ENG The LE GRAY is located in Beirut's fashionable historic district. The new luxury hotel on the square bears the signature of architect Kevin Dash. Its interior design is the result of a collaboration between Mary Fox Linton and Gordon Campbell Gray. It offers no-frills modern luxury, generous rooms and extravagant suites, plus views of the Mediterranean, Mount Lebanon and beautiful Beirut.

DEU Das LE GRAY liegt in der vornehmen historischen Altstadt von Beirut. Das neue Luxushotel am Platz trägt die Handschrift von Architekt Kevin Dash. Das Interior Design ist das Ergebnis der Zusammenarbeit von Mary Fox Linton und Gordon Campbell Gray. Es bietet modernen Luxus, ohne Schnörkel, großzügige Räume und extravagante Suiten und dazu einen Blick auf das Mittelmeer, den Mount Lebanon und das schöne Beirut.

FR LE GRAY se trouve dans le quartier historique et très en vogue de Beyrouth. Ce nouvel hôtel de luxe porte la signature de l'architecte Kevin Dash tandis que son design intérieur est le résultat de la collaboration entre Mary Fox Linton et Gordon Campbell Gray. Il offre un luxe moderne et sans fioritures, des chambres généreuses comme des suites extravagantes, sans compter les différentes vues sur la Méditerranée, le Mont Liban et la splendide Beyrouth.

NED Het LE GRAY ligt in de voorname historische oude stad van Beiroet. Het nieuwe luxehotel aan het plein is van de hand van architect Kevin Dash. Het interieurontwerp is het resultaat van de samenwerking van Mary Fox Linton en Gordon Campbell Gray. Het biedt moderne luxe, zonder franje, royale ruimtes en extravagante suites met daarbij een blik op de Middellandse Zee, Mount Lebanon en het mooie Beiroet.

W RETREAT & SPA-MALDIVES
MALDIVES | NORTH ARI ATOLL | HOTELS

ENG The W RETREAT & SPA-MALDIVES in the northern Ari Atoll is exclusive and stylish, luxurious and trendy. The design of the 78 villas is sophisticated and avant-garde—private pool, glass floor, tropical outdoor showers, and a barbecue lounge. There is also a starkly designed below-sea-level bar, called "15 Below", and a spa on its own platform in the middle of the lagoon. A remarkable synthesis of design, luxury, and nature.

DEU Das W RETREAT & SPA-MALDIVES im nördlichen Ari Atoll ist exklusiv und stylish, luxuriös und trendy. Die 78 Villen sind avantgardistisch und mondän eingerichtet – Privatpool, gläserner Boden, tropische Outdoor-Duschen, eine Barbecue-Lounge. Dazu eine puristische Bar unter dem Meeresspiegel – „15 Below" – und ein Spa auf einer eigenen Plattform inmitten der Lagune. Eine bemerkenswerte Synthese aus Design, Luxus und Natur.

FR Le W RETREAT & SPA-MALDIVES au nord de l'atoll Ari est à la fois sélect, élégant, luxueux et branché. Le design sophistiqué et avant-gardiste de ses 78 villas prévoit piscines privées, sols de verre, douches extérieures tropicales ou encore salon barbecue. Cet hôtel est une synthèse remarquable de design, de luxe et de nature. On peut également se rendre dans un bar étonnant, situé sous le niveau de la mer et appelé le « 15 Below », ou encore se faire chouchouter au spa, installé sur sa propre plate-forme en plein milieu du lagon.

NED Het W RETREAT & SPA-MALDIVES op de noordelijke Ari Atoll is exclusief en stijlvol, luxueus en trendy. De 78 villa's zijn avantgardistisch en mondain ingericht – privézwembad, glazen vloer, tropische openluchtdouches, een barbecuelounge. Met verder nog een puristische bar onder de zeespiegel – '15 Below' – en een kuuroord op een eigen platform midden in de baai. Een opmerkelijke synthese van ontwerp, luxe en natuur.

RAINTREE MISIBIS BAY

PHILIPPINES | ALBAY | HOTELS

ENG A small but elegant resort right on the beach. Just 38 luxury rooms, with high ceilings and large panorama windows that blur the boundaries between interior and exterior, between room and ocean. The architecture is sleek, modern, and no-frills. Large terraces and sun decks, a spa, three pools, and the white sand beach at your feet. Underwater you will find a fantastic, mysterious world, while above water a helicopter waits to take guests to the Mayon Volcano.

DEU Ein kleines aber feines Resort, direkt am Strand. Nur 38 Luxuszimmer mit hohen Decken und großen Panoramafenstern, die die Grenzen zwischen Innen und Außen, zwischen Raum und Ozean auflösen. Die Architektur ist modern, geradlinig und ohne Schnörkel. Große Terrassen und Sonnendecks, ein Spa, drei Pools und der weiße Sandstrand zu Füßen. Dazu unter Wasser eine phantastische geheimnisvolle Welt und über Wasser ein Helikopter, der die Gäste zum Mayon Volcano bringt.

FR Ce complexe de petite taille mais très élégant semble avoir été planté sur la plage. On y trouve seulement 38 chambres luxueuses, dont les plafonds hauts et les fenêtres panoramiques font disparaître toute limite entre l'intérieur et l'extérieur : la chambre et l'océan ne font presque plus qu'un. L'architecture très fluide, moderne et sans fioritures compte de larges terrasses et leur solarium, un spa, trois piscines et une plage de sable blanc s'étendant littéralement à vos pieds. Le fantastique et mystérieux monde sous-marin recèle des trésors que seule une escapade en hélicoptère en direction du volcan Mayon saurait faire oublier.

NED Een klein maar fijn resort, direct aan het strand. Slechts 38 luxekamers met hoge plafonds en grote panoramavensters, die de grenzen tussen binnen en buiten, tussen kamer en oceaan tenietdoen. De architectuur is modern, rechtlijnig en zonder opsmuk. Grote terrassen en zonnedekken, een kuuroord, drie zwembaden en het witte zandstrand aan de voeten. Met onder water een fantastische geheimzinnige wereld en boven water een helikopter die de gasten naar de Mayon-vulkaan brengt.

ESKAYA BEACH RESORT & SPA

PHILIPPINES | BOHOL | HOTELS

ENG Nature reached deep into her treasure chest here: a five-kilometer (three-mile) sand beach, a cliff, flatlands, a gorge, caves, and views of the lush vegetation and the ocean. And all that in an area of only 16 hectares (40 acres). Here you will find 15 villas which form a boutique resort perfectly integrated into this diverse landscape. "Eskaya" is the name of the indigenous people of Bohol, and the resort's architecture is modeled after their building style. Thatched villas, called balai, are sturdily constructed from local materials: bamboo, wood and cogon grass. Filipino and ultra-modern to boot.

DEU Die Natur hat hier in ihr Schatzkästchen gegriffen: fünf Kilometer Sandstrand, ein Kliff, flache Landschaften, eine Schlucht, Höhlen, der Blick in die üppige Vegetation der Berge und aufs Meer. All das auf einer Fläche von 16 Hektar. Darauf nur 15 Villen, ein Boutique-Resort, das sich in diese abwechslungsreiche Landschaft perfekt einfügt. „Eskaya" heißen die Einheimischen von Bohol. Ihrer Bauweise nachempfunden ist die Architektur der Anlage: Schilfgedeckte Villen, so genannte Balai, robust konstruiert, unter Verwendung einheimischer Materialien: Bambus, Holz und Cogongras. Philippinisch und dazu ultramodern.

FR La nature a rassemblé ici toutes les richesses possibles : une plage de sable de cinq kilomètres, une falaise, une gorge, des grottes ainsi qu'une vue sur la végétation luxuriante et sur l'océan. Tous ces trésors sont regroupés sur seulement 16 hectares, dans un complexe-boutique parfaitement intégré à ces différents paysages. « Eskaya » est le nom du peuple indigène de Bohol dont le style de construction a inspiré l'architecture du resort. Les 15 solides villas au toit de chaume, appelés balai, sont construites à l'aide de matériaux locaux comme le bambou, le bois et la paille de dys, pour former un ensemble aux allures à la fois phi lippines et ultramodernes.

NED De natuur heeft hier een greep in haar juwelenkistje gedaan: vijf kilometer zandstrand, een klif, vlakke landschappen, een kloof, grotten, de blik op de weelderige vegetatie van de bergen en op de zee. Dit alles op een oppervlakte van 16 hectaren. Hierop slechts 15 villa's, een boetiekresort, dat volmaakt in dit afwisselende landschap past. 'Eskaya' heten de inheemsen van Bohol. De architectuur van het complex is een nabootsing van hun bouwwijze. Rietgedekte villa's, zogeheten balai, robuust gebouwd, gebruikmakend van inheemse materialen: bamboe, hout en cogongras. Filippijns en tegelijk ultramodern.

NAUMI HOTEL

ENG The façade, a gray steel origami trellis, is ten stories high and covered in living plants. The interior has "Calligari Isola seaters" and "Dora armchairs". The three-story installation, constructed of mirrors, glass, and steel with flowers, frogs, and butterflies, is entitled "Garden". The color changes from lavender to violet, blue to fuchsia, peach to red—depending on the time of day. The rooms are equipped with Italian designer furniture, the most costly marble, freestanding bathtubs, and luxury lighting, plus a rooftop pool with spectacular views. The creators: Eco-id Architecture and Design.

DEU Die Fassade aus grauen Origami-Stahlgittern ist zehn Stockwerke hoch und mit Pflanzen bewachsen. Innen, „Caligari's Isola Seater" und „Dora Armchairs". „Garden" heißt die Installation aus drei Ebenen mit Spiegeln, Glas und Stahl, mit Blumen, Fröschen und Schmetterlingen. Sie wechselt die Farbe von lavendel zu violett, blau zu fuchsie, pfirsich zu rot – abhängig von der Tageszeit. Die Zimmer sind mit italienischen Designer-Möbeln, dem teuersten Marmor, freistehenden Badewannen und Luxusleuchten ausgestattet, dazu ein Hotelpool auf dem Dach mit spektakulärer Aussicht. Und die Macher: Eco-id Architecture and Design.

FR La façade végétalisée de cet hôtel de dix étages est un treillis gris fait d'acier imitant l'origami. On peut trouver à l'intérieur les célèbres fauteuils « Calligari Isola » et « Dora » ainsi qu'une installation en triptyque intitulée « Garden », faite de miroirs, de verre et d'acier comprenant aussi fleurs, grenouilles et papillons. La palette des couleurs passe de lavande à violet, bleu, fuchsia, pêche ou rouge suivant l'heure de la journée. Les chambres sont décorées de mobilier design italien, de marbre de la meilleure qualité, de vasques et de luminaires luxueux, tandis que sur le toit, la piscine offre une vue spectaculaire sur les environs. Cet hôtel fantastique est une création Eco-id Architecture and Design.

NED De voorgevel van grijze stalen origamiroosters is tien verdiepingen hoog en begroeid met planten. Binnen 'Calligari's Isola Seater' en 'Dora Armchairs'. 'Garden' heet de constructie van drie niveaus met spiegels, glas en staal met bloemen, kikkers en vlinders. Ze wisselt van kleur van lavendel tot violet, blauw tot fuchsia, perzik tot rood – afhankelijk van de tijd van de dag. De kamers zijn uitgerust met Italiaanse designermeubels, het duurste marmer, losstaande badkuipen en luxelichten, en op het dak een hotelzwembad met spectaculair uitzicht. En de makers: Eco-id Architecture and Design.

NEW MAJESTIC HOTEL

REPUBLIC OF SINGAPORE | SINGAPORE | HOTELS

ENG As soon you enter the lobby you will be greeted by a peculiar and equally fascinating mix of futuristic design and architectural remnants from the colonial era. Vintage and designer furniture from the 1920s to the 1960s. 30 rooms, each a remarkable blend of art and architecture. Singapore's emerging artists' movement played a significant role in the design. Choosing one of the four room varieties depends on the guest's design preferences and individual openness to experimentation: Mirror, Hanging Bed, Aquarium or Loft Room, plus pop art paintings and hidden messages.

DEU Bereits in der Lobby findet sich ein eigentümliches und gleichermaßen faszinierendes Gemisch aus futuristischem Design und architektonischen Überbleibseln aus der Kolonialzeit: Vintage und Designer-Möbel aus den 1920er- bis 1960er-Jahren. 30 Zimmer, jedes eine bemerkenswerte Verschmelzung von Kunst und Architektur. Maßgeblich daran beteiligt war die aufstrebende Künstlerbewegung Singapurs. Die Entscheidung für einen der vier Zimmertypen hängt hier an Design-Vorlieben und der individuellen Experimentierfreudigkeit des Gastes: Mirror-, Hanging Bed-, Aquarium- oder Loftroom, dazu Pop-Art-Gemälde und versteckte Botschaften.

FR L'hôtel éveille curiosité et fascination dès son entrée, où sont mêlés design futuriste et vestiges de l'ère coloniale. Si le mouvement artistique émergeant à Singapour a joué un rôle important dans sa création, le mobilier vintage et design des années 1920 à 1960 est aussi une caractéristique notable. Art et d'architecture forment la toile de fond de chacune des 30 chambres de l'établissement. Suivant ses goûts en matière de design et sa capacité à accepter l'inconnu, chaque client est libre de choisir parmi quatre catégories de chambres : Miroir, Lit suspendu, Aquarium ou Loft, sont également décorées d'œuvres pop art et de messages cachés.

NED De lobby vertoont een eigenzinnig en al evenzeer fascinerend mengsel van futuristisch design en architectonische overblijfselen uit de koloniale tijd: vintage- en designermeubelen uit de jaren 1920 tot 1960. Dertig kamers, elk een opmerkelijke versmelting van kunst en architectuur. De vooruitstrevende kunstenaarsbeweging van Singapore heeft hier grote invloed op uitgeoefend. De keuze voor een van de vier kamertypen hangt hier af van de designvoorkeuren en de individuele experimenteerlust van de gast: mirror-, hanging bed-, aquarium- of loftroom, inclusief popartschilderijen en verborgen boodschappen.

VILLA MAGGONA

SRI LANKA | MAGGONA | HOTELS

ᴱᴺᴳ The VILLA MAGGONA is a "little secret" far from the tourist crowds, built on the ruins from the tsunami and designed for outdoor living. The rooms can be opened all the way, and there are 30-meter (98-foot) verandas, a 30-meter (98-foot) pool and sun terraces. The interior design is rustic yet contemporary—polished concrete floors, wooden shutters, and pergolas. All constructed to appeal to the environmentally conscious traveler.

ᴰᴱᵁ Die VILLA MAGGONA ist ein „kleines Geheimnis", fernab vom lauten Tourismus, erbaut auf den Ruinen des Tsunami und designt für ein Leben im Freien. Die Räume können komplett geöffnet werden, dazu 30 Meter Veranden, 30 Meter Pool und Sonnenterrassen. Die Innenausstattung ist rustikal aber zeitgenössisch – polierte Betonböden, Holzläden und Pergolen. Das Ganze in einer Bauweise, die den umweltbewusst Reisenden anspricht.

ᶠᴿ La VILLA MAGGONA est un « petit paradis » situé à l'abri des touristes. Construit sur des ruines après le passage du tsunami et créé dans l'idée d'une vie au grand air, les chambres sont totalement ouvertes sur l'extérieur. Chacune compte une véranda de 30 mètres, une piscine de même dimension et un solarium. L'ensemble de l'édifice saura aussi charmer le voyageur éco-citoyen. La décoration intérieure est à la fois rustique et contemporaine, faite de revêtements en béton poli ou de volets et de pergolas en bois.

ᴺᴱᴰ De VILLA MAGGONA is een 'klein geheim', ver van het luidruchtige toerisme, gebouwd op de ruïnes van de tsunami en ontworpen voor een leven in de openlucht. De ruimten kunnen geheel worden geopend, met 30 meter aan veranda's, 30-meter zwembad en zonneterrassen. De inrichting is rustiek maar eigentijds – glimmende betonvloeren, houten luiken en pergola's. En dat alles gebouwd op een manier die de milieubewuste reiziger aanspreekt.

LEBUA AT STATE TOWER

THAILAND | BANGKOK | HOTELS

ENG The hotel tower with its golden dome resembles an oriental palace taken flight. The interior is elegant, luxurious, and fanciful in places, the grand exterior magnificent. The LEBUA AT STATE TOWER luxury hotel is the second highest building in Bangkok. The view from the suites, with or without a balcony, is unparalleled. The view from the gourmet restaurant Sirocco and the Sky Bar is endless.

DEU Der Hotelturm mit seiner goldenen Kuppel mutet an wie ein in die Höhe geschossener orientalischer Palast. Innen elegant, luxuriös und bisweilen verspielt, außen prachtvoll. Das LEBUA AT STATE TOWER Luxushotel ist das zweithöchste Gebäude Bangkoks. Der Blick aus den Suiten, ob mit oder ohne Balkon, ist unvergleichlich. Aus dem Gourmet-Restaurant Sirocco und der Sky-Bar ist er grenzenlos.

FR Avec son dôme doré, la tour de cet hôtel prend l'apparence d'un palais oriental. L'intérieur n'est qu'élégance, luxe et fantaisie, tandis que de l'extérieur, l'hôtel s'érige vers le ciel de toute sa magnificence. Le luxueux LEBUA AT STATE TOWER est la deuxième plus haute tour de Bangkok. La vue qu'offrent les suites, dont certaines possèdent un balcon, n'a pas d'égal tandis que le restaurant gastronomique Sirocco et le Sky Bar présentent un panorama infini.

NED De hoteltoren met zijn gouden koepel doet aan als een omhoog geschoten oosters paleis. Van binnen elegant, luxueus en soms speels, van buiten prachtig. Het luxehotel LEBUA AT STATE TOWER is het op een na hoogste gebouw van Bangkok. Het uitzicht vanuit de suites, met of zonder balkon, is onvergetelijk. Vanuit het gourmetrestaurant Sirocco en de Sky Bar is het eindeloos.

151

METROPOLITAN BANGKOK HOTELS

THAILAND | BANGKOK | HOTELS

ENG No-frills modern design accentuated with Asiatic ornamentation: the METROPOLITAN BANGKOK's approach is not one of contrasts, but rather the balancing of opposing forces and elements. It strives towards an equilibrium between East and West, between ornamentation and clean lines, a balance that acts as mediator between extremes. Interior designer Kathryn Kng has struck this visual balance perfectly.

DEU Schnörkelloses modernes Design akzentuiert mit asiatischer Ornamentik: Nicht die Gegensätze, sondern das Gleichgewicht entgegenwirkender Kräfte und Aspekte ist das Anliegen des METROPOLITAN BANGKOK HOTELS. Es geht um die Ausgewogenheit zwischen Ost und West, Geradlinigkeit und Schnörkel, um die Balance als den Mittler zwischen den Extremen, visuell perfekt in Szene gesetzt von der Innenarchitektin Kathryn Kng.

FR Un design moderne sans fioritures mis en avant par une décoration aux accents asiatiques : le METROPOLITAN BANGKOK ne cherche pas les contrastes, mais plutôt l'équilibre des forces et des éléments. Cet établissement aspire à un équilibre entre l'orient et l'occident, entre l'ornementation et les lignes épurées ; il aspire à un équilibre qui se veut médiateur entre les extrêmes. Kathryn Kng, l'architecte d'intérieur en charge du projet, a su parfaitement créer équilibre visuel.

NED Strak modern design naast Aziatische ornamentiek: Niet de tegenstellingen maar het evenwicht van tegenwerkende krachten en aspecten is de hartenwens van het METROPOLITAN BANGKOK HOTEL. Het gaat om de evenwichtigheid tussen Oost en West, rechtlijnigheid en opsmuk, om de balans als bemiddelaar tussen de uitersten, visueel volmaakt in scène gezet door binnenhuisarchitecte Kathryn Kng.

MILLENNIUM HILTON BANGKOK

THAILAND | BANGKOK | HOTELS

ENG The view will make you forget everything you've ever seen. The Chao Phraya and Bangkok are stunning during the day, and at night they are unsurpassable. Each room of the luxurious MILLENNIUM HILTON BANGKOK comes with a panorama window that makes this incomparable view possible. Even from the outside, the extravagant 32-story hotel tower, with its ultra-modern architecture, is enrapturing. Inside, modern elegance is king.

DEU Der Blick lässt alles in Vergessenheit geraten. Der Chao Phraya und Bangkok sind schon bei Tage umwerfend, bei Nacht unübertrefflich. Jedes Zimmer des luxuriösen MILLENNIUM HILTON BANGKOK verfügt über Panoramafenster, die diesen unvergleichlichen Ausblick ermöglichen. Der extravagante Hotelturm mit seinen 32 Stockwerken besticht schon von außen durch seine ultramoderne Architektur. Und innen herrscht moderne Eleganz.

FR La vue sur le Chao Phraya et Bangkok vous fera oublier tout ce que vous connaissiez. Étonnants de jour, le fleuve et la ville deviennent indétrônables de beauté à la nuit tombée. Dans les chambres du luxueux MILLENNIUM HILTON BANGKOK, une fenêtre panoramique offre cette vue grandiose sur un plateau d'argent. L'architecture ultramoderne de cet extravagant hôtel de 32 étages est envoûtante. Elle laisse place, à l'intérieur, à l'élégance et à la modernité.

NED Door het uizicht raakt alles in vergetelheid. De Chao Phraya en Bangkok zijn overdag al overweldigend, 's nachts onovertroffen. Elke kamer van het luxueuze MILLENNIUM HILTON BANGKOK beschikt over panoramavensters, die dit onvergelijke uitzicht mogelijk maken. De extravagante hoteltoren met zijn 32 verdiepingen bekoort buiten al door zijn ultramoderne architectuur. En binnen heerst moderne elegantie.

KIRIMAYA

ENG The two-story resort and spa, consisting of indoor and outdoor pavilions, has a certain chic that's more urban than tropical rustic, even if it does make use of local natural materials. Straw-covered paths, an antique carved Indian door, roofs with cedar shaped shingles, travertine floors, a bamboo daybed. It all characterizes the successful combination of innovative architecture and contemporary luxury with Asian accents. And the best part of all: camping in a luxury tent.

DEU Das zweigeschossige Resort und Spa, bestehend aus Outdoor- und Indoor-Pavillons, besitzt einen eher urbanen als tropisch-rustikalen Chic, obgleich es sich lokaler natürlicher Materialien bedient. Strohbedeckte Wege, eine antike geschnitzte indische Tür, Dächer mit Schindeln in Zedernform, Travertinböden oder ein Daybed aus Bambus. All das kennzeichnet die gelungene Kombination aus innovativer Architektur und zeitgenössischer Luxusausstattung mit asiatischen Akzenten. Und der Clou: Campen im Luxuszelt.

FR En dépit de l'usage de matériaux naturels locaux, l'élégance de ce complexe et spa de deux étages est plus urbaine que tropicale. Les pavillons sont reliés par des sentiers recouverts de paille. Grâce à des éléments très visuels, comme une porte indienne sculptée, des toits aux bardeaux imitant la forme du cèdre, des sols de tuf calcaire ou des banquettes en bambou, l'ensemble est résolument harmonieux. Même si l'établissement combine une architecture innovante et un faste contemporain aux accents asiatiqués, le plus beau reste encore de camper sous une tente de luxe.

NED Het twee verdiepingen tellende resort en kuuroord, bestaande uit buiten- en binnenpaviljoens, bezit eerder een stedelijke dan een tropisch-rustieke elegantie, hoewel er gebruik is gemaakt van plaatselijke natuurlijke materialen. Met stro bedekte paden, een antieke bewerkte Indiase deur, daken met dakspanen in cedervorm, travertijnvloeren of een bank van bamboe. Dit alles kenmerkt de geslaagde combinatie van innovatieve architectuur en eigentijdse luxe inrichting met Aziatische accenten. En het klapstuk: kamperen in een luxetent.

THE RACHA

THAILAND | KOH RACHA YAI | HOTELS

ENG Modern, for the modern nomad. Sparse, purist, and no-frills with clean lines and Asian accents, nestled in the untouched natural landscape. Nothing was altered, nothing removed. The resort was harmoniously incorporated into its natural surroundings, without harming the trees. Great care was taken to observe proper treatment of the environment, on land as well as in the water. The walls are double layered to reduce the need for air conditioning, no water or energy goes to waste, the pool is treated with ozone rather than chlorine. All that without making any sacrifices when it comes to luxury. A perfect example that you can have the best of both worlds: top-notch luxury, design, and architecture, with a pristine natural landscape on all sides.

DEU Modern, für moderne Nomaden. Schlicht, geradlinig, puristisch, schnörkellos, mit asiatischen Akzenten, eingebettet in die unberührte Landschaft. Nichts wurde entfernt oder aufgeschüttet. Das Resort wurde harmonisch in die Natur eingefügt, Bäume erhalten. Sorgfältig achtete man auf den verantwortungsvollen Umgang mit der Umwelt, an Land und im Wasser. Zweifache Mauern, um die Klimatisierung zu reduzieren, keine Verschwendung von Wasser und Energie, statt Chlor Ozon in den Pools. All das bedeutet keinerlei Verzicht in Sachen Luxus. Ein perfektes Beispiel dafür, dass es geht: Luxus, Design und Architektur der Extraklasse, unberührte Landschaften und der Mensch mittendrin.

FR La modernité s'offre ici aux nomades modernes. Au cœur d'un environnement préservé, cet hôtel au style épuré et sans fioritures mise sur des lignes nettes aux accents asiatiques. Le complexe a été harmonieusement intégré à son environnement naturel, dans le plus grand respect de la flore préexistante et sans modification profonde du lieu. Une attention toute particulière a été portée au développement durable : les murs, dont l'épaisseur a été doublée, réduisent les besoins en climatisation, l'eau et l'énergie sont réutilisées et la piscine est traitée à l'ozone pour éviter le chlore. Le luxe n'en pâtit pas pour et l'hôtel allie ainsi le meilleur de deux mondes : luxe haut de gamme, design et architecture se fondent dans un cadre naturel absolument immaculé.

NED Modern, voor moderne nomaden. Eenvoudig, rechtlijnig, puristisch, zonder franje, met Aziatische accenten, ingebed in het ongerepte landschap. Niets is er verwijderd of opgehoogd. Het resort is harmonisch in de natuur ingepast, bomen zijn behouden gebleven. Zorgvuldig is erop gelet verantwoordelijk met het milieu om te gaan, op het land en in het water. Dubbele muren, om de ontluchting te verminderen, geen verspilling van water en energie, in plaats van chloor ozon in de zwembaden. Dit alles betekent niet dat er tekort aan luxe heerst. Een volmaakt voorbeeld van dat het kan: luxe, design en architectuur van buitengewone kwaliteit, ongerepte landschappen en er middenin de mens.

VILLA BEIGE

THAILAND | KOH SAMUI | HOTELS

ENG The VILLA BEIGE, a 5,000-square-meter (53,820-square-foot) private resort, is situated in the middle of tropical jungle and offers a fantastic view of the Koh Samui coast. The snow-white cubes with their ceiling-high window panes seem like dice that were rolled and came to rest here. The interiors are of an exclusive design: ebony, Thai silk, snakeskin, and design classics. This luxury villa can accommodate up to eight people, with the added service of an attached 5-star hotel.

DEU Inmitten des tropischen Dschungels, mit einem phantastischen Blick über die Küste von Koh Samui, liegt die VILLA BEIGE, ein 5 000 Quadratmeter großes Privatresort. Wie hingewürfelt wirken die schneeweißen Kuben, die über deckenhohe Fensterflächen verfügen. Die Einrichtung ist exklusiv: Ebenholz, Thai-Seide, Schlangenleder und dazu Designklassiker. Platz für bis zu acht Personen bietet diese Luxusvilla mit dem angeschlossenen Service eines 5-Sterne-Hotels.

FR La VILLA BEIGE, complexe privatif de 5 000 mètres carrés, se trouve au cœur d'une jungle tropicale et offre une vue fantastique sur la côte de Koh Samui. Les cubes d'une blancheur immaculée percés de fenêtres s'étirant sur toute leur hauteur, ressemblent à des dés jetés par une main de géant et venus rouler jusque-là. Ébène, soie thaïe, peaux de serpent et classiques de designers composent le design unique de cette luxueuse villa, pouvant accueillir jusqu'à huit personnes et offrant les services d'un cinq étoiles.

NED Midden in de tropische jungle, met een fantastisch uitzicht over de kust van Koh Samui, ligt de VILLA BEIGE, een 5000 vierkante meter groot privéresort. De sneeuwwitte kubussen, die over plafondhoge vensters beschikken, lijken net dobbelstenen. De inrichting is exclusief: ebbenhout, Thaise zijde, slangenleer en designklassiekers. Deze luxevilla biedt plaats aan wel acht personen en de service van een vijfsterrenhotel is inbegrepen.

X2 KUI BURI

THAILAND | PRACHUAB KHIRI KHAN | HOTELS

ENG X2, pronounced "cross to", refers to a switch or changeover to a complete new dimension of luxury, one based on design. The X2 KUI BURI's architecture functions as a link between man and nature. Clear, minimalist, and free of superfluous flourishes, it fits seamlessly into the landscape. By shunning the spotlight, this architectural design makes it possible to see things in their true beauty and to absorb them as they are.

DEU X2, gesprochen „cross-to", meint ein Sich-Hinwenden oder Hinüberwechseln zu einer völlig neuen Dimension von Luxus, die auf Design basiert. Dabei fungiert die Architektur des X2 KUI BURI als Verbindung zwischen Mensch und Natur. Klar, minimalistisch ohne jeden Schnörkel fügt sie sich in die Landschaft. Sie möchte die Aufmerksamkeit nicht für sich und ermöglicht so, die Dinge in ihrer Schönheit zu erfassen und in sich aufzunehmen.

FR X2, à prononcer « cross to », renvoie à une rupture radicale du luxe vers sa dimension nouvelle, fondée sur le design. L'architecture du X2 KUI BURI se veut lien entre l'homme et la nature. Claire, minimaliste et exempte de toute fioriture, elle se fond intégralement dans le paysage. Loin de chercher la reconnaissance et le faste, ce design architectural permet d'apprécier et d'absorber la beauté profonde des choses.

NED X2, uitgesproken als 'cross-to', betekent zich wenden naar of overgaan op een volledig nieuwe dimensie van luxe die op design berust. Hierbij fungeert de architectuur van het X2 KUI BURI als verbinding tussen mens en natuur. Helder en minimalistisch zonder enige franje voegt het zich in het landschap. Het eist de aandacht niet voor zichzelf op, waardoor men de schoonheid van de dingen kan ervaren en in zich kan opnemen.

ALILA CHA-AM

THAILAND | CHA AM | HOTELS

ENG Duangrit Bunnag, one of Thailand's leading architects, designed this tropical getaway. His aim was to defy conventions. He creates a peaceful atmosphere and private sphere using clear shapes and clean lines. You feel as if you have the place to yourself. An impression created by the connections between open spaces and areas with private paths and details that promote intimacy, such as cabanas that act as retreats for couples. The most out-of-the-ordinary element, though, is a massive staircase, the entryway to the resort, which leads into stunning gardens, pool landscapes, and a labyrinth of private terraces and courtyards, all stretching all the way to the ocean.

DEU Duangrit Bunnag, einer der führenden Architekten Thailands, entwarf dieses tropische Getaway. Sein Ziel war es, sich den Konventionen zu widersetzen. Mit klaren Formen und Linien erzeugt er Ruhe und Privatsphäre. Es ist, als hätte man den Ort für sich allein. Ein Eindruck, der durch die Verknüpfungen von offenen Räumen und Flächen mit Privatwegen und Intimität erzeugenden Details wie Cabanas als Rückzugsorte für Paare entsteht. Das Ungewöhnlichste aber ist eine mächtige Treppe, der Eingang zum Resort, die in wunderschöne Gärten, Pool-Landschaften und ein Labyrinth privater Terrassen und Höfe führt, die sich allesamt bis zum Ozean erstrecken.

FR Duangrit Bunnag, l'un des plus plus grands architectes thaïlandais, et a imaginé ce refuge tropical. Son objectif était de défier les conventions en créant une atmosphère paisible et une sphère intime grâce à des formes et des lignes claires. Le lieu semble nous appentenir. Cette impression naît des connections entre espaces ouverts et zones privées dont certains détails invitent à l'intimité, comme de petits pavillons permettant une retraite paisible. L'élément le plus extraordinaire reste cependant un escalier monumental, permettant l'entrée au complexe et conduisant vers des jardins étonnants. Il domine la piscine et un labyrinthe de petites cours et de terrasses privées, disséminées sur le sentier menant jusqu'à l'océan.

NED Duangrit Bunnag, een van de toonaangevende architecten van Thailand, ontwierp dit tropische ontsnappingsoord. Zijn doel was zich te verzetten tegen de conventies. Met heldere vormen en lijnen wekt hij rust en een huiselijke sfeer op. Het lijkt alsof men het oord voor zichzelf heeft. Een indruk die ontstaat door de aaneensluitingen van open ruimten en oppervlakken met eigen wegen en details die intimiteit oproepen. Het meest ongewone is echter een enorme trap, de ingang tot het resort, die leidt naar wondermooie tuinen, zwembad-landschappen en een labyrint van besloten terrassen, die zich helemaal tot de oceaan uitstrekken.

SONEVA KIRI & SIX SENSES SPA

THAILAND | KOH KOOD | HOTELS

ENG This luxury resort extends over 50 hectares (124 acres) on Koh Kood, a gorgeous and pristine island in eastern Thailand. 46 pool villas, each 400 to 770 square meters (4,305 to 8,288 square feet) in size, are spread out over the beach and hillside with views of the Gulf of Thailand and arranged around pools of water. Preserving the environment and harmonizing with the surroundings were the defining criteria for the resort's architecture and design, and for the means of transportation within the resort. Guests walk, cycle, or use an electric vehicle—or swing, in ecological swinging daybeds. A paradisiacal resort with "true-to-nature" comfort and a simple yet refined design.

DEU Auf Koh Kood, einer wunderschönen unberührten Insel im Osten Thailands, liegt dieses Luxusresort auf einer Fläche von 50 Hektar. 46 Pool Villas, jeweils 400 bis 770 Quadratmeter groß, verteilen sich an Strand und Hang mit Blick über den Golf von Thailand und umgeben von Wasserbecken. Der Erhalt der Umwelt und der Einklang mit der Umgebung waren die bestimmenden Kriterien für Architektur und Design, aber auch für die Fortbewegung innerhalb des Resorts. Man läuft, fährt Rad oder nutzt ein Elektrofahrzeug – oder man lässt sich bewegen, im swingenden Öko-Daybed. Eine paradiesische Anlage mit „naturbelassenem" Komfort und einem schlichten und doch raffinierten Design.

FR Koh Kood est une île préservée du tourisme à l'est de la Thaïlande, où s'étend sur plus de 50 hectares ce luxueux complexe. Les 46 villas de 400 à 770 mètres carrés, entourées de piscines et disséminées sur la plage ou la colline offrent toutes une vue sur le magique golfe de Thaïlande. Le projet souhaitait essentiellement préserver environnement et harmoniser l'établissement et le cadre naturel. Les hôtes se déplacent ainsi à pied, en vélo ou à l'aide d'un véhicule électrique, mais peuvent aussi se balancer sur des banquettes mobiles. Ce complexe paradisiaque au design simple et raffiné est doté d'un confort « proche de la nature ».

NED Op Koh Kood, een wondermooi ongerept eiland in het oosten van Thailand, ligt dit luxeresort op een oppervlak van 50 hectare. 46 pool villa's, 400 tot 770 vierkante meter groot, verspreiden zich langs het strand en op de helling met uitzicht over de Golf van Thailand en zijn omringd door waterbekkens. Milieubehoud en harmonie met de omgeving waren de bepalende criteria voor architectuur en design, maar ook voor de voortbeweging binnen het resort. Men loopt, fietst of gebruikt een elektrisch voertuig of laat zich bewegen in het schommelende eco-daybed. Een paradijselijk complex met 'zuiver' comfort en een eenvoudig doch geraffineerd design.

DESERT PALM

UNITED ARAB EMIRATES | DUBAI | HOTELS

ENG This luxury retreat, consisting of 24 elegant suites and villas, is located in the heart of the Polo Estate, surrounded by lush vegetation and shaded by palm trees. The design was inspired by a modern Arabian aesthetic. Inside, you will be enchanted by the generous rooms, the unique effects created by light and fabric, the wooden and ceramic elements, and the huge windows providing views of the polo fields. High-tech luxury, designer furnishings, and artisan craftsmanship are all locally inspired. Secluded yet close to the city, simultaneously urban and yet as rural as a country estate.

DEU Im Herzen des Polo Estates liegt dieses Luxus-Retreat aus 24 eleganten Suiten und Villen, umgeben von üppiger Vegetation und im Schatten von Palmen. Das Design ist inspiriert von einer modernen arabischen Ästhetik. Im Innern bestechen großzügige Räume, besondere Effekte aus Licht und Stoffen, Elemente aus Holz und Keramik und großflächige Fenster mit Blick über das Pologelände. Hightech-Luxus, Designer-Ausstattung und Kunsthandwerk sind lokal inspiriert. Nah an der Stadt und doch abgeschieden, urban und wie ein privater Landsitz zugleich.

FR Cette retraite luxueuse entourée d'une végétation luxuriante et de palmiers ombreux se trouve au cœur d'un domaine consacré au polo. L'esthétique arabe moderne a largement inspiré le design de ses 24 suites et villas d'élégance. L'enchantement est ainsi garanti par les chambres généreuses, les effets inimitables de la lumière, les tissus, les éléments de bois et de céramique ainsi que les baies vitrées permettant d'observer les terrains de polo. Le luxe high-tech, les meubles de designer et les objets d'artisanat s'inspirent tous des traditions locales. Sous ses airs de domaine de campagne, c'est une adresse urbaine très prisée.

NED In het hart van het Polo Estate ligt dit luxetoevluchtsoord van 24 elegante suites en villa's, omringd door weelderige vegetatie en in de schaduw van palmen. Het ontwerp is geïnspireerd door een moderne Arabische esthetiek. Binnen zijn er zeer aantrekkelijke grote ruimten, speciale effecten van licht en stoffen, elementen van hout en keramiek en grote vensters met uitzicht op het poloterrein. Hightechluxe, designerinrichting en kunstnijverheid zijn plaatselijk geïnspireerd. Dicht bij de stad en toch apart ervan, stedelijk en tegelijk een privébuitenverblijf.

AL MAHA DESERT RESORT & SPA

UNITED ARAB EMIRATES | DUBAI | HOTELS

ENG This desert resort, in the middle of a 25-square-kilometer (10 square mile) nature reserve, is named after the native oryx, the "maha". The surroundings inspire a certain Bedouin atmosphere, which can't be said for the resort itself. It's far too luxurious for that. Its devotion to nature, however, makes it one of the first eco projects in the United Arab Emirates. The main building houses the "majlis", traditional Arabian rooms. Ancient Arabian traditions with modern refinements, incorporated into an unusual ambience and surrounded by a desert that stretches as far as the eye can see.

DEU Dieses Wüstenresort, inmitten eines 25 Quadratkilometer großen Naturreservats, trägt den Namen der heimischen Oryx-Antilope, der „Al Maha". Die Umgebung lässt Beduinenfeeling aufkommen, das eigentliche Resort nicht. Dazu ist es zu luxuriös. Aber der Natur verschrieben, gilt es als erstes Öko-Projekt der Vereinigten Arabischen Emirate. Im Haupthaus finden sich typische arabische Räume, die „Majlis". Arabischer Ursprung modern verfeinert, eingefügt in ein außergewöhnliches Ambiente, und dazu die Wüste, soweit das Auge reicht.

FR Ce resort dans le désert, au beau milieu d'une réserve naturelle de 25 kilomètres carrés, doit son nom à l'oryx, appelé ici « maha ». Même si l'on est d'abord frappé par la délicate présence du luxe, le lieu évoque aussi à sa manière le peuple bédouin. Entièrement dévoué au respect de la nature, il est l'un des premiers éco-projets lancé aux Émirats arabes unis. Le bâtiment principal accueille les « majlis », les pièces principales traditionnelles de la région. Une tradition arabe ancestrale alliée à un raffinement des plus modernes participent à créer l'ambiance inhabituelle de ce lieu unique, entouré par le désert.

NED Dit woestijnresort, midden in een natuurreservaat van 25 vierkante kilometer, draagt de naam van de inheemse orynx-antilope, de 'al maha'. De omgeving roept een bedoeïenengevoel op, het eigenlijke resort niet. Daar is het veel te luxueus voor. Maar gewijd aan de natuur als het is, geldt het als eerste ecoproject van de Verenigde Arabische Emiraten. In het hoofdhuis bevinden zich typische Arabische ruimten, de 'majlis'. Verfijnde Arabische oorsprong, ingepast in een buitengewone ambiance, met de woestijn erbij, zo ver het oog reikt.

ONE & ONLY ROYAL MIRAGE

UNITED ARAB EMIRATES | DUBAI | HOTELS

ENG It's as if the ancient glory of old Arabia has returned. At the ONE & ONLY ROYAL MIRAGE, the name says it all. This resort has a storybook quality, with its intricate arches, domes, and towers, its gardens complete with fountains and magnificent flowerbeds. The hotel grounds consist of three separate areas: the Palace, the Arabian Court, and the Residence & Spa. And what they all have in common is overwhelming opulence. The image of tales from the *Arabian Nights* is an old cliché, no doubt about it. But the fact of the matter is: it's spot on.

DEU Es ist, als wäre die Pracht des Arabiens vergangener Tage zurückgekehrt. Beim ONE & ONLY ROYAL MIRAGE ist der Name Programm. Märchenhaft wirkt dieses Resort mit seinen verwinkelten Bögen, Kuppeln und Türmen, den herrlichen Gärten mit Springbrunnen und prächtigen Blumenbeeten. Drei voneinander getrennte Bereiche umfasst die Hotelanlage: Palace, Arabian Court und Residence & Spa. Allen gemein ist eine unermessliche Pracht. Ohne Zweifel, es klingt banal, das Bild vom Märchen aus 1001 Nacht. Tatsache aber ist: Es trifft den Kern.

FR On dirait que la gloire historique de l'Arabie d'antan a refait surface. Le nom du ONE & ONLY ROYAL MIRAGE se suffit à lui-même pour faire rêver. Avec ses arches complexes, ses dômes et tours, ses jardins ornés de fontaines et de magnifiques parterres de fleurs, ce complexe respecte une tradition architecturale séculaire. L'hôtel est constitué de trois zones séparées : le Palais, la Cour arabe et la Résidence & Spa. Face à une telle opulence, penser aux Mille et une nuits serait presque un cliché, il n'en fait aucun doute... mais il n'en reste pas moins qu'on s'y croirait.

NED Het is alsof de Arabische luister van de dagen van weleer terugkeert. Bij het ONE & ONLY ROYAL MIRAGE is de naam een programma. Met zijn talloze bogen, koepels en torens, de heerlijke tuinen met fonteinen en prachtige bloemperken doet dit resort sprookjesachtig aan. Het complex omvat drie van elkaar gescheiden gebieden: Palace, Arabien Court en Residence & Spa. Alle hebben ze een onmetelijke schoonheid gemeen. Ongetwijfeld, hoe banaal het ook klinkt, het beeld van het sprookje van 1001 nacht. Feit is echter: het raakt de kern.

INTERCONTINENTAL HANOI WESTLAKE AND RESORT

VIETNAM | HANOI | HOTELS

ENG It's as if this place is immune to the din of the metropolis. The INTERCONTINENTAL HANOI WESTLAKE is an oasis of tranquility. Traditional Vietnamese elements and modern design blend into a harmonious whole here. And when you sit at twilight on one of the balconies with their unparalleled sea views, you might just catch a glimpse of it out there—the golden dragon that, according to legend, rose here from the mist of the Red River.

DEU Es ist, als könne die lärmende Großstadt diesem Ort nichts anhaben. Eine Oase der Ruhe ist das INTERCONTINENTAL HANOI WESTLAKE. Hier fügen sich traditionelle vietnamesische Elemente und modernes Design zu einem harmonischen Ganzen. Und sitzt man in der Dämmerung auf einem der Balkone mit dem unvergleichlichen Seeblick, könnte man meinen, man sähe ihn – den goldenen Drachen, der hier der Legende nach aus den Nebeln des Roten Flusses aufgestiegen ist.

FR L'endroit semble totalement coupé du vacarme de la métropole. L'INTERCONTINENTAL HANOI WESTLAKE est une oasis de tranquillité. Les éléments traditionnels vietnamiens côtoient un design moderne pour former un tout des plus harmonieux. S'asseoir sur l'un des balcons pour regarder le coucher du soleil sur le lac permet parfois d'apercevoir ce dragon d'or qui, selon la légende, aurait ici transpercé les brumes du fleuve Rouge.

NED Het lijkt wel alsof het lawaai van de grote stad dit oord niet kan deren. Gewoon een oase van rust is het INTERCONTINENTAL HANOI WESTLAKE. Hier voegen traditionele Vietnamese elementen en modern design zich samen tot een harmonisch geheel. En wie in de schemering op een van de balkons met het onvergetelijke uitzicht op het meer zit, zou kunnen denken dat hij hem zag – de gouden draak, die hier volgens de legende is opgerezen uit de nevelen van de Rode Rivier.

THE GRAND TOWER – SHERATON SAIGON HOTEL & TOWERS

VIETNAM | SAIGON | HOTELS

ENG THE GRAND TOWER, part of the SHERATON SAIGON HOTEL & TOWERS, is a "hotel in a hotel", designed for particularly discerning business guests. It comprises 112 luxurious studios and suites, each between 55 and 83 square meters (592 and 893 square feet), just six on each level, all served by their own personal butler. Totally unique, totally apart from the rest. Modern, stylish, and equipped with the latest high-tech touches. Plus a fascinating view of Saigon right from the bathtub, the entire city in all its raw glory.

DEU THE GRAND TOWER, Teil des SHERATON SAIGON HOTEL & TOWERS, ist ein „Hotel im Hotel", gedacht für besonders anspruchsvolle Businessgäste. Er umfasst 112 luxuriöse Studios und Suiten, nur sechs pro Stockwerk, 55 bis 83 Quadratmeter groß, mit eigenem Butlerservice. Ganz eigen, völlig abseits vom Rest. Modern, stylish und mit den neuesten Hightech-Finessen ausgestattet. Dazu ein faszinierender Blick über Saigon aus der Badewanne, unverstellt und unbegrenzt.

FR THE GRAND TOWER, petit protégé du SHERATON SAIGON HOTEL & TOWERS, est un « hôtel dans l'hôtel », créé pour des hommes d'affaires particulièrement connaisseurs. Il compte 112 studios et suites de luxe, chacun mesurant entre 55 et 83 mètres carrés. Chaque étage n'en comprend que six, tous desservis par un maître d'hôtel attitré. Cet hôtel est absolument unique, totalement différent de ce qui existe déjà. Moderne, élégant et équipé des dernières technologies, la vue sur Saigon depuis la baignoire embrasse la ville entière, dans son état le plus brut.

NED THE GRAND TOWER, onderdeel van het SHERATON SAIGON HOTEL & TOWERS, is een 'hotel in het hotel', ontworpen voor zeer veeleisende zakengasten. Het omvat 112 luxueuze studio's en suites, slechts zes per verdieping, 55 tot 83 vierkante meter groot, met eigen butlerservice. Helemaal voor de gast zelf, ver van de rest. Modern, stijlvol en met de nieuwste hightechsnufjes uitgerust. Met ook nog een fascinerend uitzicht over Saigon vanuit het ligbad, ongeveinsd en onbegrensd.

RESTAURANTS
GOURMET-TEMPLES AND CAFES

BEI

ENG The BEI is a characteristic Asian restaurant in the "Opposite House", a hotel designed by Kengo Kuma. The space's division between a large public area and intimate private areas is modeled after traditional Chinese restaurants. A classic concept, re-interpreted by Lydon Neri & Rossana Hu. A little forest of trees greets guests as they enter and also acts as a screen to the outside. In the public dining area, lamps hang from the ceiling like birds fluttering in excitement. An additional five private dining rooms are separated from the main room, each of a different design and with heavy bronze doors that can be closed for privacy.

DEU Das BEI ist ein typisches asiatisches Restaurant im „The Opposite House", einem Hotel, das von Kengo Kuma entworfen wurde. Dem traditionellen chinesischen Restaurant nachempfunden ist die Aufteilung in einen großen öffentlichen und in intime private Bereiche. Ein klassisches Konzept, neu interpretiert von Lyndon Neri und Rossana Hu. Ein kleiner Wald aus Bäumen, zugleich Sichtschutz von außen, begrüßt den Gast am Eingang. Im öffentlichen Dining-Bereich hängen Leuchten von der Decke, die wie aufgeregt flatternde Vögel wirken. Davon separiert befinden sich fünf private Speiseräume, die jeweils individuell gestaltet sind und mit schweren bronzenen Türen geschlossen werden können.

FR Le BEI est un restaurant asiatique situé dans « l'Opposite House », un hôtel pensé par Kengo Kuma. La partition de l'espace entre vastes zones publiques et salons privés plus intimes imite la disposition des restaurants chinois traditionnels. C'est un véritable classique, revisité par Lydon Neri & Rossana Hu. Une petite forêt accueille les hôtes à leur arrivée mais sert également à cacher ce diamant des regards extérieurs. Dans le salon principal, les lampes tombent du plafond comme de petits oiseaux virevoltants. Les cinq salons privés, dont les lourdes portes de bronze peuvent être fermées pour davantage d'intimité, sont séparés de la salle principale et possèdent chacun leur propre ambiance.

NED Het BEI is een typisch Aziatisch restaurant in 'The Opposite House', een hotel dat door Kengo Kuma werd ontworpen. De verdeling in een grote openbare ruimte en intieme privéruimten is gebaseerd op het traditionele Chinese restaurant. Een klassiek concept, op nieuwe wijze geïnterpreteerd door Lyndon Neri & Rossana Hu. Een klein bosje met bomen, dat tegelijk bescherming tegen inkijk biedt, begroet de gast bij de ingang. In de publieke dining-sector hangen lampen aan het plafond die het effect van opgewonden fladderende vogels hebben. Apart hiervan zijn er nog vijf privé-eetzalen, die allemaal anders zijn vormgegeven en met zware bronzen deuren kunnen worden gesloten.

ᴱᴺᴳ The client wanted a traditional Chinese restaurant, yet something that had never been done before. The Danish designers at Johannes Torbe Studios provided one answer: "airport atmosphere". The roof had to be visually lowered to give the space a more intimate feel overall, and it needed to have an eye-catcher. Five arches over the dining area ensure that SUBU is visible from a distance. The other answer is the "cocoon", a modern form of the traditional Chinese private room in a Scandinavian interpretation. One room, one element. Everything, from the furniture to the tablecloths, has been made exclusively for this location.

ᴰᴱᵁ Der Kunde wollte ein traditionelles chinesisches Restaurant, aber zugleich etwas noch nie Dagewesenes. Eine Antwort der dänischen Designer von Johannes Torbe Studios lautete: „Flughafenatmosphäre". Das Dach musste optisch niedriger, insgesamt der Platz intimer wirken, und es bedurfte eines Eyecatchers. Fünf Bögen über dem Essensbereich machen das SUBU weithin sichtbar. Die andere Antwort ist der „Cocoon", die moderne Form des chinesischen Separee, skandinavisch interpretiert. Ein Raum, ein Element. Alles, von den Möbeln bis zur Tischwäsche, ist ausschließlich für diesen Ort gemacht.

ᶠᴿ Le propriétaire de ce restaurant chinois souhaitait quelque chose de traditionnel, mais qui n'avait jamais été vu auparavant. Les designers danois du Johannes Torbe Studios lui proposèrent une idée unique : « une atmosphère d'aéroport ». Il fallait descendre le plafond pour créer un sentiment d'intimité, tout en le rendant attractif. Cinq arceaux surplombant la salle principale ont donc été installés pour assurer à SUBU une visibilité maximale. La seconde proposition des architectes fut l'idée de « cocon », une forme moderne du salon privé chinois traditionnel, interprété à la mode scandinave où une pièce met en relief un élément. Cet endroit est absolument unique, car tout ce qui le compose, du mobilier aux nappes, est le fruit d'une commande spéciale pour le restaurant.

ᴺᴱᴰ De klant wilde een traditioneel Chinees restaurant, maar tegelijk iets geheel nieuws. Een antwoord van de Deense ontwerpers van Johannes Torbe Studios luidde: 'luchthavensfeer'. Het dak moest visueel lager, de plek moest als geheel intiemer aandoen en er was een blikvanger nodig. Door de vijf bogen boven het eetgedeelte is het SUBU tot op grote afstand zichtbaar. Het andere antwoord is de 'cocoon', de moderne vorm van de Chinese chambre séparée, Scandinavisch uitgelegd. Een ruimte, een element. Alles, van de meubels tot het tafellinnen, is uitsluitend voor dit restaurant gemaakt.

AQUA

ENG One Peking Road, Kowloon—that's where you'll find AQUA. A blend of ultra-stylish interior, breathtaking views of the harbor and downtown, and an innovative combination of Italian and Japanese cuisine. AQUA has two dining areas: the Aqua Roma, a contemporary tribute to Italian design, and the Aqua TokyO, hip and trendy with tatami floors and slate and granite accents. And now there's the Aqua Spirit, a new mezzanine-level chill zone. Buddha Bar style and sound, plus plush lounge seating, and a fabulous panorama.

DEU One Peking Road, Kowloon – da befindet sich das AQUA. Eine Mischung aus ultra-stylishen Interieurs, atemberaubenden Hafen- und Cityblicken und einer innovativen Kombination aus italienischer und japanischer Küche. Zwei Dining-Bereiche umfasst das AQUA: das Aqua Roma, ein zeitgenössischer Tribut an italienisches Design, und das Aqua TokyO, hip und trendy mit Tatami-Böden und Akzenten in Granit und Schiefer. Und auf einem Zwischengeschoss die neue Chill-Zone – das Aqua Spirit. Buddha-Bar-Style & Sound und plüschiges Lounge-Seating mit einer phantastischen Aussicht.

FR Sur Peking Road, à Kowloon : c'est là que vous trouverez AQUA. Cet endroit combine une décoration très élégante, une vue imprenable sur le port et le centre ville, ainsi qu'un mélange novateur de cuisines italienne et japonaise. AQUA compte deux salles, dont l'Aqua Roma, hommage contemporain au design italien, et l'Aqua TokyO, une salle branchée où le sol d'ardoise recouvert de tatamis contraste avec la couleur claire du granit. Vient ensuite l'Aqua Spirit, un nouvel étage-mezzanine dédié à la détente, dans le style et l'ambiance Buddha Bar, agrémenté de banquettes confortables et d'un panorama fabuleux.

NED One Peking Road, Kowloon – hier bevindt zich het AQUA. Een mengeling van ultrachique interieurs, adembenemende uitzichten op haven en stad en een innovatieve combinatie van Italiaanse en Japanse keuken. Het AQUA heeft twee dining-sectoren: Aqua Roma, een eigentijds eerbetoon aan Italiaans design, en Aqua TokyO, hip en trendy met tatami-vloeren en accenten in graniet en leisteen. En op een tussenverdieping de nieuwe chill-zone - Aqua Spirit. Buddha-Bar-Style & Sound en pluche loungebekleding met een fantastisch uitzicht.

ENG The 28th floor of the Hotel Peninsula Hong Kong, an unrivalled panorama of the harbor and skyline, with gourmet cuisine, exclusive bars, and interior design by Philippe Starck. We're talking about FELIX, one of the most stylish and exclusive bar/lounge and gourmet restaurant combinations in the world. Wood, metal, glass, aluminum, crystal—Starck's unparalleled style both divides and unites this ultra-modern restaurant and entertainment level.

DEU Die 28. Etage des Hotel Peninsula Hong Kong, ein unvergleichlicher Panoramablick auf Hafen und Skyline, mit Gourmetküche, exklusiven Bars und dem Interior Design von Philippe Starck: Die Rede ist vom FELIX, einer der stilvollsten und exklusivsten Kombinationen aus Barlounge und Gourmetrestaurant weltweit. Holz, Metall, Glas, Aluminium, Kristall – der unvergleichliche Stil von Starck trennt und vereint diese ultramoderne Restaurant- und Unterhaltungsebene.

FR Au 28ème étage de l'Hôtel Peninsula Hong Kong, le panorama sur le port et les gratte-ciels de la ville est inégalable. Tout comme les mets raffinés, le bar sélect et le design intérieur créé par Philippe Starck que l'on peut y trouver. Il est ici question du FELIX, le seul bar/lounge des plus élégants et sélects au monde à s'associer à un restaurant gastronomique. Bois, métal, verre, aluminium et cristal sont de mise, mais le style inégalé de Starck divise et unit encore une fois ce restaurant ultramoderne et le monde du divertissement.

NED De 28e etage van hotel Peninsula Hong Kong, een onvergelijkelijk panorama op haven en skyline, met gourmetkeuken, exclusieve bars en het interieurontwerp van Philippe Starck. We hebben het over FELIX, een van de stijlvolste en exclusiefste combinaties van barlounge en gourmetrestaurant ter wereld. Hout, metaal, glas, aluminium, kristal – de onnavolgbare stijl van Starck scheidt en verenigt dit ultramoderne restaurant- en ontspanningsgedeelte.

HUTONG

CHINA | HONG KONG | RESTAURANTS

ENG The HUTONG, located on the 28th floor of "One Peking", is a reflection of ancient China. The interior, with its traditional carved screens, silk curtains, and red lanterns, is reminiscent of the imperial suites of old. But with a fabulous view of the Hong Kong skyline. The space combines historical charm with the achievements of the modern age. And the cuisine: traditional northern Chinese dishes with a contemporary touch.

DEU Ein Spiegel des alten China ist das HUTONG, das sich im 28. Stock des „One Peking" befindet. Das Interieur erinnert an königliche Gemächer mit den traditionellen geschnitzten Wandschirmen, seidenen Vorhängen und roten Laternen. Dazu ein phantastischer Blick auf die Skyline von Hongkong. Der Charme der Geschichte ist hier geknüpft an die Errungenschaften der Moderne. Und die Küche: traditionelle nordchinesische Gerichte mit einem zeitgenössischen Touch.

FR Le HUTONG, situé au 28ème étage du « One Peking », reflète une Chine millénaire. Des panneaux traditionnels sculptés y côtoient rideaux de soie et lampions rouges pour rappeler les suites impériales des temps anciens. Grâce à une vue fabuleuse sur Hong Kong, le lieu combine le charme historique aux accomplissements de l'ère moderne. En cuisine, des plats traditionnels du nord de la Chine agrémentés d'une touche contemporaine ravissent les papilles.

NED Een afspiegeling van het oude China is het HUTONG, dat zich op de 28e verdieping van 'One Peking' bevindt. Het interieur doet denken aan koninklijke vertrekken met de traditionele bewerkte kamerschermen, zijden gordijnen en rode lantaarns. Met daarbij een fantastisch uitzicht op de skyline van Hongkong. De charme van de geschiedenis is hier gekoppeld aan de verworvenheden van de moderne tijd. En de keuken: traditionele Noord-Chinese gerechten met een eigentijdse touch.

MATSUBISHI JAPANESE RESTAURANT

ENG This characteristic Japanese restaurant has been renovated by Yasumichi Morita. The cuisine is traditional Hong Kong fare, the Teppanyaki cooking area is also traditional, as are the chosen themes: origami and Noh theater. The origami theme is reflected in the bold and expressive, straight and polygonal shapes on the oak walls. The Teppanyaki zone is constructed like a Noh stage, only instead of watching actors you can marvel at the artistry of the cooks. All the classical elements are here, the stage backdrop with pine trees, the expressive masks. "Matsu" is the Japanese word for pine tree, "MATSUBISHI" is the name of the restaurant. We've come full circle.

DEU Yasumichi Morita hat dieses typische japanische Restaurant renoviert. Hongkong-traditionell ist die Küche, traditionell die Teppanyaki-Cooking-Area und die gewählten Themen: Origami und Noh-Theater. Origami-Anklänge finden sich in den ausdrucksstarken geraden und polygonalen Formen auf den Eichenholzwänden. Die Teppanyaki-Zone ist aufgebaut wie eine Bühne für das Noh-Theater, denn wie dort die Schauspieler, bestechen hier die Köche durch ihre Kunstfertigkeit. Es finden sich die klassischen Elemente, das Bühnenbild mit Kiefern und die ausdrucksstarken Masken. „Matsu" bedeutet auf japanisch Kiefer, „MATSUBISHI" heißt das Restaurant. Der Kreis schließt sich.

FR La rénovation de ce restaurant japonais typique est signée Yasumichi Morita. On y cuisine à la mode traditionnelle Hongkongaise. Le Teppanyaki, la cuisine ouverte, témoigne lui aussi de la tradition, tout comme les thèmes choisis que sont l'origami et le théâtre Nô. On retrouve l'origami dans les formes vives et expressives, droites et polygonales des parois de chêne. Le Teppanyaki est quant à lui construit sur le modèle de la scène Nô, à la seule différence que l'on y admire des artistes culinaires plutôt que tragiques. L'ensemble des éléments classiques du théâtre sont présents, des fresques de pins formant le décor de scène jusqu'aux fameux masques d'expression. « Matsu », qui signifie pin en japonais, a entraîné « MATSUBISHI », le nom de ce restaurant.

NED Yasumichi Morita heeft dit typisch Japanse restaurant gerenoveerd. Traditioneel Hongkongs is de keuken, traditioneel het Teppanyaki-kookgedeelte en de gekozen thema's: origami en noh-theater. Sporen van origami bevinden zich op de expressieve rechte en veelhoekige vormen op de eikenhouten wanden. De Teppanyaki-zone is gebouwd als een toneel voor het noh-theater, want net als daarbij de toneelspelers, fascineren hier de koks met hun vakmanschap. De klassieke elementen worden er aangetroffen: het decor met pijnbomen en de expressieve maskers. 'Matsu' betekent in het Japans pijnboom, 'MATSUBISHI' heet het restaurant. De cirkel is gesloten.

THE KITCHEN – W HONG KONG

CHINA | HONG KONG | RESTAURANTS

ENG On one side are the cooks as they prepare cuisine that's truly a cut above the rest, and on the other is Hong Kong Harbor. The nucleus of this bright and lively restaurant is a large communal table for individual guests. Of course, there are also private tables for parties of two or more. Wide hallways, generous space between tables, fanciful installations, fabulous harbor views. The off-beat collection of designer furniture, lamps, and art pieces is characteristic of the entire W HONG KONG. Audacious, imaginative, brilliant—with or without limit.

DEU Auf der einen Seite die Köche bei der Zubereitung eines wahrlich nicht durchschnittlichen Menüs, auf der anderen Hong-kongs Hafen. Nukleus des hellen und lebhaften Restaurants ist ein großer Tisch für Gäste ohne Begleitung. Dazu gibt es natürlich auch private Tische für zwei und mehr Personen. Weite Gänge, großzügiger Platz zwischen den Tischen, verspielte Installationen, phantastische Hafenansichten. Die ausgefallene Sammlung von Designer-Mobiliar, Leuchten und Kunstobjekten ist kennzeichnend für das ganze W HONG KONG. Verwegen, phantasievoll, genial – mit und ohne Grenzen.

FR Vous découvrez d'un côté les cuisiniers attelés à la préparation de mets sortant de l'ordinaire et de l'autre le port de Hong Kong. Le centre névralgique de ce restaurant clair et animé est une large table commune. Des tables plus intimes sont également disponibles pour les repas à deux ou en groupe. De larges allées, un espace généreux entre les tables, des installations fantaisistes et une vue surprenante sur le port composent un décor agréable. Une collection excentrique de meubles, lampes et œuvres d'art caractérise aussi le W HONG KONG, dont le style est audacieux, imaginatif et brillant.

NED Aan de ene kant de koks die een menu bereiden dat beslist niet alledaags is, aan de andere kant de haven van Hongkong. Middelpunt van het lichte en levendige restaurant is een grote tafel voor gasten zonder gezelschap. Verder zijn er natuurlijk ook privétafels voor twee of meer personen. Brede gangen, ruim plaats tussen de tafels, speelse constructies, fantastische uitzichten op de haven. De buitenissige verzameling designermeubilair, lampen en kunstvoorwerpen is kenmerkend voor het hele W HONG KONG. Vermetel, fantasievol, geniaal – met en zonder grenzen.

TIVO

ENG TIVO, short for "aperitivo", is an Italian-style bar. Like a typical Italian bar, it strives to be the center of social life. And, like Italy, everything here is bathed in warm colors, inviting and comfortable. Interior designer David Yeo provided two central features: wooden hanging lamps against the backdrop of back-lit wine racks and an oval-shaped central bar with concave sides, inspired by the inside of a wine barrel. It's the perfect place for a quick espresso on your feet, or sitting and lingering awhile.

DEU Das TIVO, kurz für „Aperitivo", ist eine Bar nach italienischem Vorbild. Es will, wie die typische italienische Bar, Zentrum des sozialen Lebens sein. Wie in Italien ist auch hier alles in warme Farben getaucht, einladend und behaglich. Innenarchitekt David Yeo sah zwei zentrale Features vor: Hängeleuchten aus Holz vor dem Hintergrund von hinterleuchteten Weinregalen und eine ovale zentrale Bar mit konkaven Seitenflächen, inspiriert von dem Inneren eines Weinfasses. Entstanden ist ein Ort für den schnellen Espresso im Stehen oder zum Verweilen.

FR TIVO, diminutif d' « aperitivo », est un bar à l'ambiance italienne. Comme en Italie, tout n'est que chaleur des coloris et invitation au confort pour ce lieu qui se veut centre de la vie sociale. L'architecte d'intérieur David Yeo lui a créé deux caractéristiques particulières : des suspensions lumineuses en bois sur fond de casiers à bouteilles et un bar central de forme ovale dont l'extérieur est concave, rappelant ainsi l'intérieur d'une barrique. C'est le lieu idéal pour un expresso sur le pouce ou une pause un peu plus longue.

NED Het TIVO, afkorting van 'Aperitivo', is een bar naar Italiaans voorbeeld. Het is bedoeld om net als de typische Italiaanse bar het middelpunt van het sociale leven te zijn. Net als in Italië baadt ook hier alles in warme kleuren, uitnodigend en behaaglijk. Binnenhuisarchitect David Yeo heeft twee centrale elementen ontworpen: hanglampen van hout tegen de achtergrond van vanachter verlichte wijnrekken en een ovale centrale bar met holle zijvlakken, geïnspireerd op de binnenkant van een wijnvat. Zo is een plek ontstaan voor een snelle espresso die staande wordt opgedronken, of om te verpozen.

HONEYCOMB

CHINA | SHENZHEN | RESTAURANTS

ENG The HONEYCOMB in Shenzhen is true to its name. A large room and a smaller one are modeled after traditional Chinese restaurants. The small room is traversed by transparent surfaces, the large room by white opaque surfaces. These white, honeycombed structures function like a partition, demarcating intimate VIP areas. The surfaces are covered in over 1000 oval holes, like the holes in a honeycomb, some back-lit, some arched, some flat. These give rise to organic shapes reminiscent of an organism of gigantic proportions. The brilliant mind behind this idea: architect Keiichiro Sako.

DEU Der Name bedeutet Honigwabe, und so sieht das HONEYCOMB in Shenzhen auch aus. Ein großer und ein kleiner Raum sind dem Aufbau des traditionellen chinesischen Restaurants nachempfunden. Transparente Flächen durchziehen den kleinen, weiße undurchsichtige den großen Raum. Diese weißen, wabenförmigen Gebilde grenzen ähnlich einem Raumteiler intime VIP-Bereiche ein. Über 1 000 ovale Löcher, Waben, durchziehen die Flächen, mal hinterleuchtet, mal gewölbt, mal flach. Es entstehen organische Formen, die an einen Organismus gigantischen Ausmaßes erinnern. Der geniale Kopf dieser Idee: Architekt Keiichiro Sako.

FR Le HONEYCOMB de Shenzhen porte bien son nom. Des structures blanches et alvéolaires servent à structurer le restaurant, en proposant des espaces VIP plus intimes. Les deux salles de taille très différentes, séparées par des parois transparentes ou opaques, rappellent les restaurants traditionnels du pays. Ces parois sont percées de milliers d'ovales, semblables aux alvéoles d'une ruche : certaines sont rétro-éclairées, d'autres allongées ou encore droites. Semblable à un organisme géant, cet ensemble sort de l'esprit étonnant de l'architecte Keiichiro Sako.

NED De naam betekent honingraat en zo ziet de HONEYCOMB in Shenzhen er ook uit. Een grote en een kleine ruimte zijn gebouwd naar het voorbeeld van het traditionele Chinese restaurant. Transparante vlakken vullen de kleine ruimte, witte ondoorzichtige de grote. Deze witte, honingraatvormige bouwsels omgrenzen net als een scheidingswand intieme VIP-gedeelten. Ruim 1000 ovale gaten, raten, zitten in de vlakken, soms van achteren verlicht, soms gewelfd, soms vlak. Er ontstaan organische vormen, die doen denken aan een organisme van gigantische afmetingen. Het brein achter dit idee: architect Keiichiro Sako.

SAFFRON

ENG In its nearly four-decade history, "the Park" has gone through a considerable number of different styles and interiors. Today, architects Prakash Mankar, Made Wijaya, and Carl Ettensperger give the hotel its contemporary touch. The SAFFRON is known for excellent contemporary Indian cuisine. The same applies to the ambience. A refined cosmic look has been combined with highly sophisticated modern elements, all deeply rooted in Indian tradition and with a pronounced sense of modern art.

DEU In seiner fast vier Jahrzehnte währenden Geschichte hat „The Park" eine stattliche Zahl an Stilrichtungen und Interieurs durchlaufen. Heute geben die Architekten Prakash Mankar, Made Wijaya und Carl Ettensperger dem Hotel seine zeitgenössische Note. Das SAFFRON steht für exzellente zeitgenössische indische Küche. Wie die Küche, so das Ambiente: Ein raffinierter kosmischer Look wurde mit sehr edlen modernen Elementen kombiniert, alles tief verwurzelt in der indischen Tradition und mit einem ausgeprägten Sinn für moderne Kunst.

FR Au cours de ces presque quarante ans d'histoire, « the Park » a changé de style et de décoration à de nombreuses reprises. Aujourd'hui, ce sont les architectes Prakash Mankar, Made Wijaya et Carl Ettensperger qui ont donné à l'hôtel son allure contemporaine. Le SAFFRON propose une cuisine indienne contemporaine d'excellence et il en va de même pour l'ambiance qui y règne. Son apparence cosmique raffinée est liée à un goût certain pour l'art moderne ainsi qu'à des éléments modernes et sophistiqués, tous profondément ancrés dans la tradition indienne.

NED In zijn bijna vier decennia lange geschiedenis heeft 'The Park' een behoorlijk aantal stijlrichtingen en interieurs doorlopen. Nu geven de architecten Prakash Mankar, Made Wijaya en Carl Ettensperger het hotel zijn eigentijdse cachet. Het SAFFRON biedt een uitmuntende eigentijdse Indiase keuken. Zo de keuken, zo de ambiance. Een geraffineerde kosmische look werd gecombineerd met heel kostbare moderne elementen, alles diep geworteld in de Indiase traditie met een uitgesproken gevoel voor moderne kunst.

243

ENG A casual bistro, a place for everyday with an out-of-the-ordinary but affordable menu, with an appealing and low-key design, a bar, and a restaurant—the LOEWY is all that and more. At the straight 15 meter (50 foot) bar you can get your fill of all the "old" classics as well as a selection of the finest single malts. The cuisine ranges from gourmet Asian chicken dishes to escargot, a mix of simple and exotic delicacies. And if the name of the place sounds familiar, that's because its namesake is none other than Raymond Loewy, father of industrial design.

DEU Ein legeres Bistro, ein alltagstauglicher Platz mit einem ungewöhnlichen aber bezahlbaren Angebot, ansprechend designt und ungezwungen dekoriert, Bar und Restaurant – all das ist das LOEWY. Über die schnurgerade 15 Meter lange Theke wandern die „alten" Klassiker und eine Auswahl der besten Fine-Single-Malts. Fein gemachtes orientalisches Huhn rangiert neben Schnecken, Einfaches neben Luxuriösem. Und seinen Namen hat das Ganze von einem ganz Großen: von Raymond Loewy, dem Vater des Industriedesign.

FR C'est un bistro décontracté, un lieu du quotidien dont le menu sort de l'ordinaire, tout en restant abordable; c'est un design discret et attrayant, un bar et un restaurant – le LOEWY c'est tout cela à la fois, et bien plus encore. Il est possible de s'installer à ce bar de 15 mètres de long pour commander un whisky classique comme une sélection comme une des single malts les plus fins. Le chef propose un savant mélange de simplicité et de mets raffinés allant de la gastronomie asiatique aux escargots. Si le nom de cet établissement vous est familier, c'est sans doute parce que son homonyme n'est autre que Raymond Loewy, le père du design industriel.

NED Een comfortabele bistro, een alledaagse plaats met een ongewoon maar betaalbaar aanbod, aantrekkelijk ontworpen en ongedwongen gedecoreerd, bar en restaurant – dat alles is het LOEWY. Boven de kaarsrechte 15 meter lange tapkast zwerven de oude 'klassiekers' en een keur aan de beste fine single malts. Fijn klaargemaakte oosterse kip naast slakken, eenvoud naast luxe. En de naam is afkomstig van een hele grote: van Raymond Loewy, de vader van het industrieel ontwerp.

ROSSO

ENG The ROSSO's expansion was inspired by the rolling green hills, deep-ridged fields, and oak-shaded resting places of the Yezre-el Valley in northern Israel. The architects at SO Architecture got their cue from the main motifs of this landscape, translating them into architectural form. The furrowed fields are framed by windows, a pattern continued in the ceiling and encompassing the entire restaurant. Chairs and windows are done up in plant motifs, all of which strengthens the connection to the landscape. At ROSSO guests sit inside and yet, in a way, also outside, in the midst of the beautiful landscape around Ramat Yishay.

DEU Die sanften grünen Hügel des Valley of Yezre-el im Norden Israels, seine furchigen Felder und schattige Ruheplätze unter Eichen waren die Quelle der Inspiration für die Erweiterung des ROSSO. Die Architekten von SO Architecture griffen die zentralen Motive der Landschaft auf und gaben ihnen eine architektonische Form. Die zerfurchten Felder sind durch Fenster gerahmt, ihre Form wird fortgeführt in der Decke und umfasst so das ganze Restaurant. Stühle und Fenster zieren Pflanzenmotive – all das, um die Verbindung mit der Landschaft zu verstärken. Der Gast des Rosso sitzt innen und irgendwie auch draußen inmitten der wunderschönen Landschaft rund um Ramat Yishay.

FR L'extension du ROSSO s'inspire des collines ondoyantes, des champs profondément labourés et des lieux ombragés de la vallée de Yezre-el au nord d'Israël. Les architectes de SO Architecture ont étudié les motifs dominants de ce paysage pour les traduire en une structure architecturale concrète. Les sillons des champs voisins sont encadrés par les fenêtres, dont le motif est repris au plafond et présent dans l'ensemble du restaurant. Chaises et fenêtres sont décorées de motifs floraux afin de renforcer le lien avec le paysage. Lorsque l'on s'assoit à l'intérieur du ROSSO, on se sent également d'une certaine manière, à l'extérieur, dans un paysage surplombant Ramat Yishay.

NED De zachte groene heuvels van de Yezreel-vallei in het noorden van Israël, met zijn gegroefde akkers en beschaduwde rustplaatsen onder eiken waren de inspiratiebron voor de uitbreiding van het ROSSO. De architecten van SO Architecture pakten de centrale motieven van het landschap op en gaven ze een architectonische vorm. De doorploegde velden zijn omlijst door vensters, hun vorm wordt doorgevoerd in het plafond en omvat zo het hele restaurant. Stoelen en ramen zijn versierd met plantenmotieven, alles om de verbinding met het landschap te versterken. De gast van het ROSSO zit binnen en in zekere zin ook buiten, midden in het wondermooie landschap rondom Ramat Yishay.

ENG MAN is a traditional Japanese tea room in a modern interpretation. Tea room architecture is said to be among the most challenging, despite its simplicity. The materials: wood and bamboo. Two rooms, one for preparing the tea, the other for the ceremony. The floor is covered in tatami mats, as are the walls. And then there are the shoji, the traditional sliding walls made of translucent paper in cedar frames. They filter the light, pleasantly diffusing it throughout the room. The space is sparsely decorated and contains a tokonoma alcove with an ink scroll and a simple flower arrangement. Floor lighting beautifully illuminates the dancing geishas. As the name implies, the MAN is for men only.

DEU Das MAN ist ein traditioneller japanischer Teeraum, modern interpretiert. Es heißt, die Architektur des Teeraums sei bei aller Schlichtheit mit die anspruchsvollste. Die Materialien: Holz und Bambus. Zwei Räume, einer für die Teezubereitung, einer für die Zeremonie. Der Boden ist bedeckt mit Tatamimatten, ebenso die Wände, dazu Shoji, die traditionellen Schiebewände aus mit durchscheinendem Japanpapier bespannten Zedernholzstreifen. Sie filtern das Licht und verteilen es angenehm gleichmäßig. Wenig Dekoration, eine Tokonoma-Nische mit einer Tuschezeichnung und ein einfaches Gesteck. In den Boden integriertes Licht verschönert den Tanz der Geishas. Das MAN – ein Ort nur für Männer.

FR MAN est une maison de thé traditionnelle réinterprétée par la modernité. Malgré son apparente simplicité, l'architecture des maisons de thé figure parmi les plus audacieuses en utilisant des matériaux comme le bois et le bambou. Une première pièce sert à la préparation du thé et une seconde à la cérémonie. Le sol et les murs sont recouverts de tatamis, tandis que les shoji, les parois coulissantes traditionnelles faites de papier et d'un cadre en cèdre, ouvrent sur une autre pièce. Celles-ci filtrent la lumière et la diffusent pour mettre en valeur les danses des geishas et la décoration minimaliste ; on y trouve une alcôve tokonoma ne présentant qu'un simple arrangement floral et une estampe. Comme son nom l'indique, le MAN est réservé aux hommes.

NED MAN is een traditionele Japanse theeruimte, modern geïnterpreteerd. Dat wil zeggen, de architectuur van de theeruimte behoort ondanks alle eenvoud tot de meest verfijnde. De materialen: hout en bamboe. Twee ruimten, een voor het bereiden van de thee, een voor de ceremonie. De vloer is bedekt met tantami-matten, net als de wanden, verder shoji, de traditionele schuifwanden van met doorschijnend Japans papier bespande cederhouten stroken. Ze filteren het licht en verdelen het aangenaam gelijkmatig. Weinig decoratie, een tokonoma-nis met een prent en een eenvoudig bloemstukje. In de vloer geïntegreerd licht verfraait de dans van de geisha's. MAN – een plek alleen voor mannen.

UEYANAGI

ENG A taboo violated! A geisha bar and a tea house under one roof. The execution is as traditional as the concept is audacious. Like the MAN, the UEYANAGI is based on traditional models. Kyoto is the center of Japanese geisha culture and the tea ceremony, and is also the birthplace of Noh theater. The UEYANAGI is a visual expression of this. Classic elements and traditional techniques are linked with the culture of this region and amplified by the customary Noh backdrops with their depiction of pine trees.

DEU Ein Tabubruch! Eine Geisha-Bar und ein Tee-Haus unter einem Dach. So verwegen dieser Umstand, so traditionell die Umsetzung. Wie das MAN orientiert sich auch das UEYANAGI an den traditionellen Vorgaben. Kyoto ist das Zentrum der japanischen Geisha-Kultur, der Tee-Zerenomie und die Geburtsstätte des Noh-Theaters. Das Ueyanagi ist visueller Ausdruck dafür. Klassische Elemente und traditionelle Techniken sind an die Kultur dieser Region geknüpft, ergänzt von den mit Kiefern geschmückten Bühnenbildern des Noh-Theaters.

FR Un tabou est levé ! Un bar à geishas et une maison de thé sont réunis sous un même toit et leur réalisation est aussi tradition-nelle que le concept est audacieux. À l'instar du MAN, l'UEYANAGI réinvente les modèles traditionnels. Pour le Japon, Kyoto est un véritable centre culturel : de la cérémonie du thé en passant par la présence des geishas, c'est également le lieu de naissance du théâtre Nô. L'UEYANAGI est l'expression visuelle de ce foisonnement : les éléments classiques et les techniques artistiques tra-ditionnelles sont étroitement liés à la culture locale de cette région et amplifiés par des fresques Nô représentant des pins.

NED Een doorbroken taboe! Een geishabar en een theehuis onder één dak. Zo vermetel als deze omstandigheid is, zo traditioneel is de uitvoering. Net als het MAN is ook het UEYANAGI afgestemd op de traditionele richtlijnen. Kyoto is het centrum van de Japan-se geishacultuur, de theeceremonie en de geboorteplaats van het noh-theater. Het UEYANAGI is de visuele uitdrukking ervan. Klassieke elementen en traditionele technieken zijn aan de cultuur van deze regio gekoppeld, aangevuld door de met pijnbomen versierde decors van het noh-theater.

MITSUI MURATA

ENG The award-winning MITSUI MURATA has been distinguished for its interior design, which is based on a design by Glamorous. Even from the exterior the building is stylish, with an installation of traditional Japanese roof tiles bathed in blue light. The interior is a Japanese restaurant, inviting, warm, and elegant. The walls are made of an installation of 3,000 stacked masu cups, the characteristic cubic wooden drinking vessels traditionally used to serve sake.

DEU Das MITSUI MURATA wurde für sein Interior Design, das auf einen Entwurf von Glamorous zurückgeht, ausgezeichnet. Stylish ist schon das Gebäude von außen, mit einer in blaues Licht getauchten Installation aus typischen japanischen Dachziegeln. Innen ein japanisches Speiserestaurant, einladend, warm, elegant. Die Wände bestehen aus einer Installation von 3 000 übereinander gestapelten Masu-Bechern, jenen typischen würfelförmigen Trinkbechern aus Holz, in denen traditionell der Sake gereicht wird.

FR MITSUI MURATA s'est vu maintes fois récompensé pour son design intérieur créé sur une idée de Glamorous. Le bâtiment respire l'élégance, grâce à une installation de tuiles traditionnelles japonaises baignées d'une lumière bleue. À l'intérieur, on y trouve un restaurant japonais, accueillant, chaleureux et élégant. Un imposant mur de 3 000 masus, des gobelets cubiques traditionnels en bois dans lesquels on sert généralement du saké, fait toute la différence.

NED Het MITSUI MURATA is onderscheiden voor zijn interieurontwerp, dat stamt van een ontwerp van Glamorous. Alleen al aan de buitenkant is het gebouw stijlvol, met een in blauw licht badende constructie van typische Japanse dakpannen. Binnen een Japans restaurant, uitnodigend, warm, elegant. De wanden bestaan uit een constructie van 3000 op elkaar gestapelde masu-bekers, die typische kubusvormige houten drinkbekers, waarin traditioneel sake wordt aangeboden.

TOKYO CURRY LAB

ENG TOKYO CURRY LAB: an "experimental laboratory" for curry dishes located in the Tokyo Tower. The name says it all. There's no limit to the experimentation here. It's called a "lab" and looks like one too. A clinical ultra-modern design with an "experiment table" in the middle and seating around it, each with its own monitor, and the motley assortment of curries in test tubes. Truly a unique restaurant. The innovative designers at Wonderwall are behind all of this.

DEU TOKYO CURRY LAB: Ein „Versuchslaboratorium" für Currygerichte im Tokyo Tower. Der Name sagt alles. Hier kann nach Belieben mit Curry experimentiert werden. Es heißt „Labor" und sieht auch so aus. Steril, ultramodern, im Zentrum ein „Versuchstisch", die Plätze ringsherum, je mit eigenem Bildschirm, in Reagenzgläsern die bunte Vielfalt des Curry. Wahrlich ein Restaurant der besonderen Art. Und dahinter stecken die innovativen Designer von Wonderwall.

FR TOKYO CURRY LAB est un « laboratoire expérimental » situé dans la Tokyo Tower. Son nom en dit bien assez long sur ce que l'on peut y déguster et les expérimentations autour du curry n'ont ici aucune limite. Le lieu porte le nom de « labo » car il en a aussi l'apparence. Son design est ultramoderne et aseptisé : une « table d'expériences » entourée de chaises au beau milieu de la salle, chacune possédant son propre écran, et un assortiment hétéroclite de currys dans des tubes à essai. C'est un restaurant tout bonnement unique et tout droit sorti des esprits créatifs de Wonderwall.

NED TOKYO CURRY LAB: Een 'proeflaboratorium' voor kerrieschotels in de Tokyo-toren. De naam zegt alles. Hier kan naar hartenlust met kerrie worden geëxperimenteerd. Het heet 'lab' en ziet er ook zo uit. Steriel, ultramodern, in het midden een 'proeftafel', de plaatsen rondom, elk met eigen beeldscherm, in reageerbuizen de bonte verscheidenheid aan kerrieschotels. Waarlijk een heel bijzonder restaurant. En erachter zitten de innovatieve ontwerpers van Wonderwall.

ITHAA AT ARI ATOLL – CONRAD MALDIVES RANGALI ISLAND

MALDIVES | SOUTH ARI ATOLL | RESTAURANTS

ENG The finest white sand beach, crystal clear water, plus the comfort of the ARI ATOLL CONRAD MALDIVES luxury hotel. As if that weren't enough, visitors to "Ithaa" will discover the world's first undersea restaurant—dining in the middle of a coral reef. Thanks to the latest aquarium technology, up to 14 people can enjoy an unimpeded view of the fantastical underwater world under a giant rippled acrylic-glass dome. And lest you believe the food is merely an afterthought here, rest assured that you will find the very best that Maldivian cuisine has to offer.

DEU Feinster Sandstrand, kristallklares Wasser, dazu der Komfort des Luxushotels ARI ATOLL CONRAD MALDIVES: Als wäre das alles nichts, erwartet den Reisenden im „Ithaa", dem weltweit ersten Unterwasser-Restaurant, ein Dinner mitten im Korallenriff. Unter der riesigen gewellten Acrylglashaube können dank modernster Aquariumstechnik bis zu 14 Personen einen uneingeschränkten Blick auf die phantastische Unterwasserwelt genießen. Zu essen, und das gerät schon fast zur Nebensache, gibt es nur das Beste, was die maledivische Küche zu bieten hat.

FR Le sable blanc le plus fin du monde et l'eau cristalline ne constituent qu'une infime partie de ce que le luxueux hôtel ARI ATOLL CONRAD MALDIVES peut offrir. Comme si cela ne suffisait pas, les visiteurs d' « Ithaa » découvriront le premier restaurant sous-marin au monde, où l'on peut dîner face à la barrière de corail. Grâce à une technologie de pointe, 14 personnes peuvent jouir d'un moment unique face au fantastique monde sous-marin, sous une gigantesque coupole de plexiglas. Et si vous pensez que la cuisine n'est qu'un prétexte, assurez-vous d'y trouver le meilleur de ce que les Maldives offrent aux fins gourmets.

NED Het fijnste zandstrand, kristalhelder water, en ook nog het comfort van het luxehotel ARI ATOLL CONRAD MALEDIVES: alsof het allemaal niets is, wacht de reiziger in het 'Ithaa', het eerste onderwaterrestaurant ter wereld, een diner midden in het koraalrif. Onder de reusachtige gewelfde kap van acrylglas kunnen dankzij de modernste aquariumtechniek tot veertien personen van een onbeperkte blik op de fantastische onderwaterwereld genieten. Om te eten, en dat wordt al gauw bijzaak, is er alleen het beste wat de Maldivische kust te bieden heeft.

JING

ENG A contemporary Chinese restaurant in the "One Fullerton Building" on the shore of Marina Bay, created by Atela Eraso Architectes. The dining area is separated into a main room and two smaller private areas. The interaction between accessories, furnishings and contemporary art is captivating. The ceiling is of geometric design with recessed lights that bathe the room in shades of gold. The floor is volcanic rock, with light from modular strips of rice paper, plus wooden ornamentation and a red palette of luxurious silk fabrics. The furniture and fixtures are reminiscent of 1930s China, while the seats number a lucky 88.

DEU Ein zeitgenössisches chinesisches Restaurant im „One Fullerton Building," am Ufer der Marina Bay, gemacht von Atela Eraso Architectes. Der Speisebereich ist in einen Hauptraum und zwei kleinere Separees unterteilt. Bestechend die Interaktion von Accessoires, Möbeln und zeitgenössischer Kunst. Die Decke ist geometrisch dekomponiert, mit verborgenen Leuchtkörpern, die den Raum in Schattierungen von Gold tauchen. Der Boden aus Vulkanstein, das Licht aus modularen Reispapier-Strecken, dazu Holzverzierungen und eine rote Palette luxuriöser Seidenstoffe. Möbel und Armaturen erinnern an das China der 1930er-Jahre, die Anzahl der Plätze, 88, an Glück.

FR Voici un restaurant chinois contemporain situé dans le « One Fullerton Building », le long de Marina Bay, créé par Atela Eraso Architectes. Une pièce principale et deux salons privés sont le cadre d'une interaction captivante entre les accessoires, le mobilier et de l'art contemporain, grâce aux motifs géométriques du plafond et à des luminaires discrets baignant la pièce de reflets dorés. Le sol en pierre volcanique contraste avec la lumière traversant des bandes de papier de riz. Une frise de bois et un camaïeu de luxueux tissus dans les tons rouges donnent une touche inimitable au lieu. Le mobilier rappelle la Chine des années 1930, tandis que le nombre de chaises (88) sert de porte-bonheur.

NED Een eigentijds Chinees restaurant in het 'One Fullerton Building', aan de oever van de Marina Bay, gemaakt door Atela Eraso Architectes. Het eetgedeelte is in een hoofdruimte en twee kleinere chambres séparées onderverdeeld. Aantrekkelijk is de interactie van accessoires, meubels en moderne kunst. Het plafond valt geometrisch uiteen, met verborgen lichtgevende voorwerpen die de ruimte doen baden in goudschakeringen. De vloer van vulkaansteen, het licht van modulaire banen rijstpapier, met verder houtversieringen en een rood palet luxueuze zijden stoffen. Meubels en armaturen herinneren aan het China van de jaren 1930, het aantal plaatsen, 88, aan geluk.

ENG TRISARA means "third garden of heaven", but you're not forbidden from entering this divine space. This luxury resort with individual villas is situation on Naithorn Bay in the northwest of Phuket, nestled in the thick tropical rain forest. The details: open day beds for lounging in the shade of coconut palms, marble, teak, a private pool. A sleeping Buddha angel in front of the door conveys a stern "Do not disturb". There is an al fresco restaurant on the ocean-front teak deck, with the philosophy of preparing the finest ingredients in such a way that their flavor and unique characteristics are perfectly preserved. And if you prefer a more intimate dining experience, you can always reserve a personal cook for dinner at your private pool.

DEU TRISARA bedeutet „Dritter Garten des Himmels", und sein Betreten ist nicht verboten. Im Nordwesten Phukets, an der Naithorn Bay, befindet sich dieses Luxusresort mit einzelnen Villen, eingebettet in den dichten tropischen Regenwald. Die Details: offene Ruhebetten im Schatten von Kokospalmen, Marmor, Teakholz und Außenduschen im privaten Pool. Ein schlafender Buddha-Engel vor der Tür vermittelt verbindlich: „Bitte nicht stören". Und auf dem Oceanfront-Teak-Deck ein Restaurant im Freien, das sich der Philosophie verschrieben hat, das Feinste so zuzubereiten, dass Geschmack und Besonderheit erhalten bleiben. Wer es gerne intimer hat, reserviert einen eigenen Koch für ein abendliches Menü am Privatpool.

FR TRISARA signifie « troisième jardin paradisiaque », mais personne ne vous empêchera d'entrer dans cet espace divin. Ce luxueux complexe doté de villas individuelles se situe à Naithorn Bay, au nord-ouest de Phuket, niché au cœur d'une dense forêt tropicale. Il propose des banquettes à l'ombre des cocotiers, du marbre, du teck ou une piscine privée. Un Bouddha endormi garde la porte d'entrée en chuchotant « Ne pas déranger ». Un restaurant ouvert sur une terrasse en teck fait face à l'océan et la philosophie du lieu est de préparer les ingrédients les plus raffinés afin que leur saveur et leur caractéristique unique en soient totalement préservées. Si vous préférez dîner plus intimement au bord de votre piscine privée, il est toujours possible de réserver un cuisinier.

NED TRISARA betekent 'Derde Tuin van de Hemel' en hij mag betreden worden. In het noordwesten van Phuket, aan de Naithornbaai, bevindt zich dit luxeresort met afzonderlijke villa's, verscholen in het dichte tropische regenwoud. De details: open rustbedden in de schaduw van kokospalmen, marmer, teakhout en buitendouches in het privézwembad. Een slapende Boeddha-engel voor de deur deelt vriendelijk mede: 'Gelieve niet te storen'. En op het teakhouten stranddek een restaurant in de openlucht, dat de filosofie huldigt altijd het allerbeste zo te bereiden, dat de smaak en het bijzondere ervan behouden blijven. Wie van meer intimiteit houdt, kan een eigen kok reserveren voor een avondmenu aan het privézwembad.

NIGHTLIFE
BARS, LOUNGES AND CLUBS

SHIRO

CHINA | HONG KONG | NIGHTLIFE

ENG This is a stylish version of a traditional Japanese kaiten sushi restaurant with reflections on the fashion world. Here you will find delicate, creative Japanese cuisine and a 25-seat bar with quite an extensive selection of sake and innovative cocktails. The interior, by David Yeo, is as unconventional as its sushi dishes. A stylized samurai motif pervades the entire space. There is a sushi "runway" and for those on the go: "sushi prĐt-à-porter".

DEU Es ist die stylishe Variante des traditionellen japanischen Kaiten-Sushi-Restaurants mit Anklängen an die Welt der Mode. Dazu delikate, ausgefallene japanische Küche und eine Bar mit 25 Plätzen mit einer geradezu extensiven Auswahl an Sake und innovativen Cocktails. Das Interieur von David Yeo ist ausgefallen wie die Sushi-Variationen. Überall finden sich stilisierte Symbole der Samurai. Dazu ein Sushi-„Laufsteg", und für die Rastlosen: „Sushi prêt-à-porter".

FR Cette version élégante des traditionnels restaurants à sushi japonais, les kaiten, fait aussi référence au monde de la mode. On trouve ici une cuisine japonaise délicate et créative ainsi qu'un bar de 25 places où déguster une sélection interminable de sakés et de cocktails innovants. L'intérieur, pensé par David Yeo, est aussi peu conventionnel que les sushis proposés. Un motif samurai stylisé envahit tout l'espace et le « tapis roulant » propose des sushis à déguster sur place et des « sushis prêt-à-emporter » pour les plus pressés.

NED Het is de chique variant van het traditionele Japanse kaiten-sushi restaurant met lichte overeenkomsten met de wereld van de mode. Verder een delicate, buitenissige Japanse keuken en een bar met 25 plaatsen mel een bijna extensieve keuze aan sake en innovatieve cocktails. Het interieur van David Yeo is net zo buitenissig als de sushi-variaties. Overal bevinden zich gestileerde symbolen van de samoerai. Verder een sushi-'plankier' en voor rusteloze personen: 'sushi prêt-à-porter'.

UMAMI AT LE MERIDIEN CYBERPORT

CHINA | HONG KONG | NIGHTLIFE

ENG "Umami" is a Japanese word which roughly translates into "greatest delicacy". And that's just what you'll find at this trendy sushi bar and restaurant located in the "LE MERIDIEN CYBERPORT", an "art and tech hotel" by LRF Designers. Exquisite sushi and sashimi interpretations both inside and out. A stylish ambience inside, and a bamboo garden house outside. Both delicious and a welcome departure from the norm.

DEU „Umami" kommt aus dem Japanischen und bedeutet frei übersetzt „größte Köstlichkeit". Solches bietet das UMAMI, trendige Sushi-Bar und Restaurant, im „LE MERIDIEN CYBERPORT", einem „Art-and-Tech-Hotel" von LRF Designers. Exquisite Interpretationen von Sushi und Sashimi außen wie innen. Innen in einem stilvollen Ambiente, außen im Bamboo-Garden-House. Köstlich und ein wenig anders als sonst.

FR En japonais, « Umami » signifie « plus grand délice ». Et c'est exactement ce que vous trouverez dans ce restaurant et sushi bar très tendance, situé dans « LE MERIDIEN CYBERPORT », un « hôtel art et tech » créé par LRF Designers. Les sushis et sashimis réinterprétés y sont exquis et peuvent être dégustés à l'intérieur dans une ambiance raffinée ou à l'extérieur dans une maison de jardin construite en bambou. S'y arrêter est une véritable invitation à la sérénité.

NED 'Umami' komt uit het Japans en betekent vrij vertaald 'grote heerlijkheid'. Dit is precies wat het UMAMI biedt: een trendy sushibar en restaurant, in 'LE MERIDIEN CYBERPORT', een 'Art-Tech-Hotel' van LRF Designers. Exquise interpretaties van sushi en sashimi van buiten en van binnen. Vanbinnen in een stijlvolle ambiance, vanbuiten in het Bamboo-Garden-House. Heerlijk en een beetje anders dan anders.

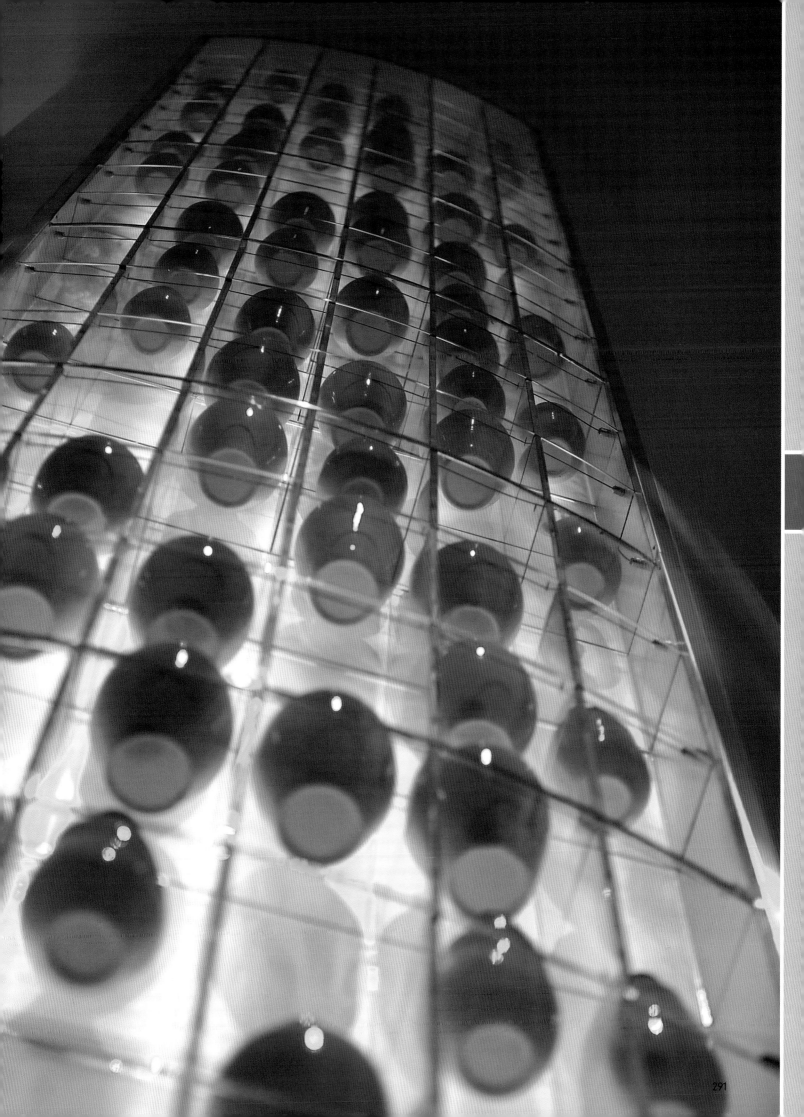

YUN FU

CHINA | HONG KONG | NIGHTLIFE

ENG The room division, with one large dining area and smaller private ones, reflects the classic Chinese dining experience. The entrance with its heavy oak doors is reminiscent of a noble estate. A steep staircase lined with Buddha statues leads to a round, tower-like room which houses the bar. The circle appears here as a symbol of unity and infinity, and again in the ceiling, in the traditional baskets, and in the arched hallway connecting the bar and main room. The wooden doors and red windows along the hallway are reminiscent of the facades one finds on the simple houses in a typical Chinese village. This location, with its deep connection to culture and tradition, is filled with symbols and inspires a wealth of associations.

DEU Die Aufteilung entspricht dem klassischen chinesischen Speiserestaurant, bestehend aus einem großen und kleinen privaten Speiseräumen. Der Eingang mit schweren Eichentüren erinnert an ein Herrschaftshaus. Eine steile, mit Buddhastatuen gesäumte Treppe führt in einen runden turmähnlichen Raum, die Bar, mit einer runden Theke. Der Kreis als Symbol von Einheit und Unendlichkeit findet sich dort, aber auch in der Decke, in den typischen Körben und in dem gebogenen Gang, der Bar und großen Saal verbindet. Die Holztüren und roten Glasfenster entlang des Ganges erinnern an die Fassaden des einfachen chinesischen Hauses in einem typischen Dorf. Dieser Ort, der tief verbunden ist mit Kultur und Tradition, ist voller Symbole und weckt viele Assoziationen.

FR La partition du lieu, proposant une vaste salle de restaurant et de petites alcôves privées, reflète les dîners classiques à la chinoise. L'entrée et ses lourdes portes de chêne rappellent une noble demeure. Les marches de l'escalier, qui présentent de nombreuses statues de Bouddha, mènent au bar, situé dans une salle ronde semblable à une tour ancienne. Le cercle est ici symbole d'unité et d'infini, notions présentes également au plafond, dans les paniers traditionnels ainsi que dans le passage vouté du bar à la salle principale. Les portes en bois et les fenêtres rouges du couloir rappellent les façades traditionnelles, de villages chinois. Ce lieu, permettant l'interaction de la culture avec la tradition, fourmille de symboles et inspire de riches associations.

NED De indeling stemt overeen met die van het klassieke Chinese restaurant, met een grote zaal en verder kleine besloten eetruimten. De ingang met zware eiken deuren doet denken aan een herenhuis. Een steile trap met Boeddhabeelden erlangs leidt naar een ronde, torenachtige ruimte, de bar, met een ronde tapkast. De cirkel als symbool van eenheid en oneindigheid bevindt zich daar, maar ook in het plafond, in de typische manden en in de gebogen gang, die de bar en de grote zaal met elkaar verbindt. De houten deuren en rode ruiten langs de gang herinneren aan de voorgevels van het eenvoudige Chinese huis in een karakteristiek dorp. Deze plaats, die diep verbonden is met cultuur en traditie, zit vol symbolen en roept veel associaties op.

ROXY

ENG The ROXY cocktail bar in Calcutta's "Park" hotel pays homage to the 1960s. Plain, spacious, free of frills and plush, the interior design is a close adaptation of the Bauhaus style. The only decoration is an installation of polished aluminum ovals, mounted on the simple brick wall. The shiny ovals reflect activities inside in all their facets, and not just figuratively.

DEU Die Cocktailbar ROXY im Hotel „The Park" in Kalkutta ist eine Hommage an die 1960er-Jahre. Schlicht, großzügig, ohne Schnörkel oder Plüsch orientiert sich das Interior Design eng am Bauhaus-Stil. Einziger Schmuck ist eine Installation aus polierten Aluminium-Ovalen, aufgebracht auf das schlichte Mauerwerk aus Ziegelstein. In den glänzenden Ovalen spiegelt sich das Innenleben, und das nicht nur sprichwörtlich, in allen seinen Facetten.

FR Le ROXY, bar à cocktails de l'hôtel « Park» de Calcutta, est un hommage aux années 1960. Simple, spacieux et sans fioritures, le design intérieur est une adaptation proche du mouvement Bauhaus. Le seul ornement est une installation constituée d'ovales d'aluminium poli, recouvrant un simple mur de briques. Ces ovales brillants reflètent de toutes leurs facettes l'activité du bar, au sens propre comme figuré.

NED De Cocktailbar ROXY in hotel 'The Park' in Kolkata is een hommage aan de jaren 1960. Het interieurontwerp is eenvoudig, royaal, zonder franje of pluche en nauw afgestemd op de Bauhausstijl. De enige versiering is een constructie van gepolijste aluminium ovalen, aangebracht op het eenvoudige metselwerk van baksteen. In de glimmende ovalen weerspiegelt zich het leven binnen, en dat niet alleen spreekwoordelijk, in al zijn facetten.

BLUE FROG

INDIA | MUMBAI | NIGHTLIFE

ENG BLUE FROG is a revolutionary music project in Mumbai. Production, sound lab, records, and a club done up in 1970s style with an almost UFO-like elegance are all spread out over 1,000 square meters (10,764 square feet) inside an old warehouse in the Mill District. Designers Chris Lee and Kaptil Gupta of Serie have created a cohesive yet provocative space in which they have reduced the number of visual stimuli in favor of fewer, and therefore bolder, elements. The stylized grinder of a mill appears in various interpretations on different levels and around the seating areas, always in mahogany.

DEU BLUE FROG ist ein revolutionäres Musikprojekt in Mumbai. Produktion, Soundlab, Records und ein im Stil der 1970er-Jahre gestylter Club, der geradezu UFOesk-elegant wirkt, verteilen sich auf 1 000 Quadratmetern in den Mauern eines alten Lagerhauses im Mill District. Die Designer Chris Lee und Kaptil Gupta von Serie schufen einen zusammenhängenden und trotzdem aufregenden Raum, indem sie die Anzahl visueller Hervorhebungen reduzierten zugunsten einiger weniger und dafür besonders starker Reize. Das Mahlwerk einer Mühle findet sich stilisiert wieder um die Sitzgruppen, auf unterschiedlichen Ebenen in verschiedenen Ausführungen – aber immer aus Mahagoni.

FR Le BLUE FROG est un projet musical révolutionnaire de Bombay. Un lieu de production et de vente de disques, un studio audio et un club inspiré des années 1970 d'une élégance quasi extraterrestre sont réunis sur environ 1 000 mètres carrés, dans un ancien entrepôt du quartier industriel. Les designers Chris Lee et Kaptil Gupta de chez Serie ont créé un espace cohésif mais provocateur dans lequel les stimuli visuels ont été réduits afin de ne privilégier que les plus audacieux. Les multiples interprétations d'un moulin stylisé apparaissent à différents niveaux et autour des banquettes en acajou.

NED BLUE FROG is een revolutionair muziekproject in Mumbai. Productie, soundlab, platen en een in de stijl van de jaren 1970 vormgegeven club, die bijna ufo-achtig elegant aandoet, bevinden zich verspreid over 1000 vierkante meter in de muren van een oud pakhuis in het Mill District. De ontwerpers Chris Lee en Kaptil Gupta van Serie schiepen een logische en toch opwindende ruimte, waarin zij de hoeveelheid visuele prikkels terugbrachten om de overblijvende juist een sterker effect te geven. Het maalwerk van een molen komt in gestileerde vorm steeds terug rond de zitgroepen, op verschillende niveaus in verschillende uitvoeringen – maar altijd van mahonie.

LEGGENDA

ISRAEL | RAMAT ISHAY | NIGHTLIFE

ᴱᴺᴳ SO Architecture is the creative force behind an ambitious renovation of the new LEGGENDA ice cream and yogurt shop. A particular challenge was posed by the nature of the space itself, a former carpenter's shop measuring 4.5 x 18.5 meters (14.5 x 60.5 feet) with a 2.3-meter-high (7.5-foot-high) ceiling, with portions of the building's foundations in the interior. The goal: a stylish shop with an airy, tranquil flair. The idea: two linear elements that draw customers into the shop. To the left is an integrated pinewood bar where customers can sit and which conceals parts of the foundation, with displays to the right, and a dark concrete floor throughout. This highlights the displays and shows customers the way into the rear portion of the shop, where they will discover "cozy" seats.

ᴰᴱᵁ SO Architecture sind die kreativen Köpfe hinter einem anspruchsvollen Umbau für den neuen Shop von LEGGENDA Ice Cream and Yogurt. Die räumlichen Gegebenheiten, eine frühere Zimmermannswerkstatt mit einer Fläche von 4,50 Meter auf 18,50 Meter, bei einer Deckenhöhe von 2,30 Meter, dazu Teile des Gebäudefundaments im Inneren, waren dabei die besondere Herausforderung. Das Ziel: ein stylisher Shop mit einem luftigen, ruhigen Flair. Die Idee: zwei lineare Elemente, die den Kunden ins Innere des Shops ziehen. Links aus Kiefernholz eine integrierte Bar zum Sitzen, die Teile des Fundaments verkleidet, rechts Displays. Ein dunkler Betonboden betont die Displays und weist dem Kunden den Weg in den hinteren Teil des Ladens.

ᶠᴿ SO Architecture a pensé et piloté la rénovation ambitieuse de la nouvelle boutique de glaces et yaourts LEGGENDA. La nature même du lieu était un défi en soi : cet ancien atelier de charpentier mesurait 4,5 x 18,5 mètres, avec une hauteur sous plafond de 2,3 mètres et une charpente apparente. L'objectif était de créer un endroit élégant, clair, spacieux et reposant. L'idée : deux éléments linéaires accompagnent le client à l'intérieur. À gauche, un bar en pin encastré dissimule une partie de la charpente (apparente à droite) et permet aux clients de s'asseoir. Du béton sombre recouvre le sol et invite les clients à découvrir l'arrière du magasin, où les attendent des fauteuils très cosy.

ᴺᴱᴰ SO Architecture is het brein achter een veeleisende verbouwing van de nieuwe winkel van LEGGENDA Ice Cream and Yogurt. De bestaande ruimtelijke omstandigheden, een voormalige timmermanswerkplaats van 4,50 bij 18,5 meter, bij een plafondhoogte van 2,30 meter, en verder delen van het fundament van het gebouw binnenin, vormden hierbij de speciale uitdaging. Het doel: een stijlvolle winkel met een luchtige, rustige uitstraling. Het idee: twee lineaire elementen die de klant helemaal de winkel in trekken. Links van grenenhout een geïntegreerde bar om aan te zitten, de delen van het fundament bekleed, rechts displays. Verder een donkere betonvloer. Deze benadrukt de displays en wijst de klanten de weg naar de 'knusse' zitplaatsen in het achterste deel van de winkel.

THEODORE

ISRAEL | RAMAT ISHAY | NIGHTLIFE

ENG Come here to dine in a very special atmosphere. The THEODORE, as cozy as your own living room, is also a cultural space. Its focus ranges from literature, music, art, and architecture to gastronomy. The architects at SO Architecture have taken the Lev Kuleshov effect and translated it into spatial design. The Kuleshov effect states that the sequence in which images appear, rather than the images themselves, is the key factor for the viewer's interpretation. And that's precisely the case here. Rather than individual elements, architectural sequences in the form of three-dimensional elements, an intense sequence of alternating zones in interaction with two-dimensional graphics, are responsible for the room's energy and density.

DEU Hier speist man in einer ganz speziellen Umgebung: Heimelig wie das eigene Wohnzimmer, ist das THEODORE zugleich ein Ort der Kultur. Es geht um Literatur, Musik, Kunst, Architektur und Kulinarisches. Den Lev-Kuleshov-Effekt haben die Architekten von SO Architecture in die Sprache der räumlichen Gestaltung übersetzt. Er besagt, die Bildersequenz sei der Hauptfaktor für die Interpretation des Betrachters, nicht das einzelne Bild. Und so ist es auch hier. Keine einzelnen Elemente, sondern architektonische Sequenzen in Gestalt dreidimensionaler Elemente, eine intensive Sequenz von wechselnden Bereichen in Interaktion mit zweidimensionaler Grafik sind für die Dichte und Energie in diesem Raum verantwortlich.

FR Venez ici dîner dans une atmosphère particulière. Le THEODORE, aussi confortable et accueillant que votre propre salon, est un lieu de culture. Il met en avant la littérature et la musique, l'art, l'architecture ou la gastronomie. Les architectes de SO Architecture ont utilisé l'effet Koulechov et l'ont transposé au design d'espace. Selon Koulechov, l'interprétation d'une image dépend davantage de l'ordre dans lequel l'image apparaît que de l'image en elle-même. C'est le cas ici. L'énergie et la densité de la pièce ne sont pas dues à des éléments singuliers, mais à des séquences architecturales alternant éléments tridimensionnels et fresques.

NED Hier eet men in een heel speciale omgeving. Het THEODORE is gezellig als de eigen woonkamer en tegelijk een cultuurplaats. Het betreft literatuur, muziek, kunst, architectuur en culinaire zaken. Het Lev Koeleshov-effect hebben de architecten van SO Architecture in de taal van de ruimtelijke vormgeving omgezet. Dit effect houdt in dat de beeldsequentie de hoofdfactor is voor de interpretatie van de toeschouwer, niet het afzonderlijke beeld. En zo is het ook hier. Geen afzonderlijke elementen, maar architectonische opeenvolgingen in de gedaante van driedimensionale elementen, een intense sequentie van wisselende sectoren in interactie met tweedimensionale grafische kunst is verantwoordelijk voor de dichtheid en energie in deze ruimte.

BAR À VINS TATERU YOSHINO

JAPAN | TOKYO | NIGHTLIFE

ENG Connoisseurs describe the atmosphere at BAR À VINS, Japan's first official society bar, as relaxed and a bit sophisticated. This smart, sleek, and modern venue is located on the 25th floor of the "Park Hotel Tokyo", created by interior designer Frederic Thomas. It's the perfect place to slip away from the hustle and bustle of Shiodome, Tokyo's new business and cultural district, and enjoy a cocktail, glass of wine or single malt.

DEU Als ruhig und ein wenig sophisticated beschreiben Kenner die Atmosphäre in der ersten offiziellen Society-Bar Japans, der BAR À VINS. Im 25. Stock des vom Innenarchitekten Frederic Thomas entworfenen „Park Hotel Tokyo" findet sich diese moderne, geradlinige und zugleich smarte Bar. Hier gelingt es bei einem Cocktail, einem Glas Wein oder einem Single Malt dem emsigen Treiben des neuen Business- und Kulturviertels Shiodome in Tokio für einen Augenblick zu entkommen.

FR Les connaisseurs décrivent l'atmosphère de BAR À VINS, le premier bar « corporate » officiel au Japon, comme un endroit cool et un brin sophistiqué. Ce lieu moderne, chic et élégant se trouve au 25ème étage du « Park Hotel Tokyo », créé par l'architecte d'intérieur Frédéric Thomas. C'est l'endroit rêvé pour fuir le bourdonnement incessant de Shiodome, le nouveau quartier d'affaires et culturel de Tokyo et pour siroter un cocktail, un verre de vin ou un single malt.

NED Als rustig en niet erg geraffineerd beschrijven kenners de sfeer in de eerste officiële societybar van Japan, de BAR À VINS. Op de 25e verdieping van het door binnenhuisarchitect Frederic Thomas ontworpen 'Park Hotel Tokyo' bevindt zich deze moderne, rechtlijnige en tegelijk chique bar. Hier lukt het om bij een cocktail, een glas wijn of een single malt even aan de drukke bedrijvigheid van de nieuwe zaken- en cultuurwijk Shiodome in Tokyo te ontkomen.

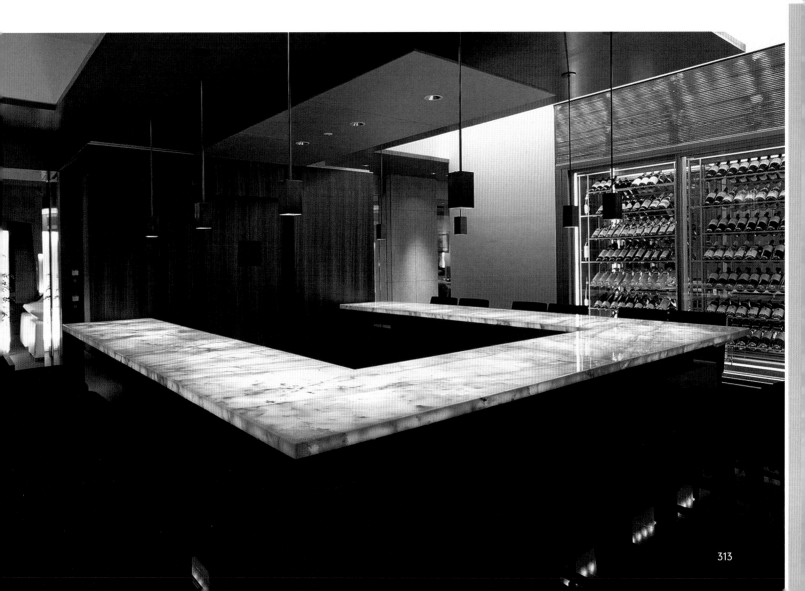

BAR THE OTHELLO

JAPAN | TOKYO | NIGHTLIFE

ENG The black and white color scheme comes from the name itself. Glittery track lighting accompanies the guest down the stairs to the entrance of this elegant and unconventional bar. The color contrast signifies two separate areas: black for the bar, which, illuminated with lights that sparkle like diamonds, is a relaxed and tranquil spot; white for the private sofa room, which, designed by Yasumichi Morita, is a nice little pick-me-up with no side effects.

DEU Das Farbkonzept aus Schwarz und Weiß ergibt sich aus dem Namen. Eine funkelnde Lichtschiene geleitet den Gast die Treppe hinab zum Eingang dieser außergewöhnlichen und eleganten Bar. Der Farbkontrast steht für zwei separate Bereiche: Schwarz für die Bar, mit wie Diamanten funkelnden Lichtern illuminiert, ein Ort der Ruhe, Weiß für den privaten Sofa-Room – ein Muntermacher ganz ohne Nebenwirkungen gestaltet von Yasumichi Morita.

FR Un éclairage scintillant accompagne le visiteur au bas des escaliers, menant à l'entrée de ce bar peu conventionnel. La thématique noir et blanc n'est qu'une conséquence logique du nom qui lui a été choisi. Le contraste des couleurs délimite deux différentes zones : le noir pour le bar, qui, éclairé par des luminaires éclatants comme des diamants, propose un endroit relaxant et tranquille ; le blanc pour le salon privé, qui, pensé par Yasumichi Morita, s'avère être un agréable petit remontant dépourvu d'effets secondaires.

NED Het kleurconcept van zwart en wit komt voort uit de naam. Een fonkelende lichttrail leidt de gast de trap af naar de ingang van deze bijzondere en elegante bar. Het kleurcontrast staat voor twee afzonderlijke gedeelten: zwart voor de bar, verlicht met als diamanten flonkerende lichten, een plaats van rust, wit voor de huiselijk sofakamer – een pepmiddel zonder bijwerkingen, vormgegeven door Yasumichi Morita.

CLUB TSUKI

JAPAN | TOKYO | NIGHTLIFE

ᴱᴺᴳ The concept: luxury and elegance. The second floor houses the TSUKI bar. From the outside two three-armed chandeliers and steel curtains are visible, shimmering in gold and champagne. The staircase is decorated with hand-painted arabesques by Masataka Kurashina. A black metal door, Phantoms by Baccarat in display windows, a central counter made from solid bubinga wood, red leather chairs, and an original wine and champagne cellar, plus nearly 200 Phantoms by Baccarat on each side, arranged like wings. Both majestic and fanciful.

ᴰᴱᵁ Das Konzept: Luxus und Eleganz. Im zweiten Stock befindet sich die Bar TSUKI. Von außen zwei dreiarmige Lüster und stählerne Vorhänge, schimmernd in Gold und Champagner. Die Treppe geschmückt mit handgemalten Arabesken, von Masataka Kurashina. Eine schwarze Metalltür, Phantoms by Baccarat in Vitrinen, ein zentraler Tresen aus massivem Bubinga-Holz, rote Lederstühle und ein Original Wein- und Champagner-Cellar, dazu fast 200 Phantoms by Baccarat auf jeder Seite, arrangiert wie Flügelschwingen. Prachtvoll und verspielt.

ᶠᴿ Le concept tient en deux mots : luxe et élégance. Depuis l'extérieur du bar TSUKI, on peut voir deux énormes chandeliers et des rideaux de métal miroitant dans des tons or et champagne. L'escalier est décoré d'arabesques peintes à la main par Masataka Kurashina. On peut aussi y admirer une porte de métal noir, des suspensions Phantoms de Baccarat présentées en vitrine, un robuste comptoir central en bois bubinga, des chaises de cuir rouge et une cave à vins originale, ainsi que 200 suspensions Phantoms de Baccarat s'étirant de chaque coté du bar, disposées telles des ailes. L'ensemble est à la fois majestueux et extravagant.

ᴺᴱᴰ Het concept: luxe en elegantie. Op de tweede verdieping bevindt zich de bar TSUKI. Van buiten twee driearmige lusters en stalen schermen, glinsterend in goud en champagne. De trap versierd met handgeschilderde arabesken, van Masataka Kurashina. Een zwarte metalen deur, phantoms van Baccarat in vitrines, een centrale tapkast van massief bubinga, roodleren stoelen en een originele wijn- en champagnekelder, met daarbij aan weerskanten bijna 200 phantoms van Baccarat, geplaatst als vleugelslagen. Prachtig en speels.

PETER AT THE PENINSULA TOKYO

JAPAN | TOKYO | NIGHTLIFE

ENG A traditional Japanese lantern was the inspiration for Kazukiyo Sato's freestanding hotel tower at the PENINSULA TOKYO. It keeps watch over Tokyo's Marunouchi business district like a "lighthouse". The PETER bar and restaurant, which is located on the 24th floor and can be accessed by its own private elevator, offers a 360° view of downtown Tokyo. You will find a remarkable combination of art and avant-garde design with fascinating interactive elements and a theatrical feel. The team at Yabu Pushelberg was responsible for the interior design.

DEU Einer dieser typischen japanischen Lampions inspirierte Kazukiyo Sato zu dem freistehenden Hotelturm des PENINSULA TOKYO. Wie ein „Leuchtturm" wacht er über das Tokioter Geschäftsviertel Marunouchi. Hier, im 24. Stock, mit eigenem privatem Lift, befindet sich das PETER, Restaurant und Bar in einem. 360 Grad umfasst der Blick auf die Innenstadt. Dazu eine bemerkenswerte Verbindung aus Kunst und avantgardistischem Design mit faszinierenden interaktiven Elementen, Bühnenfeeling inbegriffen. Das Team von Yabu Pushelberg ist verantwortlich für das Interior Design.

FR C'est un lampion traditionnel japonais qui a inspiré Kazukiyo Sato pour son hôtel flottant PENINSULA TOKYO. IL surplombe le quartier des affaires Marunouchi tel un phare et offre une vue à 360 degrés sur le centre-ville de Tokyo. Son bar et restaurant PETER, situé au 24ème étage, possède son propre ascenseur. Art et design avant-gardiste s'y côtoient de façon brillante, à travers différents éléments créant une ambiance théâtrale résolument fascinante. Son design intérieur est l'œuvre de l'équipe de Yabu Pushelberg.

NED Een van die typisch Japanse lampions inspireerde Kazukiyo Sato tot de losstaande hoteltoren van het PENINSULA TOKYO. Als een 'vuurtoren' waakt hij over de Tokyose zakenwijk Marunouchi. Hier, op de 24e verdieping, met een eigen privélift, bevindt zich het PETER, restaurant en bar ineen. Het uitzicht op de binnenstad beslaat 360 graden. Verder een opmerkelijke verbinding van kunst en avant-gardistisch ontwerp met fascinerende interactieve elementen, toneelgevoel inbegrepen. Het team van Yabu Pushelberg is verantwoordelijk voor het interieurontwerp.

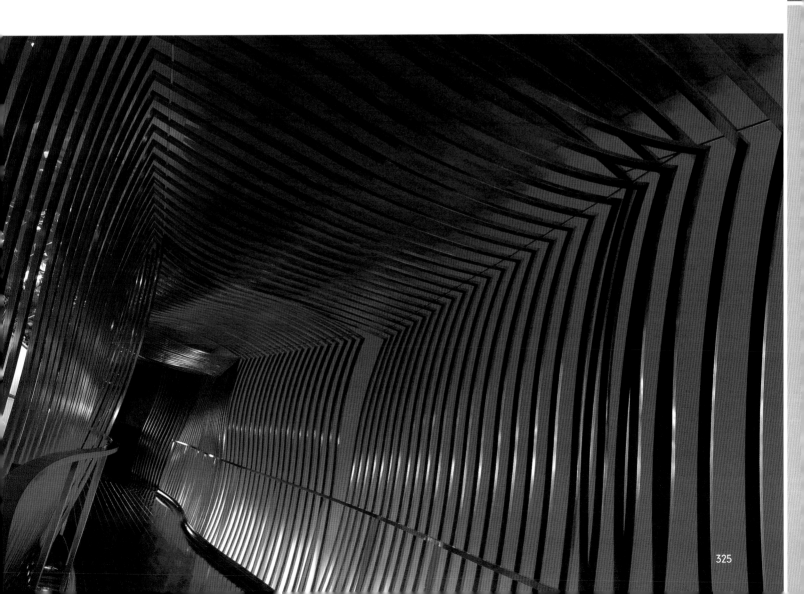

PALATE PALETTE

MALAYSIA | KUALA LUMPUR | NIGHTLIFE

ENG A restaurant, bar, café, lounge, and a place to while away bright and happy hours. Without a doubt, the PALATE PALETTE is all that and more. "Palate" refers to taste, "palette" to the artistic spectrum of colors, materials, characters, and ingredients. Taken together, they signify cooking, designing, painting, mixology, etc. PALATE PALETTE unites color for your daily life with gastronomy for your taste buds. Both are a treat for the senses and unique beyond question.

DEU Restaurant, Bar, Café, Lounge und Ort für fröhliche und farbenfrohe Stunden. Das alles ist das PALATE PALETTE ohne jeden Zweifel. „Palate" steht für den Geschmack, „Palette" für das künstlerische Spektrum von Farben, Materialien, Charakteren und Zutaten. Zusammen meinen sie das Kochen, Gestalten, Malen, Cocktails mixen etc. Im PALATE PALETTE treffen sich Farbe für den Alltag und Kulinarisches für die Geschmacksknospen. Beides ist für die Sinne und ohne Frage einzigartig.

FR Un restaurant, un bar, un café, un salon et un endroit où passer des heures délicieuses : le PALATE PALETTE est sans aucun doute tout cela et bien plus encore. « Palate » se réfère au palais, tandis que « palette » rappelle le spectre artistique des couleurs, matériaux, personnages et ingrédients. Pris dans leur ensemble, ils englobent la cuisine, le design, la peinture, l'art du cocktail et bien d'autres plaisirs. Le PALATE PALETTE unit la couleur, pour égayer le quotidien, à la gastronomie, pour le régal des papilles et les sens en redemandent.

NED Restaurant, Bar, Café, Lounge en plek voor vrolijke en bonte uurtjes. Dit alles is het PALATE PALETTE ongetwijfeld. 'Palate' staat voor de smaak, 'palette' voor het artistieke spectrum aan kleuren, materialen, karakters en extra's. Samen bedoelen ze het koken, vormgeven, schilderen, cocktails mixen, enzovoort. In PALATE PALETTE ontmoeten kleur voor alledag en culinaire zaken voor de smaakknoppen elkaar. Allebei voor de zintuigen en absoluut uniek.

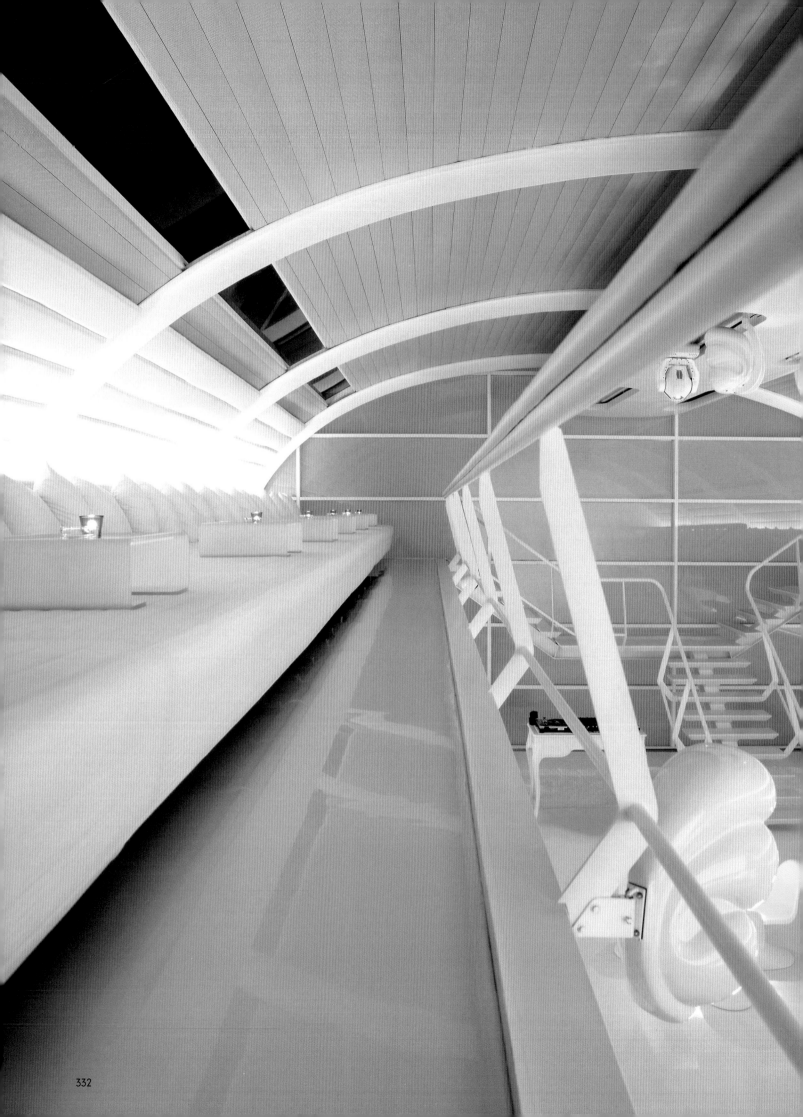

BED SUPPERCLUB

THAILAND | BANGKOK | NIGHTLIFE

[ENG] The creators of the BED SUPPERCLUB have embodied their philosophy in what may well be the most popular club in Bangkok. It's everything: a gourmet restaurant, club, bar, gallery, theater, stage—an architectural jewel on stilts that rises from the street like a UFO. The interior is dominated by a pure white that, chameleon-like, is almost completely transformed by the effects created by colored light. The BED SUPPERCLUB is a place for all the senses, a lifestyle enhancement, and the first club in the world where you can dine while lying in bed.

[DEU] Die Macher des BED SUPPERCLUB haben ihrer Philosophie eine Gestalt gegeben. Der vielleicht angesagteste Club Bangkoks ist alles: Gourmetrestaurant, Club, Bar, Galerie, Theater, Showbühne – ein architektonisches Kleinod auf Stelzen, das sich in den Straßen ausnimmt wie ein UFO. Sein Inneres dominiert ein reines Weiß, das sich einem Chamäleon gleich nahezu vollständig verändert durch den effektvollen Einsatz von farbigem Licht. Der BED SUPPERCLUB ist ein Ort für alle Sinne, eine Erhöhung des Lifestyles und der erste Club weltweit, in dem man im Bett liegend speisen darf.

[FR] Les créateurs du BED SUPPERCLUB ont apposé leur philosophie à ce qui s'avère le club le plus branché de Bangkok. C'est un peu tout à la fois : un restaurant gastronomique, un club, un bar, une galerie d'art, un théâtre, une arène et un joyau architectural aux allures d'OVNI. Un blanc immaculé domine le lieu, coloré uniquement par le jeu des lumières. Le BED SUPPERCLUB est un paradis pour les sens, une amélioration du quotidien et le premier club au monde à proposer de dîner au lit.

[NED] De makers van de BED SUPPERCLUB hebben aan hun filosofie een vorm gegeven. De misschien wel meest gepresenteerde club van Bangkok is alles: gourmetrestaurant, club, bar, galerie, theater, showtoneel – een architectonisch juweel op stelten, dat er in de straten als een ufo uitziet. Binnen overheerst zuiver wit, dat als een kameleon nagenoeg geheel verandert door het effectief gebruik van gekleurd licht. De BED SUPPERCLUB is een plek voor alle zintuigen, een verhoging van de leefstijl en de eerste club ter wereld waar je liggend op bed mag eten.

SIROCCO, THE DOME AT LEBUA

THAILAND | BANGKOK | NIGHTLIFE

ENG There's more than one spectacular bar in Bangkok, it's true. But the SKY BAR is without question among the most impressive, possibly in the world. And not just because of its privileged location. It is part of the SIROCCO, the world's highest open-air restaurant, on the 63rd floor in the dome of the Lebua at State Tower, on an extended platform with breathtaking views of the Chao Phraya River and Bangkok. You can savor the views while enjoying anything a cosmopolitan bar has to offer, plus a five-star luxury hotel.

DEU Es gibt wahrlich nicht nur eine spektakuläre Bar in Bangkok. Die SKY BAR aber gehört ohne jeden Zweifel zu den beeindruckendsten, möglicherweise weltweit. Und das liegt nicht allein an ihrer privilegierten Lage. Sie ist Teil des SIROCCO, des höchstgelegenen Open-Air-Restaurants der Welt, im 63. Stock, in der Kuppel des Lebua at State Tower, auf einem überhängenden Podest mit atemberaubendem Blick über den Chao Praya und Bangkok. Zum Blick dazu gibt es alles, was eine Bar von Welt zu bieten hat, nebst Fünf-Sterne-Luxushotel.

FR Il est de notoriété publique que Bangkok compte d'innombrables clubs sortant de l'ordinaire. En partie grâce à sa situation privilégiée, le SKY BAR est sans doute le plus impressionnant d'entre eux, et ce à l'échelle mondiale. Depuis la plateforme du SIROCCO, le plus grand restaurant à ciel ouvert au monde, situé au 63ème étage du Lebua at State Tower, la vue sur le fleuve Chao Phraya et sur Bangkok est spectaculaire. Il est ainsi possible de savourer ce panorama en sirotant un verre puis de passer la nuit dans l'hôtel cinq étoiles.

NED Er is echt niet maar één spectaculaire bar in Bangkok. De SKY BAR behoort echter zonder twijfel tot de indrukwekkendste, misschien wel ter wereld. En dat ligt niet alleen aan de bevoorrechte ligging. Hij maakt deel uit van het SIROCCO, het hoogstgelegen openluchtrestaurant ter wereld, op de 63e verdieping, in de koepel van het Lebua At State Tower, op een overhangend platform met adembenemend uitzicht over de Chao Praya en Bangkok. Behalve het uitzicht is er alles wat een bar van wereldklasse maar kan bieden, naast een vijfsterren-luxehotel.

BOBBY CHINN

VIETNAM | HANOI | NIGHTLIFE

ENG Around 450 square meters (4844 square feet), silk curtains that function as room dividers, various colors for various themes. The goal: intimacy and privacy. Three parts—a restaurant, bar, and lounge—separated by silk fabrics and special acoustics. Because who wants the neighbors listening in? Then there's the prime exhibition of contemporary art and 1,000 roses per week. All this is the signature of Bobby Chinn, including the exquisite cuisine influenced by this unconventional chef's African and Chinese roots.

DEU Größe rund 450 Quadratmeter, seidene Vorhänge als Raumteiler, unterschiedliche Farben für unterschiedliche Themen. Das Ziel: Intimität und Privatsphäre. Drei Teile – Restaurant, Bar und Lounge – voneinander getrennt durch Seidenstoffe und eine besondere Akustik. Denn das Belauschen der Nachbarn ist nicht erwünscht. Dazu eine ausgesuchte Ausstellung zeitgenössischer Kunst und 1 000 Rosen pro Woche. Neben einer exquisiten Küche, die beeinflusst ist von Bobby Chinns Wurzeln in Afrika und China, ist all das die Handschrift dieses ungewöhnlichen Küchenchefs.

FR Sur environ 450 mètres carrés, des rideaux de soie séparent les salons dont la thématique change au gré des différentes couleurs. L'objectif est l'intimité. Trois lieux – un restaurant, un bar et un salon – sont séparés par des tissus soyeux et une acoustique soignée, afin de ne pas être dérangé par la conversation du voisin. On peut y trouver aussi une exposition d'art contemporain et un décor de 1000 roses changé chaque semaine. Ce lieu d'une grande beauté est signé Bobby Chinn, tout comme la cuisine délicieuse influencée par les racines africaines et chinoises de ce chef peu conventionnel.

NED Grootte rond 450 vierkante meter, zijden gordijnen als scheidingswanden, verschillende kleuren voor verschillende thema's. Het doel: intimiteit en huiselijke sfeer. Drie delen – restaurant, bar en lounge – van elkaar gescheiden door zijden stoffen en een bijzondere akoestiek, want de buren afluisteren is ongewenst. Verder een uitgelezen tentoonstelling van eigentijdse kunst en 1000 rozen per week. Naast een exquise keuken, die is beïnvloed door Bobby Chinns wortels in Afrika en China, draagt dit alles de signatuur van deze buitengewone chef-kok.

SHOPS
MALLS AND STORES

LATTICE

ENG It's the commercial projects that have catapulted Beijing into the modern age. Projects like Sanlitun Village on Bar Street in the embassy district. Renowned architects, including Tadao Ando and Jun Aoki, are part of the select team. The master plan is by Kengo Kuma and LATTICE by Keiichiro Sako. The whole thing is a complex of shops, restaurants, offices, block-like structures, a maximum of four stories, a mix of new construction and renovation. Revolutionary for Beijing, especially the variety of façade designs. LATTICE is a commercial building with fanciful metal facades in new interpretations of traditional Chinese patterns, which change their appearance according to the time of day and how the light falls on them.

DEU Es sind die kommerziellen Projekte, die Peking in die Neuzeit katapultieren. Projekte wie das Sanlitun Village an der Bar Street im Botschaftsviertel. Renommierte Architekten wie Tadao Ando, Jun Aoki u.a. sind Teil des erlesenen Teams. Der Masterplan ist von Kengo Kuma und das LATTICE von Keiichiro Sako. Das Ganze ein Komplex aus Geschäften, Restaurants, Büros, blockähnlichen Strukturen, vier Stockwerke maximal, aus Neuem und renovierungsbedürftigem Alten. Für Peking revolutionär, insbesondere die Vielfalt der Fassadengestaltung. Das LATTICE ist ein Geschäftshaus mit verspielten Metallfassaden aus traditionellen chinesischen Mustern, die hier neu interpretiert wurden und je nach Tageszeit und Lichteinfall ihr Aussehen verändern.

FR Pékin est entrée dans l'ère moderne grâce à des projets commerciaux d'envergure. C'est le cas par exemple du Sanlitun Village sur Bar Street, dans le quartier des ambassades. De célèbres architectes tels que Tadao Ando et Jun Aoki s'y sont attelés. LATTICE est l'œuvre de Keiichiro Sako et Kengo Kuma en a dessiné les plans. Ce complexe de structures cubiques regroupe magasins, restaurants et bureaux ; il compte quatre étages au maximum et mêle savamment construction et rénovation. C'est une petite révolution pour Pékin, car LATTICE est un immeuble commercial dont la façade excentrique en métal réinterprète des motifs traditionnels chinois, qui changent d'apparence selon la lumière et l'heure de la journée.

NED Het zijn de commerciële projecten die Peking de nieuwe tijd in slingeren. Projecten als het Sanlitun Village aan de Bar Street in de ambassadewijk. Gerenommeerde architecten als Tadao Ando, Jun Aoki en andere maken deel uit van het voortreffelijke team. Het masterplan is van Kengo Kuma en het LATTICE van Keiichiro Sako. Het geheel is een complex van zaken, restaurants, kantoren, blokachtige structuren, maximaal vier verdiepingen, gedeeltelijk nieuw en gedeeltelijk oud en aan renovatie toe. Voor Peking revolutionair, vooral de verscheidenheid van de gevelvormgeving. Het LATTICE is een zakenpand met speelse metalen voorgevels met traditionele Chinese patronen, die hier opnieuw zijn geïnterpreteerd en naargelang tijd van de dag en lichtval van uiterlijk veranderen.

ENG Floor, walls, and ceiling—all white. The contours of the space disappear to place the spotlight on what's essential here: the EIFINI fashions. The central design element: a 250-meter (820-foot) pipe. It winds its way through the space, tracing shapes, constructing new ones. Secured by transparent acrylic, it seems to float. The course it follows is based on the movement of a conductor's baton. The EIFINI shop is another of the many unconventional projects created by China-based Japanese architect Keiichiro Sako.

DEU Boden, Wände und Decke – alles in Weiß. Die Konturen des Raumes verschwinden und das Wesentliche wird zum Star: die Mode von EIFINI. Das zentrale gestalterische Element: ein 250 Meter langes Rohr. Es windet sich durch den Raum, zieht Formen nach, konstruiert neue. Es wirkt, als schwebe es, denn die Befestigung ist aus transparentem Acryl. Inspiriert ist sein Verlauf von der Bahn, die ein Dirigent mit seinem Taktstock beschreibt. Der Shop von EIFINI ist ein weiteres von vielen ungewöhnlichen Projekten des in China lebenden japanischen Architekten Keiichiro Sako.

FR Des sols aux murs en passant par le plafond – tout y est blanc. La boutique disparaît au profit de ce qui est ici essentiel : les articles EIFINI. L'élément design inratable : un tuyau de 250 mètres qui serpente à sa guise à travers le lieu, formant des courbes et créant des formes. Retenu par une structure d'acrylique transparent, le tuyau semble flotter et son trajet reproduit le mouvement d'une baguette de chef d'orchestre. La boutique FIFINI n'est qu'un des nombreux projets fous pensés par l'architecte japonais Keiichiro Sako, installé en Chine.

NED Vloer, wanden en plafond – alles is wit. De contouren van de ruimte verdwijnen en de essentie wordt de ster: de mode van EIFINI. Het centrale vormgevende element: een 250 meter lange buis. Deze slingert zich door de ruimte, volgt vormen, construeert nieuwe. Het lijkt alsof hij zweeft, want de bevestiging is van transparant acryl. Het verloop ervan is geïnspireerd op de baan die een dirigent met zijn dirigeerstokje beschrijft. De winkel van EIFINI is een van de vele ongewone projecten van de in China wonende Japanse architect Keiichiro Sako.

ROMANTICISM

CHINA | HANGZHOU | SHOPS

ENG The flagship store of ROMANTICISM, a Chinese fashion label with more than 500 outlets, is for women only. It was designed by Keiichiro Sako and everything is white: the walls, floor, ceiling, and furnishings. The shapes seem to dissolve. The space is defined by a seemingly endless white net, an organic shape that envelops everything. It moves from the outside in, connecting the different levels, creating shapes, uniting the whole. It's both the defining visual element and the perfect packaging for fashion.

DEU Der Flagshipstore von ROMANTICISM, einem chinesischen Modelabel mit über 500 Stores, nur für Frauen: von Keiichiro Sako. Alles in Weiß: Wände, Böden, Decken und Ausstattung. Die Formen lösen sich auf. Bestimmt wird der Raum durch ein schier endloses weißes Netz, eine organische Form, die alles umhüllt. Es zieht sich von außen nach innen, verbindet die Stockwerke, kreiert Formen, verbindet das Ganze, ist bestimmendes optisches Moment und perfekte Verpackung für die Mode zugleich.

FR Le magasin fleuron de ROMANTICISM, marque chinoise à la tête de 500 magasins, est réservé aux femmes. Pensé par Keiichiro Sako, tout y est blanc : murs, sols, plafond et mobilier. Les formes sont comme en liquéfaction, dans cet espace défini par un filet blanc sans fin, une forme organique qui enveloppe tout sur son passage. Présent également à l'extérieur, il relie les différents étages par une forme omniprésente. C'est à la fois un élément visuel déterminant et une idée parfaite pour vendre du prêt-à-porter.

NED De vlaggenschipwinkel van ROMANTICISM, een Chinees modelabel met ruim 500 zaken, alleen voor vrouwen – van Keiichiro Sako. Alles is wit: wanden, vloeren, plafonds en uitrusting. De vormen lossen op. Een bijna eindeloos wit net bepaalt de ruimte, een organische vorm, die alles omhult. Het loopt van buiten naar binnen, verbindt de verdiepingen, creëert vormen, verbindt het geheel, is tegelijk de bepalende visuele factor en perfecte verpakking voor de mode.

SHANTANU AND NIKHIL SHOWROOM

INDIA | NEW DELHI | SHOPS

ᴱᴺᴳ The WHITE POD, a tiny shop in New Delhi that was created by Romi Khosla Design Studios for the designer duo Shantanu and Nikhil, has what it takes. Forward- and backward-moving planes conceal all of the shop's storage and electronics. The floor curves up to form the wall, which also curves to form the ceiling, the furniture, the changing rooms, and so on. It is the perfect realization of the idea of an architectural form created from seamless surfaces.

ᴰᴱᵁ Der WHITE POD, ein winziges Geschäft in New Delhi, von Romi Khosla Design Studios für das Designer-Duo Shantanu and Nikhil entworfen, hat es in sich. Nach vorne und hinten versetzte Flächen verbergen Lager und Elektronik. Der Boden wölbt sich und formt die Wand, die, indem sie sich ihrerseits wölbt, die Decke bildet, die Möbel, Umkleidekabinen und so weiter. Es ist die perfekte Umsetzung der Idee einer architektonischen Form, die sich aus nahtlosen Oberflächen entwickelt.

ᶠᴿ Le WHITE POD est une petite boutique de New Delhi créée par le duo de designers Shantanu et Nikhil du Romi Khosla Design Studios. Des panneaux mobiles permettent de dissimuler la réserve du magasin ainsi que les éléments électroniques. Le sol se transforme en mur, lui-même devenant plafond : une continuité harmonieuse apparaît alors pour former également l'ensemble du mobilier, les cabines d'essayage et ainsi de suite. L'idée est parfaitement réalisée : une forme architecturale naît d'une continuité de surfaces dépourvues d'arêtes.

ᴺᴱᴰ De WHITE POD, een klein zaakje in New Delhi, door Romi Khosla Design Studios ontworpen voor het designerduo Shantanu and Nikhil, heeft het helemaal. Naar voren en achteren geplaatste vlakken verbergen het magazijn en elektronische apparatuur. De vloer welft zich en vormt de wand, die, omdat hij zich ook welft, het plafond vormt, de meubels, de kleedhokjes enzovoort. Het is de volmaakte uitvoering van een idee van een architectonische vorm, die zich ontwikkelt vanuit naadloze oppervlakken.

SUNEET VARMA STORE

INDIA | NEW DELHI | SHOPS

[ENG] The clients wanted a shop that was exclusive and extravagant—but, above all, different from the rest. The contract was awarded to Romi Khosla Design Studios. They sought a new way to interpret luxury. The result: an idea inspired by traditional origami. Two folded white airplanes are the central elements in a dark wooden box. From the ventilation to the changing rooms, absolutely everything is invisibly housed in them. The sole contrast: hundreds of colorful acrylic flowers, a floral sea on the ceiling. And that, too, is a bit different from the norm.

[DEU] Die Auftraggeber wollten einen Shop, exklusiv und extravagant – vor allem aber anders als die anderen. Den Auftrag bekamen Romi Khosla Design Studios. Gesucht wurde eine neue Art der Interpretation von Luxus. Das Ergebnis: eine vom traditionellen Origami inspirierte Idee. Zwei gefaltete weiße Flugzeuge sind die zentralen Elemente in einer Box aus dunklem Holz. Von der Entlüftung bis zu den Umkleidekabinen, einfach alles ist in ihnen unsichtbar untergebracht. Einziger Kontrast: Hunderte von farbigen Blumen aus Acryl, ein Blumenmeer an der Decke. Und auch das ist ein bisschen anders als sonst.

[FR] Les clients souhaitaient une boutique à la fois élégante et extravagante – mais ils voulaient par-dessus tout qu'elle n'ait rien de commun. Le contrat a été remporté par le Romi Khosla Design Studios, qui cherchait une nouvelle manière d'interpréter le luxe. Le résultat, inspiré de l'origami, est probant. Deux avions pliés forment le centre d'intérêt d'un cube de bois sombre et intègrent aussi bien les conduits d'aération que les cabines d'essayage. Le seul contraste autorisé prend la forme d'une rivière florale située au plafond et composée de centaines de fleurs colorées en acrylique. Cela aussi sort un peu de l'ordinaire...

[NED] De opdrachtgevers wilden een exclusieve en extravagante winkel – maar vooral anders dan de andere. Romi Khosla Design Studios kregen de opdracht. Er werd gezocht naar een nieuwe interpretatie van luxe. Het resultaat: een op de traditionele origami geïnspireerd idee. Twee gevouwen witte vliegtuigen zijn de centrale elementen in een box van donker hout. Van het ventilatiesysteem tot de kleedhokjes, gewoon alles is er onzichtbaar in ondergebracht. Het enige contrast: honderden gekleurde bloemen van acryl, een bloemenzee aan het plafond. En ook dat is een beetje anders dan anders.

BIASA BOUTIQUE AND ART GALLERY

INDONESIA | JAKARTA | SHOPS

ENG This minimalist cube was designed by Giovanni D'Ambrosio for Biasa, the Balinese fashion label, and occupies four floors: the first and second floors house the boutique, the third and fourth the art gallery. The centerpiece is a staircase constructed of G-shaped elements. The stairway doubles as an exhibition space, corresponding to the levels in height and size. Employing an optical device, a 23-meter-long (75-foot-long) bronzed mirror wall, measuring 125 square meters (1345 square feet) in all, serves both to visually double the staircase and to enlarge the space, while concealed closets create even more room. Biasa's designers are known for their versatile fashion, and the same applies to the architecture here.

DEU Vier Stockwerke misst dieser minimalistische Kubus von Giovanni D'Ambrosio für Biasa, der Modemarke aus Bali: der erste und zweite Stock für die Boutique, der dritte und vierte für die Kunstgalerie. Herzstück ist eine Treppe aus G-Profilen. In Höhe und Größe den Stufen folgend ist sie Treppe und Ausstellungsfläche zugleich. Durch einen optischen Kunstgriff, eine brünierte Spiegelwand, 23 Meter lang und mit einer Gesamtfläche von 125 Quadratmetern, wird nicht nur die Treppe optisch verdoppelt, sondern der Raum scheinbar vergrößert und Platz geschaffen durch versteckte Wandschränke. Biasas Designer sind bekannt für ihre wandelbare Mode. Wie die Mode, so die Architektur.

FR Ce cube minimaliste est l'œuvre de Giovanni D'Ambrosio pour Biasa, la marque balinaise de prêt-à-porter, et s'étend sur quatre étages : le premier et le second sont réservés à la boutique tandis que les troisième et quatrième accueillent une galerie d'art. La pièce maîtresse est un escalier dont chaque marche est une lettre G. Il devient alors espace d'exposition, à mesure que s'élèvent les étages. Grâce à un procédé optique, un miroir de bronze de 23 mètres de long mesurant 125 mètres carrés, la taille de l'escalier est doublée et l'espace est ainsi agrandi. Les cabines d'essayage dissimulées accentuent encore davantage cet aspect. La réputation des stylistes de Biasa est ici égalée par l'architecture du lieu.

NED Vier verdiepingen groot is deze minimalistische kubus van Giovanni D'Ambrosio voor Biasa, het modemerk uit Bali: de eerste en tweede verdieping voor de boetiek, de derde en vierde voor de kunstgalerie. Hoofdbestanddeel is een trap van G-profielen. In hoogte en grootte de treden volgend is deze trap en tentoonstellingsoppervlak tegelijk. Door een visuele kunstgreep, een gebronsde spiegelwand, 23 meter lang en met een totaaloppervlak van 125 vierkante meter, wordt niet alleen de trap visueel verdubbeld, maar ook de ruimte schijnbaar vergroot en plaats gecreëerd voor verborgen wandkasten. De ontwerpers van Biasa staan bekend om hun veranderlijke mode. Zo de mode, zo de architectuur.

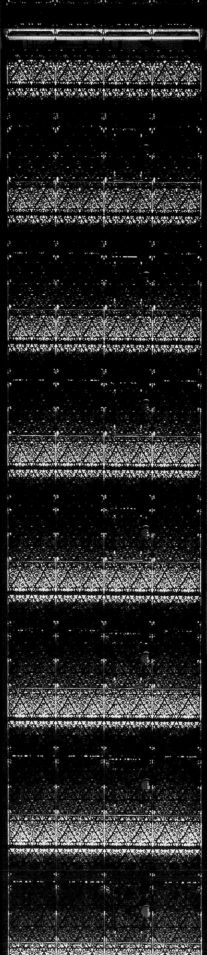

ᴱᴺᴳ Two floors in the ten-story building located in the fashionable Ginza district are reserved for the boutique of watchmaker AUDEMARS PIGUET, the others for customer service and offices, with a VIP suite on the top floor. The façade is complete with a watch mechanism, Japanized, stylized on the front, with the watch dial on the reverse. All illuminated by LED lighting systems, a modern interpretation of traditional Japanese Andon lanterns. The creative brain behind this is Japanese shooting star Yasumichi Morita.

ᴰᴱᵁ Zwei Stockwerke des zehnstöckigen Gebäudes im angesagten Ginza-Bezirk sind für die Boutique des Uhrenherstellers AUDEMARS PIGUET reserviert, die anderen für Kundenservice, Büro und VIP-Suite im obersten Stock. An der Fassade ein Uhrwerk, japanisiert, stilisiert auf der Frontseite, das Uhrenrad auf der Rückseite. Alles beleuchtet von LED-Leuchtsystemen, einer modernen Interpretation der traditionellen japanischen Andon-Laterne. Der kreative Kopf dahinter ist der japanische Shooting Star Yasumichi Morita.

ᶠᴿ Deux étages de cet immeuble, situé dans le quartier très en vogue de Ginza, sont réservés à la boutique de l'horloger AUDEMARS PIGUET ; les autres étages accueillent le service client et les bureaux, ainsi qu'une suite VIP au dernier étage. La fa-çade représente un mécanisme de montre stylisé à la japonaise, tandis que l'arrière du bâtiment rappelle quant à lui un cadran d'horloge. L'illumination par LED est une interprétation moderne des lampions traditionnels japonais, appelés Andon, et l'esprit génial à l'initiative de ce projet est la star japonaise Yasumichi Morita.

ᴺᴱᴰ Twee verdiepingen van het tien verdiepingen tellende gebouw in het bekende Ginza-district zijn voor de boetiek van de uur-werkfabrikant AUDEMARS PIGUET gereserveerd, de andere voor klantenservice, kantoor en vip-suite op de bovenste verdieping. Op de voorgevel een uurwerk, gejapaniseerd, gestileerd aan de voorkant, het opwindmechaniek aan de achterkant. Alles is ver-licht met led-verlichting, een moderne uitleg van de traditionele Japanse andon-lantaarn. De creatieve kop erachter is de Japan-se rijzende ster Yasumichi Morita.

CHRISTIAN DIOR OMOTESANDO BUILDING

JAPAN | TOKYO | SHOPS

ᴱᴺᴳ It's the perfect match: the team of architects at Sanaa, acclaimed for creating a visible relationship between a building's interior and exterior, and Kumoki Inui, the architect renowned for her façade designs. The CHRISTIAN DIOR OMOTESANDO BUILDING gleams through its "architectural skin" as through translucent wrapping paper. Constructed of two layers, clear glass on the exterior and translucent acrylic on the interior, and a second façade of perforated steel, the building's "skin" becomes a projection surface for both temporary and permanent decorative elements.

ᴰᴱᵁ Die Mischung macht's: Das Architektenteam Sanaa, mit dem Anspruch, eine sichtbare Beziehung zwischen dem Inneren und dem Äußeren eines Gebäudes herzustellen, und die für ihre Fassaden berühmte Architektin Kumoki Inui. Das CHRISTIAN DIOR OMOTESANDO BUILDING scheint durch seine „Gebäudehaut" hindurch wie durch ein durchsichtiges Geschenkpapier. Bestehend aus zwei Schichten, klarem Glas außen und einem transluzenten Acryl innen, und einer zweiten Fassade aus gelöchertem Stahl wird die „Gebäudehaut" zur Projektionsfläche für temporäre und dauerhafte dekorative Elemente.

ᶠᴿ C'est la rencontre parfaite : l'équipe des architectes de Sanaa, acclamés pour leur traitement ingénieux des intérieurs-extérieurs et Kumoki Inui, architecte reconnue pour son travail sur les façades de bâtiments. Le CHRISTIAN DIOR OMOTESANDO BUILDING luit à travers sa « peau architecturale » comme à travers un papier cadeau transparent. Il est composé d'une couche de verre et d'une couche d'acrylique transparent, ainsi que d'une seconde façade de métal perforé. La « peau » du bâtiment accueille la projection d'éléments décoratifs temporaires ou permanents.

ᴺᴱᴰ De mengeling doet het 'm: Het architectenteam Sanaa, met als eis een zichtbare relatie tussen binnen- en buitenkant van het gebouw tot stand te brengen, en de om haar gevels beroemde architecte Kumoki Inui. Het CHRISTIAN DIOR OMOTESANDO BUILDING schijnt door zijn 'gebouwhuid' als transparant cadeaupapier. De uit twee lagen bestaande 'gebouwhuid', helder glas van buiten en doorzichtig acryl van binnen en een tweede gevel van staal met gaten, wordt een projectievlak voor tijdelijke en blijvende decoratieve elementen.

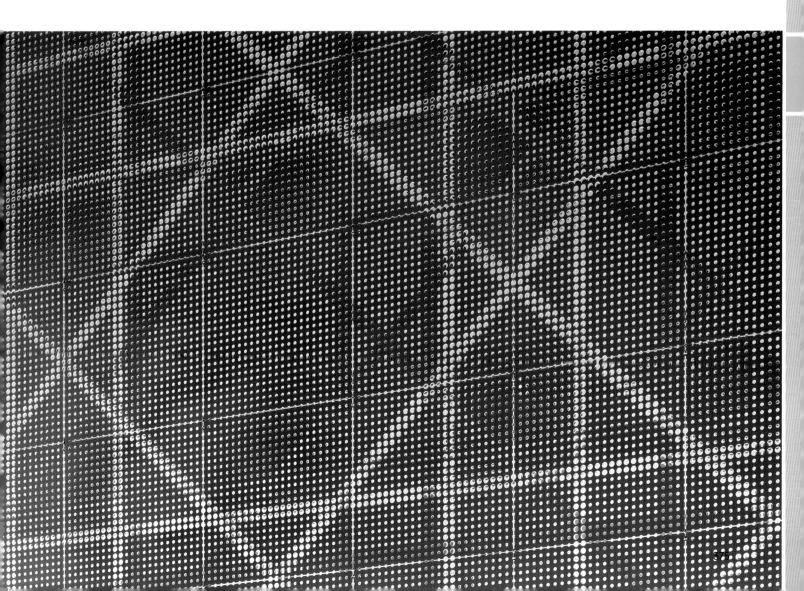

ENG The TOKIA shopping zone in the Tokyo Building is designed to enliven the Marunoushi business district. It contains 29 shops, bars, and restaurants serving Kansai-inspired cuisine, as well as a jazz club. Some restaurants are at street level. A lively spot visible from the outside, right in the midst of offices. The TOKIA has its own hallmarks: the audacious lighting incorporated into sculptures to the right and left of the corridors, and a clerestory strip in the underground mall that passes through the long corridor, sometimes up above, sometimes down below, angled in some places, in others a bench or a sign.

DEU Die Einkaufszone TOKIA im Tokyo Building soll dem Businessquartier Marunoushi mehr Leben verleihen. Hier finden sich 29 Shops, Bars und Restaurants mit Kansai-basierter Küche und ein Jazz-Club. Einige der Restaurants befinden sich auf Straßenniveau. Ein von außen sichtbarer, belebter Ort inmitten von Büros. Markenzeichen des TOKIA sind eigenwillige Leuchtkörper, eingebaut in Skulpturen rechts und links der Korridore, und ein Lichtband in der Underground-Mall, das sich durch den langen Korridor zieht, mal oben, mal unten, mal abgewinkelt, mal Ruhebank, mal Hinweisschild.

FR La zone commerciale TOKIA, au cœur du Tokyo Building a été créée pour redonner vie au quartier des affaires de Marunoushi. Elle regroupe 29 boutiques, bars et restaurants servant une cuisine d'inspiration Kansai, ainsi qu'un club de jazz. Certains restaurants donnent directement sur la rue et cette zone animée est visible depuis l'extérieur, en plein milieu des bureaux. TOKIA est unique et reconnaissable par ses luminaires audacieux intégrés à des sculptures et par un gigantesque bandeau, semblable à une claire-voie, circulant le long des couloirs et formant à certains endroits un angle, un banc ou un panneau.

NED Het winkelgebied TOKIA in het Tokyo Building moet de zakenwijk Marunouschi verlevendigen. Hier bevinden zich 29 winkels, bars en restaurants met een op Kansai gebaseerde keuken en een jazzclub. Enkele van de restaurants bevinden zich op straatniveau. Een van buiten zichtbare, levendige plek te midden van kantoren. Handelsmerken van het TOKIA zijn eigenzinnige verlichtingselementen, ingebouwd in sculpturen rechts en links van de gangen en een lichtband in het ondergrondse winkelcentrum, die door de lange gang loopt, soms boven, soms onder, soms gebogen, soms rustbank, soms aanwijzingsbord.

KYNN

STATE OF KUWAIT | KUWAIT CITY | SHOPS

ENG The design of the KYNN shop, a product of the interior designers at Design Squared, is meant to stand out from the many high-end furniture stores in Kuwait's booming industrial district. The concept: The chosen materials are contrasted in their original raw form against objects of perfect refinement. The result is extremely evocative and beautiful, creating a harmony between the internal and the external. A place has been created here where the transcendent qualities of art are combined with entrepreneurial spirit.

DEU Der KYNN-Shop ist ein Produkt der Innenarchitektinnen von Design Squared. Er sollte sich in seinem Design abheben von den vielen Möbelgeschäften der Luxusklasse im boomenden Industriebezirk Kuwaits. Das Konzept: Die gewählten Materialien werden in ihrer ursprünglichen, unverfälschten Form mit perfekt veredelten Objekten kontrastiert. Das Ergebnis ist von besonderer Ausdruckskraft und Schönheit, denn es stellt eine Harmonie her zwischen dem Inneren und dem Äußeren von Dingen. Entstanden ist ein Ort, an dem die transzendenten Qualitäten der Kunst geknüpft sind an Unternehmergeist.

FR Ce design, projet des architectes d'intérieur de Design Squared, a été pensé pour démarquer la boutique KYNN des nombreux magasins d'ameublement haut de gamme du quartier industriel montant de Koweït City. Son concept : les matériaux sélectionnés sont mis en opposition, dans leur forme brute originelle, avec des objets extrêmement raffinés. Il en résulte une harmonie esthétique et extrêmement évocatrice entre intérieur et extérieur. Cet endroit permet ainsi de combiner les qualités propres à l'art et un certain esprit d'entreprise.

NED De KYNN-winkel is een product van de binnenhuisarchitectes van Design Squared. Het ontwerp moet de winkel laten afsteken bij de vele meubelzaken in de luxeklasse in het sterk opbloeiende industriegebied van Koeweit. Het concept: de gekozen materialen worden in hun oorspronkelijke, onvervalste vorm gecontrasteerd met perfect veredelde voorwerpen. Het resultaat is buitengewoon indrukwekkend en fraai, want er is harmonie tot stand gekomen tussen het innerlijk en het uiterlijk van dingen. Er is een plek ontstaan waar de transcendente eigenschappen van de kunst zijn gekoppeld aan ondernemersgeest.

CHOCOLATE RESEARCH FACILITY

REPUBLIC OF SINGAPORE | SINGAPORE | SHOPS

ENG The CHOCOLATE RESEARCH FACILITY is a candy store for connoisseurs, offering over 100 types of chocolate. The store's appearance is ultra-modern, stylish, as clean and sparse as a pharmacy. And that's just how the chocolate is packaged. And what's it all for? Because chocolate makes you happy. So it stands to reason that it should be prescribed to men, women, and children in a pharmacy. The brains at the Asylum are behind the realization, while the idea originated, it might not surprise you to learn, from a chocolate lover.

DEU Die CHOCOLATE RESEARCH FACILITY ist ein Süßwarenladen für Kenner mit über 100 Sorten Schokolade. Das Aussehen des Ladens ist ultramodern, stylish, so clean und schnörkellos wie eine Apotheke. Und so ist die Schokolade auch verpackt. Und warum das Ganze? Weil Schokolade glücklich macht. Es liegt daher nahe, sie in einer Apotheke an Mann, Frau und Kind zu bringen. Hinter der Umsetzung stecken die Köpfe von The Asylum, hinter der Idee, und das kann nicht überraschen, ein Schokoladen-Liebhaber.

FR La CHOCOLATE RESEARCH FACILITY est un magasin de sucreries pour fins gourmets, offrant plus de 100 chocolats différents. La boutique offre une apparence ultramoderne, élégante, aussi nette et épurée qu'une pharmacie. C'est également le cas pour l'emballage des chocolats. Quelle en est la raison ? Le chocolat rend heureux, il peut donc aussi être vendu en pharmacie. Les cerveaux de chez Asylum se sont attelés à sa réalisation, tandis que l'idée originale provient, sans surprise, d'un amoureux du chocolat.

NED De CHOCOLATE RESEARCH FACILITY is een zoetwarenwinkel voor kenners met ruim 100 soorten chocolade. Het uiterlijk van de winkel is ultramodern, stijlvol, zo clean en strak als een apotheek. En zo wordt de chocolade ook verpakt. En waarom dit alles? Omdat chocolade gelukkig maakt. Het ligt daarom voor de hand deze in een apotheek aan de man, vrouw en kind te brengen. Achter de uitvoering zit het brein van The Asylum, achter het idee – en dat zal geen verrassing zijn – een chocoladeliefhebber.

ENG "Fro-" as in "frozen" and "-lick" as in "lick one's lips"—that's where this frozen yogurt bar gets its name. All white with pastel features—both the yogurt and the design, which is by the Asylum. The gleeful message is to satisfy your sweet tooth without expanding your hips at the same time. No preservatives, hardly any sugar, and not much fat, and a great flavor to boot. This shop, with its thousands and thousands of bright colorful buttons, is cheerful and offbeat. One percent of the profits go to the non-profit organization "1 Percent for the Planet".

DEU „Fro-" wie „frozen" und „-lick" wie „lick one's lips" – daher der Name dieser Frozen-Yogurt-Bar. Ganz in Weiß mit pastelligen Features, wie das Joghurt so das Design von The Asylum. Den Hunger auf Süßes zu stillen – ohne gleichzeitige Vergrößerung des Hüftumfangs – ist die frohe Botschaft. Keine Haltbarmacher, kaum Zucker und wenig Fett und das bei tollem Geschmack. Fröhlich und verschroben ist dieser Laden mit seinen abertausenden bunten Buttons. Ein Prozent des Umsatzes wandert zu der Non-Profit-Organisation „1 Percent For The Planet".

FR « Fro » comme dans « frozen » (glacé) et « lick » comme dans « lick one's lips » (s'en lécher les babines) : voilà d'où ce bar à yaourts glacés tient son nom. Tout y est blanc et pastel, des produits vendus au design, pensé par the Asylum. Les amateurs savent qu'ils peuvent satisfaire leurs envies de sucré sans jouer sur leur tour de taille. Pas d'additifs, un zeste de sucre et très peu de graisses donnent pour couronner le tout un goût incroyable aux yaourts glacés de la boutique. Des milliers de boutons colorés confèrent à cet endroit une aura sympathique et un pourcent du chiffre d'affaire est reversé à une ONG du réseau « 1% pour la planète ».

NED 'Fro-' van 'frozen' en '-lick' van 'lick one's lips' – vandaar de naam van deze Frozen-Yogurt-Bar. Geheel wit met pastelkleurige elementen, zo de yoghurt, zo het design van The Asylum. De trek in zoete dingen stillen – zonder tegelijk de heupomvang te vergroten – dat is de blijde boodschap. Geen conserveermiddelen, nauwelijks suiker en weinig vet en ook nog een verrukkelijke smaak. Vrolijk en vreemd is deze winkel met zijn duizenden bonte buttons. Eén procent van de omzet gaat naar de non-profitorganisatie '1 Percent For The Planet'.

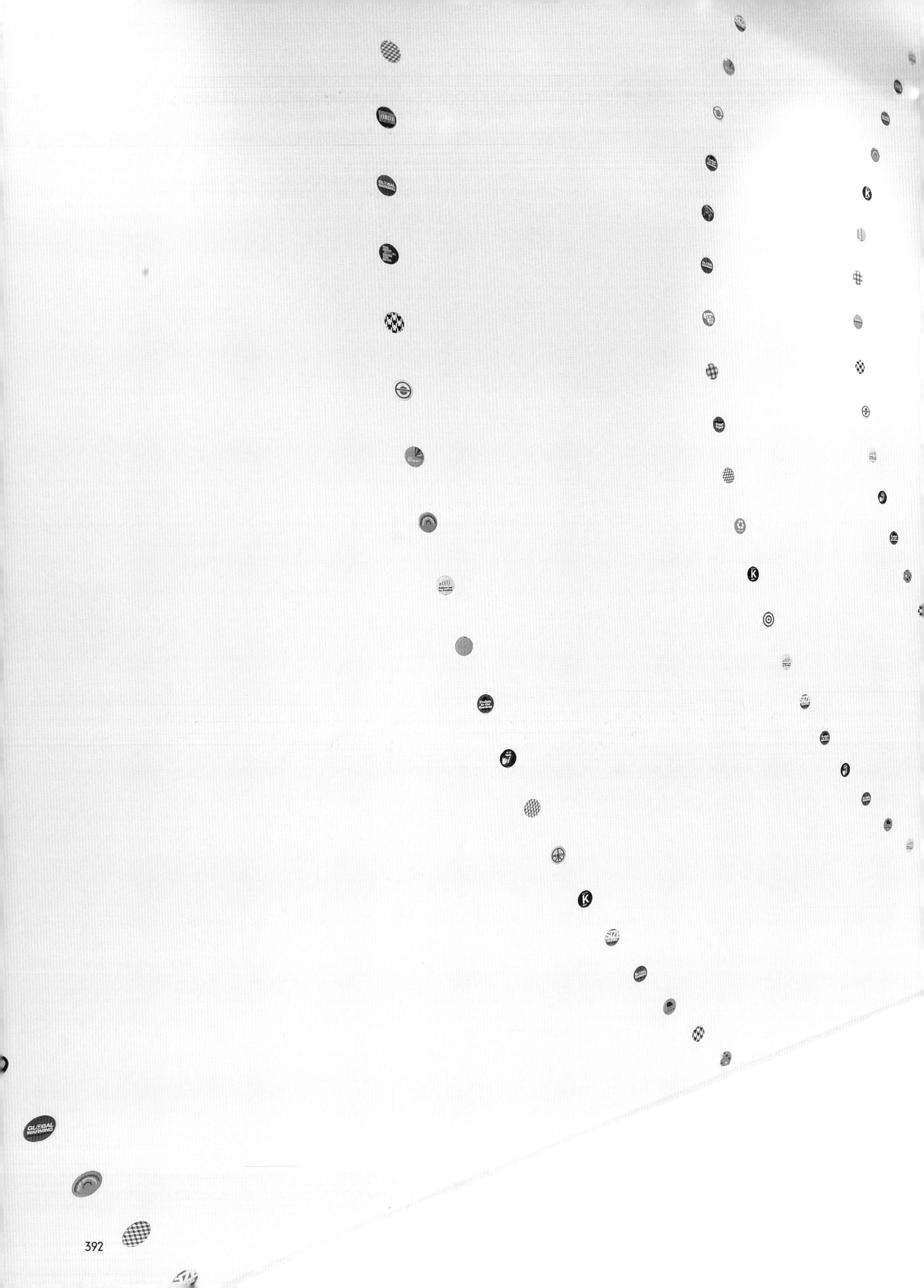
GLOBAL WARMING

ANN DEMEULEMEESTER FLAGSHIP STORE

SOUTH KOREA | SEOUL | SHOPS

ᴱᴺᴳ The ANN DEMEULEMEESTER FLAGSHIP STORE in Seoul comes across as an artificial grassy hill. It's a must for any fan of "botanical architecture". Minsuk Cho and Kisu Park of Mass Studies have created a multi-level building clad in moss and herbaceous plants for the renowned fashion designer. Green roofs and living walls cover both the interior and exterior walls. The structure embodies a convergence of dualities, natural and artificial, interior and exterior.

ᴰᴱᵁ Der ANN DEMEULEMEESTER FLAGSHIP STORE in Seoul wirkt wie ein künstlicher Grashügel. Er ist ein Muss für jeden Fan „botanischer Architektur". Minsuk Cho und Kisu Park von Mass Studies haben für die renommierte Modedesignerin ein in Moos und Kräuter gehülltes Gebäude mit verschiedenen Ebenen entworfen. Grüne Dächer und lebende Wände verkleiden die Innen- wie Außenwände. Es ist Gestalt gewordener Ausdruck für eine Annäherung der Dualitäten, zwischen natürlich und künstlich, innen und außen.

ᶠᴿ L'ANN DEMEULEMEESTER FLAGSHIP STORE de Séoul se dévoile au regard sous la forme d'une colline herbeuse. C'est un must imaginé par Minsuk Cho et Kisu Park de Mass Studies pour tout amoureux d'architecture « verte » : pour la célèbre styliste, les architectes ont créé un bâtiment à plusieurs étages recouvert de mousses et de plantes herbacées. Sur le toit comme sur les murs, les végétaux couvrent l'intérieur et l'extérieur et la structure incarne ainsi la convergence de deux opposés, la nature et l'artifice, l'intérieur et l'extérieur.

ᴺᴱᴰ De ANN DEMEULEMEESTER FLAGSHIP STORE in Seoul ziet eruit als een kunstmatige grasheuvel. Hij is een must voor elke fan van 'botanische architectuur'. Minsuk Cho en Kisu Park van Mass Studies hebben voor de gerenommeerde modeontwerpster een in mos en kruiden gehuld gebouw met verschillende niveaus ontworpen. Groene daken en levende wanden bedekken de binnen- en buitenmuren. Het is de vormgegeven uiting van een toenadering van de dualiteiten, tussen natuurlijk en kunstmatig, binnen en buiten.

PRADA TRANSFORMER

ᴱᴺᴳ It can be rotated or tilted, depending on the task. Rem Koolhaas constructed this marvel for Prada in Seoul. The structure consists of four welded geometric steel sections covered in a white membrane. 20 meters (66 feet) tall and weighing 180 tons. It actually has no walls, ceiling, or floor. Depending on the desired use, one side can be transformed into a wall or ceiling by rotating or tilting the entire structure. Rem Koolhaas is known for clean shapes and buildings that have a function. Not for eternity, just six months, because that's when it will be dismantled again.

ᴰᴱᵁ Er lässt sich drehen und kippen, abhängig von seiner Aufgabe. Gebaut hat ihn Rem Koolhaas für Prada in Seoul. Seine Konstruktion besteht aus vier geschweißten geometrischen Stahlteilen, die mit einer weißen Membran überzogen sind: 20 Meter hoch und 180 Tonnen schwer. Wände, Böden, Decken gibt es eigentlich nicht. Je nach Belieben ist eine Seite durch Drehen oder Kippen mal Wand, mal Decke. Rem Koolhaas steht für klare Formen und Gebäude mit einer Funktion. Nicht für die Ewigkeit, nur für sechs Monate, denn nach deren Ablauf wird der Shop wieder abgebaut.

ᶠᴿ Pour Prada, Rem Koolhaas a construit à Séoul cette merveille qui peut être tournée ou inclinée suivant le besoin. Réputé pour ses formes épurées et ses bâtiments fonctionnels, il signe ici une structure consistant en quatre sections géométriques métalliques soudées entre elles et recouvertes d'une membrane blanche. D'une hauteur de 20 mètres et d'un poids de 180 tonnes, elle ne possède en réalité ni murs, ni plafond, ni sol. Suivant l'utilisation souhaitée, l'une des parois peut devenir mur ou plafond par simple rotation ou inclinaison de l'ensemble de la structure. Celle-ci ne durera malheureusement pas éternellement, car elle sera à nouveau démontée après six mois.

ᴺᴱᴰ Hij kan worden gedraaid en gekanteld, afhankelijk van zijn taak. Door Rem Koolhaas is hij voor Prada in Seoul gebouwd. De constructie bestaat uit vier gelaste geometrische stalen delen, die met een wit membraan zijn bekleed: 20 meter hoog en 180 ton zwaar. Wanden, vloeren, plafonds zijn er eigenlijk niet. Naar believen is een zijde door draaien en kantelen soms wand, soms plafond. Rem Koolhaas staat voor heldere vormen en gebouwen met een functie. Niet voor de eeuwigheid, slechts voor een halfjaar, want na afloop daarvan wordt hij weer gedemonteerd.

HEALTH & BEAUTY
WELLNESS AND SPA RESORTS

UMA PARO – COMO HOTELS AND RESORTS

BHUTAN | PARO | HEALTH & BEAUTY

ENG Among Bhutan's unique characteristics is this odd but immediately perceptible feeling of peace. A place as if made for yoga and eastern-inspired therapies for body and soul. Built by traditional local craftsmen under the direction of architect Cheong Yew Kwan and interior designer Kathryn Kng, the UMA PARO is captivating with its sleek modern aesthetic constructed from local materials: stone and wood, lovingly accentuated with Bhutanese detail work. At once fresh, original, and entirely in the Bhutanese style—that's the architects' credo.

DEU Es gehört wohl zu den Besonderheiten Bhutans, dieses eigentümliche und sofort spürbare Empfinden von Frieden. Ein Platz wie geschaffen für Yoga und fernöstlich inspirierte Therapien für Körper und Seele. Gebaut von traditionellen heimischen Handwerkern unter Leitung von Architekt Cheong Yew Kwan und Innenarchitektin Kathryn Kng, besticht das UMA PARO durch seine moderne geradlinige Ästhetik aus heimischen Baustoffen. Stein und Holz, liebevoll akzentuiert mit bhutanischen Detailarbeiten. Frisch, originell und zugleich ganz im Stil des Landes – das Credo der Architekten.

IT Le Bhoutan possède de nombreuses qualités, mais sa caractéristique unique reste cette étrange sensation de paix, immédiatement perceptible. Voici un endroit qui semble avoir été conçu pour le yoga et les thérapies orientales pour l'âme et le corps. Construit par des artisans locaux sous la direction de l'architecte Cheong Yew Kwan et l'architecte d'intérieur Kathryn Kng, l'UMA PARO captive par son esthétique moderne et épurée. Les matériaux locaux, pierre et bois, sont joliment mis en valeur par des motifs bhoutanais. Ce lieu est à la fois rafraîchissant, original et 100% bhoutanais – c'est ce que désiraient les architectes.

NED Het behoort beslist tot de bijzonderheden van Bhutan, deze kenmerkende en direct merkbare ervaring van vrede. Een plaats geschapen voor yoga en oosterse therapieën voor lichaam en ziel. Het UMA PARO is gebouwd door traditionele ambachtslieden uit het land zelf onder leiding van architect Cheong Yew Kwan en binnenhuisarchitecte Kathryn Kng. De speciale aantrekkingskracht ervan is de moderne rechtlijnige esthetiek van bouwmaterialen uit de streek: steen en hout, liefdevol geaccentueerd met Bhutaans detailwerk. Fris, origineel en tegelijk geheel in de stijl van het land – het credo van de architecten.

ORIENTAL SPA AT THE LANDMARK MANDARIN ORIENTAL

CHINA | HONG KONG | HEALTH & BEAUTY

ᴱᴺᴳ The perfect balance of yin and yang rests on a combination of the five elements: wood, fire, earth, metal, and water. The coherently designed ORIENTAL SPA at the LANDMARK MANDARIN ORIENTAL luxury hotel is influenced by this philosophy not only in the way it's used, but in its interior as well. The interaction between bamboo, natural stone, gold leaf, fire, and water make this luxury spa, all 21,000 square meters (226,042 square feet) of it, a place of tranquility where you can forget the bustling metropolis of Hong Kong for a moment.

ᴰᴱᵁ Die perfekte Balance von Yin und Yang beruht auf der Kombination der fünf Elemente Holz, Feuer, Erde, Metall und Wasser. Diese Auffassung beeinflusst nicht nur die Art der Anwendungen, sondern auch das Interieur des ganzheitlich ausgerichteten ORIENTAL SPA des Luxushotels THE LANDMARK MANDARIN ORIENTAL. Das Zusammenspiel von Bambus, Naturstein, Blattgold, Feuer und Wasser macht dieses Spa der Luxusklasse auf insgesamt 21 000 Quadratmetern zu einem Ort der Ruhe, der die tosende Metropole Hongkong für eine Weile vergessen macht.

ᶠᴿ L'équilibre parfait entre le yin et le yang repose sur une combinaison de cinq éléments : le bois, le feu, la terre, le métal et l'eau. L'ORIENTAL SPA, situé dans le luxueux hôtel LANDMARK MANDARIN ORIENTAL, a été pensé en toute cohérence avec cette philosophie, non seulement dans son organisation, mais aussi dans son aspect intérieur. L'interaction du bambou, de la pierre naturelle, des feuilles d'or, du feu et de l'eau font de ce spa de luxe, s'étendant sur 2,1 hectares, un havre de tranquillité où l'on peut mettre de côté l'espace d'un moment le stress de la bourdonnante Hong Kong.

ᴺᴱᴰ Het volmaakte evenwicht van yin en yang berust op de combinatie van de vijf elementen hout, vuur, aarde, metaal en water. Deze opvatting beïnvloedt niet alleen de soort behandelingen, maar ook het interieur van de holistisch ingerichte ORIENTAL SPA van het luxehotel THE LANDMARK MANDARIN ORIENTAL. Het samenspel van bamboe, natuursteen, bladgoud, vuur en water maken van dit kuuroord in de luxeklasse op in totaal 21.000 vierkante kilometer een oord van rust, dat het lawaai van de metropool Hongkong even doet vergeten.

RAMBAGH PALACE

INDIA | JAIPUR | HEALTH & BEAUTY

ENG In times past, this form of luxury and extravagance was reserved only for kings, and later the maharajas. Formerly the Queen's hunting estate, later the Maharaja's residence, RAMBAGH PALACE is the embodiment of the rich culture and history of Rajastan's former rulers. As an architectural masterpiece, it is a mixture of the Rajput and Mughal building styles. Now painstakingly restored, today even uncrowned heads will find accommodation and a little peace of mind and body here in the palace's hotel and spa with their verandas, courtyard fountains, magnificent gardens, and serene terraces.

DEU Diese Form von Luxus und Extravaganz war in früheren Zeiten nur Königen, später den Maharadschas vorbehalten. Als ehemaliges Jagdschloss der Königin, danach Residenz des Maharadscha, ist der RAMBAGH PALACE die Verkörperung der reichen Kultur und Geschichte der einstigen Herrscher Rajasthans. Als architektonisches Meisterwerk ist er eine Mischung aus den Baustilen der Rajputen und Mogeten. Sorgsam restauriert finden heute auch ungekrönte Häupter Unterkunft und Ruhe für Körper und Seele im Palasthotel und Spa mit seinen Veranden, brunnenbesäumten Innenhöfen, prächtigen Gärten und verträumten Plätzen.

FR Cette forme de luxe et d'extravagance était jadis le domaine privé des rois. Ancien pavillon de chasse de la Reine devenu résidence du Maharaja, RAMBAGH PALACE incarne la culture et l'histoire flamboyantes des anciens dirigeants du Rajasthan. Ce chef-d'œuvre architectural est un mélange des styles Rajput et Mughal ; soigneusement restauré, il accueille aujourd'hui des têtes non couronnées qui trouveront une certaine paix spirituelle et corporelle dans ce palais doté d'un spa, de vérandas, de fontaines, de jardins envoûtants et de calmes terrasses.

NED Deze vorm van luxe en extravagantie was in vroeger tijden alleen voorbehouden aan koningen, en later aan de maharadja's. Als voormalig jachtslot van de koningin, daarna zetel van de maharadja, is het RAMBAGH PALACE de belichaming van de rijke cultuur en geschiedenis van de heersers van Rajastan van weleer. Als architectonisch meesterwerk is het een mengeling van de bouwstijlen van de rajputs en mogols. Het is zorgzaam gerestaureerd en ongekroonde hoofden krijgen nu ook onderdak en rust voor lichaam en ziel in het paleishotel en kuuroord met zijn veranda's, binnenhoven met fonteinen, prachtige tuinen en dromerige pleinen.

ANANDA – IN THE HIMALAYAS

INDIA | NARENDRA NAGAR | HEALTH & BEAUTY

ENG "Ananda" is the Sanskrit word for "bliss". A condition that appears easy to achieve when you see the magnificent palace of the Maharaja of Tehri Garhwal. Majestically situated, the palace offers a fabulous view of the Ganges and the Himalayas. "Ananda" also means "contentment". And that's exactly what this spa promotes. All treatments are based on the principles of yoga, ayurveda, and meditation. The ANANDA—IN THE HIMALAYAS, a royal and almost mystical place, is the perfect synthesis of the storybook splendor of an Indian palace and the luxury of modern life.

DEU „Ananda" bedeutet im Sanskrit „Seligkeit". Ein Zustand, der angesichts des prachtvollen Palastes des Maharadschas von Tehri Garhwal erreichbar scheint. Majestätisch gelegen bietet er einen phantastischen Blick über Ganges und den Himalaya. Zugleich bedeutet „Ananda" „Selbstzufriedenheit". Diese zu fördern ist der Ansatz des Spa. Die Prinzipien von Yoga, Ayurveda und Meditation sind die Basis aller Anwendungen. Das ANANDA – IN THE HIMALAYAS, ein königlicher und fast mystischer Ort, ist die perfekte Synthese aus der märchenhaften Pracht eines indischen Palastes und dem Luxus des modernen Lebens.

FR « Ananda » est la traduction en sanskrit du mot félicité. Cet état semble on ne peut plus facile à atteindre à la vue du magnifique palais du Maharaja de Tehri Garhwal. Son emplacement majestueux offre une vue fabuleuse sur le Gange et la chaîne de l'Himalaya. Mais « Ananda » signifie également contentement et le spa ne propose que du plaisir. Tous les traitements suivent les principes millénaires du yoga, de l'ayurveda et de la méditation. L'ANANDA – IN THE HIMALAYAS, et son aura royale presque mystique, est la synthèse parfaite de la splendeur passée des palais indiens et du luxe de la vie moderne.

NED 'Ananda' betekent in het Sanskriet 'zaligheid'. Een toestand die bij de aanblik van het prachtige paleis van de maharadja van Tehri Garhwal bereikbaar lijkt. Majestueus gelegen biedt het een fantastisch uitzicht over de Ganges en Himalaya. Tevens betekent 'ananda' 'zelfvoldaanheid'. Het bevorderen hiervan is de opzet van het kuuroord. De principes van yoga, ayurveda en meditatie vormen de basis van alle therapieën. Het ANANDA – IN THE HIMALAYAS, een koninklijk en bijna mystiek oord, is de perfecte synthese van de sprookjesachtige pracht van een Indiaas paleis en de luxe van het moderne leven.

BANYAN TREE SPA AT OBEROI UDAIVILAS

INDIA | UDAIPUR | HEALTH & BEAUTY

ENG Situated on the shore of Lake Pichola in Udaipur, the "Venice of India", the OBEROI UDAIVILAS is a royal palace in a fascinating setting. Open colonnades lined with 450 hand-chiseled stone columns, golden towers, frescoes, arches and fountains, marble terraces, and a spa for all the senses. The OBEROI UDAIVILAS is the synthesis of an adaptation of the cultural legacy of a royal era and the modern luxury of contemporary life.

DEU An den Gestaden des Lake Pichola in Udaipur, dem „Venedig Indiens", residiert das OBEROI UDAIVILAS, ein königlicher Palast in faszinierender Umgebung. Offene Kolonnaden flankiert von 450 handgemeißelten Steinsäulen, goldene Türme, Fresken, Bögen und Brunnen, Terrassen aus Marmor und ein Spa für alle Sinne. Das OBEROI UDAIVILAS ist die Synthese aus der Adaption des kulturellen Erbes einer königlichen Ära und dem modernen Luxus unserer Tage.

FR Situé sur les rives du lac Pichola en Udaipur, la « Venise indienne », l'OBEROI UDAIVILAS est un palais royal situé dans un cadre onirique. On y trouve des colonnades à ciel ouvert ponctuées de 450 piliers de pierre sculptés à la main, des tours dorées, des fresques, des arches et des fontaines, des terrasses de marbre et un spa pour tous les sens. L'OBEROI UDAIVILAS marie l'héritage culturel de la royauté au luxe moderne de la vie contemporaine.

NED Aan de oevers van het Pichola-meer in Udaipur, het 'Venetië van India', zetelt het OBEROI UDAIVILAS, een koninklijk paleis in een fascinerende omgeving. Open colonnades geflankeerd door 450 met de hand gemetselde stenen pilaren, gouden torens, fresco's, bogen en fonteinen, terrassen van marmer en een kuuroord voor alle zintuigen. Het OBEROI UDAIVILAS is de synthese van de aanpassing van het culturele erfgoed van een koninklijk tijdperk en de moderne luxe van onze tijd.

MINAMI-NAGANO DENTAL CLINIC

JAPAN | NAGANO | HEALTH & BEAUTY

ENG For patients with dental phobia, a pleasant, unclinical atmosphere and setting can be found here. Hiroki Tanabe has created three single-story buildings, arranged in a zigzag structure, out of 30 centimeter thick (12 inch thick) concrete. The three buildings are situated next to each other like slightly protruding cubes. The doctor's living quarters, clinic, waiting room—all contained in 280 square meters (3014 square feet). Two open courtyards are situated between the buildings. Glass boxes that function as connecting paths enhance the impression of walking through the open air. Doctor's chairs with views of greenery provide a relaxed feel. Everything, both interior and exterior, is white.

DEU Für Patienten mit Dentophobie bietet sich hier eine angenehme, unklinische Atmosphäre und Umgebung. Hiroki Tanabe gestaltete aus 30 Zentimeter dickem Beton drei eingeschossige Gebäude in Zickzack-Struktur. Wie leicht nach vorn geneigte Kuben stehen die drei Gebäude nebeneinander: Wohnraum des Arztes, Klinik, Wartezimmer, und alles auf 280 Quadratmetern. Zwischen den Gebäuden befinden sich zwei offene Innenhöfe. Glasboxen als Verbindungswege verstärken den Eindruck, man laufe durchs Freie. Behandlungsstühle mit Aussicht ins Grüne – für ein entspanntes Gefühl. Alles in Weiß, außen wie innen.

FR Les patients qui ont développé une phobie du dentiste vont trouver ici un cadre et une atmosphère agréables et peu cliniques. Hiroki Tanabe a créé ces trois immeubles de plain-pied en béton de 30 centimètres d'épaisseur. Les trois immeubles reposent en quinconce, comme trois cubes légèrement espacés. Ils accueillent la résidence du docteur, la clinique et la salle d'attente, toutes trois contenues dans 280 mètres carrés. Tout y est blanc, à l'intérieur comme à l'extérieur, et deux cours intérieures relient les bâtiments. Ces boîtes de verre fonctionnant comme des connecteurs intensifient l'impression de plein air, tandis que les fauteuils de soins donnant sur la verdure aident à la relaxation.

NED Voor patiënten met dentofobie biedt zich hier een aangename, onklinische sfeer en omgeving aan. Hiroki Tanabe maakte van 30 centimeter dik beton drie één verdieping tellende gebouwen in zigzagstructuur. Als licht naar voren hellende kubussen staan de drie gebouwen naast elkaar: woonruimte van de arts, kliniek, wachtkamer en alles op 280 vierkante meter. Tussen de gebouwen bevinden zich twee open binnenhoven. Glazen boxen als verbindingswegen versterken de indruk buiten te lopen. Behandelstoelen met uitzicht op het groen – voor een ontspannen gevoel. Alles wit, zowel buiten als binnen.

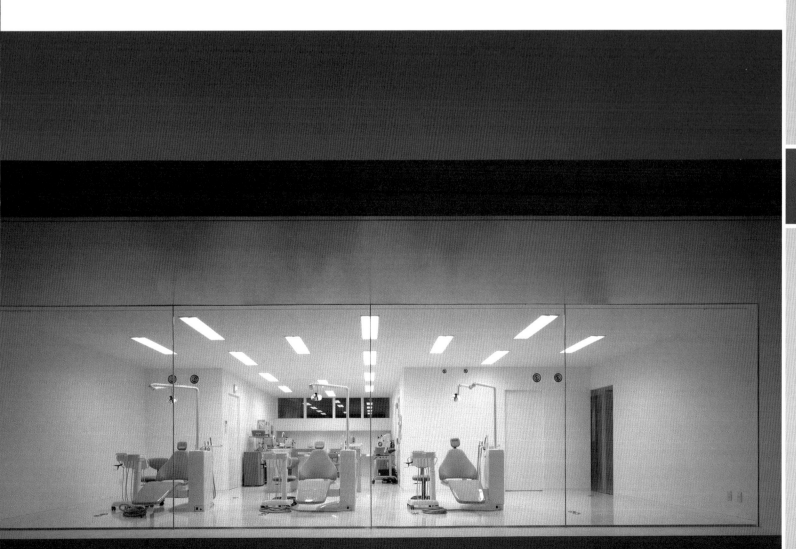

NIKI CLUB

JAPAN | NASU | HEALTH & BEAUTY

ENG Classical Ryokan elements re-interpreted: The room division and bathing ritual are traditional Japanese, while the architecture is ultra-modern. It took over 20 years for four renowned Japanese architects to design the NIKI CLUB's original buildings. Terence Conran completed the east wing, with a "network" of wood-clad guesthouses, a restaurant, and spa. This luxury oasis, hidden in the forests on the edge of the Nikko National Park, is characterized by clean lines, natural materials, large windows, and overgrown paths and bridges, along with some little design treasures.

DEU Klassische Elemente der Ryokan, neu interpretiert: Traditionell japanisch sind Raumaufteilung und Baderitual, ultramodern die Architektur. Vier renommierte japanische Architekten entwarfen vor mehr als 20 Jahren die Originalgebäude des NIKI CLUB. Und Terence Conran vollendete den Ostflügel, mit einem „Geflecht" aus holzverkleideten Gästehäusern, einem Restaurant und dem Spa. Klare Linien, natürliche Materialien, große Fensterflächen, überwucherte Pfade und Brücken und dazu kleine Designkostbarkeiten machen sie aus, diese Luxusoase versteckt in den Wäldern am Rand des Nikko-Nationalparks.

FR Le ryokan classique a été réinterprété : la répartition des pièces et le lieu dédié aux bains suivent la tradition japonaise et font face à une architecture générale ultramoderne. Il aura fallu plus de 20 ans à quatre célèbres architectes japonais pour créer les bâtiments du NIKI CLUB. Terence Conran a constitué l'aile est en un « réseau » de maisonnettes de bois, un restaurant et un spa. Cette oasis de luxe, cachée dans la forêt en bordure du Nikko National Park, n'est faite que de lignes pures, de matériaux naturels, de larges fenêtres, de ponts et de sentiers restés sauvages ; l'ensemble est délicatement ponctué de petits trésors design.

NED Klassieke elementen van de ryokan, opnieuw geïnterpreteerd: Traditioneel Japans zijn de ruimte-indeling en het badritueel, ultramodern is de architectuur. Vier gerenommeerde Japanse architecten ontwierpen meer dan 20 jaar geleden het oorspronkelijke gebouw van de NIKI CLUB. En Terence Conran voltooide de oostelijke vleugel, met een 'vlechtwerk' van met hout beklede gastenverblijven, een restaurant en het kuuroord. Heldere lijnen, natuurlijke materialen, grote raamvlakken, overwoekerde paden en bruggen en verder kleine designkostbaarheden kenmerken deze in de bossen aan de rand van het nationaal park Nikko verborgen luxeoase.

EVASON MA'IN HOT SPRINGS & SIX SENSES SPA

JORDAN | MA'IN | HEALTH & BEAUTY

ENG Situated on a thermal waterfall, quiet and secluded in the idyllic Ma'in Valley, surrounded by mountains, between the Dead Sea and Madaba. 264 meters (866 feet) below sea level, directly beneath the Ma'in hot springs, that's where travelers will find the SIX SENSES SPA with its two thermal pools, beauty salon, and Roman bath. The hotel combines unconventional design with natural materials. Accentuated with wood, candles, and soft pillows. The restaurant provides stunning views of the Dead Sea from its position on the rock plateau. And for the soul: yoga on the mountaintop, next to the waterfall.

DEU Es liegt an einem Thermalwasserfall, ruhig und versteckt im idyllischen Ma'in-Tal, umgeben von Bergen, zwischen dem Toten Meer und Madaba. 264 Meter unter dem Meeresspiegel, direkt unter den heißen Quellen von Ma'in findet der Gast das SIX SENSES SPA mit zwei Thermalpools, Beautysalon und römischem Bad. Im Hotel wurde unkonventionelles Design mit natürlichen Materialien kombiniert. Dazu Holz, Kerzen und weiche Kissen. Das Restaurant auf dem Felsplateau gibt einen herrlichen Blick auf das Tote Meer frei. Und für die Seele: Yoga auf dem Berggipfel, nebenan der Wasserfall.

FR Situé au pied d'une cascade d'eau thermale, dans la quiétude et le retrait de l'idyllique Ma'in Valley, ce spa est entouré de montagnes, entre la mer Morte et Madaba. À 264 mètres sous le niveau de la mer, directement au pied des sources chaudes de Ma'in, c'est ici que les voyageurs trouveront le SIX SENSES SPA et ses deux piscines thermales, son salon de beauté et ses thermes romains. L'hôtel combine un design inhabituel à des matériaux naturels, créant une ambiance accueillante accentuée par la présence de bois, de bougies et de coussins moelleux. Depuis son plateau rocheux, le restaurant offre une vue étourdissante sur la mer Morte et, pour nourrir les âmes, le yoga se pratique au sommet de la montagne, à proximité de la cascade.

NED Het ligt aan een thermale waterval, rustig en verscholen in het idyllische Ma'in-dal, omringd door bergen, tussen de Dode Zee en Madaba. 264 meter onder de zeespiegel, direct onder de hete bronnen van Ma'in treft de gast de SIX SENSES SPA aan met twee thermale zwembaden, schoonheidssalon en Romeins bad. In het hotel is onconventioneel design met natuurlijke materialen gecombineerd. Verder hout, kaarsen en zachte kussens. Het restaurant op het rotsplateau biedt een heerlijk vrij uitzicht op de Dode Zee. En voor de ziel: yoga op de bergtop, naast de waterval.

ANDAMAN SPA

MALAYSIA | LANGKAWI | HEALTH & BEAUTY

[ENG] THE ANDAMAN is nestled in a million-year-old tropical rainforest on Langkawi between the Andaman Sea and the majestic Mat Cincang mountain range. Its creators made it their main objective to achieve harmony between the architecture and its natural surroundings. They created a resort & spa that visibly accomplishes this. The architecture is inspired by the traditional Malaysian building style, elegantly accentuated and luxurious. A place full of peace and tranquility, in harmony with that mystical island whose unique beauty has stimulated the imagination since time immemorial.

[DEU] Auf Langkawi, zwischen der Andamanen-See und der majestätischen Mat-Cincang-Gebirgskette, liegt THE ANDAMAN eingebettet in einen Millionen Jahre alten tropischen Regenwald. Seinen Erbauern ging es vor allem darum, die Harmonie zwischen der Architektur und der sie umgebenden Natur herzustellen. Entstanden ist ein Resort & Spa, das diesen Anspruch sichtbar erfüllt. Die Architektur ist inspiriert von der traditionellen malaiischen Bauweise, elegant akzentuiert, luxuriös. Ein Ort voller Frieden und Ruhe, im Einklang mit jener mystischen Insel, die aufgrund ihrer besonderen Schönheit die Phantasie der Menschen von jeher auf so besondere Weise beflügelt.

[FR] THE ANDAMAN est nichée au cœur d'une forêt humide vieille d'un million d'années sur l'île de Langkawi, entre la mer d'Andaman et la majestueuse chaîne de montagnes de Mat Cincang. Ses créateurs avaient pour principal objectif d'harmoniser l'architecture du bâtiment avec son cadre naturel. Ils ont fait sortir de terre un complexe & spa répondant visiblement à leur problématique, car l'architecture tire son inspiration des constructions traditionnelles malaisiennes et s'enrichit d'éléments élégants et luxueux. Cet endroit semble empli de calme et de tranquillité, en harmonie avec cette île mystique dont la beauté unique stimule les imaginations depuis des temps immémoriaux.

[NED] Op Langkawi, tussen de Andamanse Zee en de majestueuze Mat Cincang-bergketen, ligt THE ANDAMAN verscholen in een miljoenen jaren oud tropisch regenwoud. Het ging er de bouwers vooral om harmonie tussen architectuur en de omringende natuur te bewerkstelligen. Er kwam een resort & spa tot stand dat aan deze eis duidelijk voldoet. De architectuur is geïnspireerd door de traditionele Maleise bouwwijze, elegant geaccentueerd, luxueus. Een oord vol vrede en rust, in harmonie met dat mythische eiland, dat door zijn buitengewone schoonheid de fantasie van de mensen van weleer op zo'n bijzondere wijze stimuleert.

437

THE DATAI SPA

MALAYSIA | LANGKAWI | HEALTH & BEAUTY

ENG Langkawi is a mystical island with jungle-covered mountains, lakes, caves, and waterfalls. Walking trails lead through pristine centuries-old rainforests, up into the mountains, down to white sand beaches and to the resort's freestanding villas. 110 rooms and suites in the traditional Malaysian style are spread out through the wings of the main house as well as in freestanding villas, with or without a pool, jacuzzi, and day bed. Then there's the 18-hole Datai Bay golf course and a spa equipped with the very finest, at once luxurious and purist. Testaments to modern life on this island full of secrets and fantastic tales.

DEU Langkawi ist eine mystische Insel mit dschungelbedeckten Bergen, Seen, Höhlen und Wasserfällen. Fußwege führen durch jahrhundertealte unberührte Regenwälder, in die Berge, an weiße Strände und zu den freistehenden Villen des Resorts. 110 im landestypischen Stil gebaute und eingerichtete Zimmer und Suiten sind untergebracht teils in den Flügeln des Haupthauses, teils in freistehenden Villen, mit oder ohne Pool, Jacuzzi und Daybed. Dazu der 18-Loch-Datai-Bay-Golf Course und ein Spa, ausgestattet mit dem Feinsten, luxuriös und puristisch zugleich. Zeugen des modernen Lebens auf dieser Insel voller Geheimnisse und phantastischer Geschichten.

FR Langkawi est une île mythique recouverte de jungles, de montagnes, de lacs, de grottes et de chutes d'eau. Suivre ses sentiers conduit inévitablement à pénétrer des forêts humides séculaires et à gravir des montagnes pour rejoindre des plages de sable blanc mais aussi à acceder aux villas indépendantes de ce complexe. Les 110 chambres et suites issues de la plus pure tradition malaisienne sont disséminées dans les ailes du bâtiment principal ou dans des villas indépendantes, avec ou sans piscine, jacuzzi et banquette extérieure. On y trouve également un parcours de golf de 18 trous et un spa doté des meilleurs équipements où tout respire le plus grand luxe. Le témoignage unique de la vie moderne sur cette île regorge de secrets et de récits fantastiques.

NED Langkawi is een mythisch eiland met door oerwoud bedekte bergen, meren, grotten en watervallen. Voetpaden leiden door eeuwenoude ongerepte regenwouden, naar de bergen, witte stranden en de vrijstaande villa's van het resort. 110 ingerichte kamers en suites die gebouwd werden in de stijl van het land zijn deels ondergebracht in de vleugels van het hoofdgebouw, deels in vrijstaande villa's, met of zonder zwembad, jacuzzi en daybed. Verder nog Datai Bay Golfbaan met 18 holes en een kuuroord, uitgerust met het allerbeste, luxueus en puristisch tegelijk. Getuigen van het moderne leven op dit eiland vol geheimen en fantastische verhalen.

TAJ EXOTICA RESORT & SPA

MALDIVES | SOUTH MALE ATOLL | HEALTH & BEAUTY

ENG There are water villas, bungalows built on stilts in the lagoon that boast Italian marble and Indonesian teak, opulent Indian mirrors, crimson silk pillows, and the GRANDE JIVA SPA. Even the path to the spa is something for body and soul, leading through luxuriant gardens and shaded pathways. Guests come here to be pampered with traditional Indian treatments—both inside and out. It was constructed according to the principles of Vastu, the holistic Indian philosophy that teaches living in harmony with natural and cosmic laws.

DEU Es gibt Wasservillen, Bungalows, die auf Stelzen in die Lagune gebaut wurden, ausgestattet mit italienischem Marmor und indonesischem Teak, prunkvollen indischen Spiegeln und purpurnen Seidenkissen, und das GRANDE JIVA SPA. Schon der Weg zum Spa ist etwas für Körper und Seele. Er führt auf schattigen Wegen durch üppige Gärten. Hier werden Gäste mit traditionellen indischen Anwendungen verwöhnt – innen wie außen. Erbaut ist es nach den Regeln der Vastu-Philosphie, der ganzheitlichen Lehre Indiens vom Wohnen und Leben in Harmonie mit den Gesetzmäßigkeiten der Natur und dem Kosmos.

FR Au GRANDE JIVA SPA, les villas ont les pieds dans l'eau, des bungalows sur pilotis mouillent dans le lagon, le marbre italien se mêle au teck indonésien et d'opulents miroirs indiens reflètent des coussins de soie pourpre. Passage forcé à travers les jardins luxuriants et sur des allées ombragées, le chemin vers le spa est en lui-même un soin bienfaisant. On vient ici se faire dorloter à l'aide de remèdes traditionnels indiens, pour le corps comme pour l'esprit. Construit selon les principes du Vastu, la philosophie holistique indienne, cet établissement suit les préceptes d'une vie en harmonie avec la nature et les lois cosmiques.

NED Er zijn watervilla's, bungalows, die op stelten in de baai zijn gebouwd, uitgerust met Italiaans marmer en Indonesisch teak, luisterrijke Indiase spiegels, purperen zijden kussen en de GRANDE JIVA SPA. Alleen al de weg naar het kuuroord is heilzaam voor lichaam en ziel. Hij loopt via beschaduwde paden door weelderige tuinen. Hier worden de gasten traditioneel met Indiase behandelingen verwend – van binnen en van buiten. Het geheel is gebouwd volgens de regels van de Vastu-filosofie, de holistische Indiase leer van het wonen en leven in harmonie met de wetmatigheden van de natuur en de kosmos.

THE ANANTI KUMGANG MOUNTAIN SPA

NORTH KOREA | KUMGANG MOUNTAIN | HEALTH & BEAUTY

ENG This is North Korea's first international golf & spa resort. Surrounded by the picturesque mountain scenery of Kumgangsan, with views of the East Sea, it's certainly one of the most beautiful as well. 1,650,000 square meters (17,760,452 square feet) with an 18-hole championship golf course. A spa and hot springs provide perfect relaxation. Each room is fitted with handcrafted furniture designed by Jaya Ibrahim. High ceilings, a panoramic view of the golf course, mountains, or sea from every room, and a spa with everything worthy of the term state-of-the-art.

DEU Es ist das erste internationale Golf- & Spa-Resort Nordkoreas. Umringt von den malerischen Gebirgszügen von Kumgangsan, mit Blick über die East Sea, ist es gewiss auch eines der schönsten. 1 650 000 Quadratmeter mit einem 18 Loch-Championship-Golf-Kurs. Ein Spa und heiße Quellen dienen der perfekten Entspannung. Jedes Zimmer ausgestattet mit handgefertigten Möbeln, designt von Jaya Ibrahim. Hohe Decken, alle Zimmer mit Panoramablick über Golfplatz, Berge oder das Meer und ein Spa mit allem, was man wenigstens State-of-the-art nennen kann.

FR C'est le premier resort golf & spa international de Corée du Nord. Entouré par les cimes pittoresques des monts Kumgangsan et donnant sur la mer du Japon, ce spa suréquipé est également l'un des plus beaux au monde. Sur 165 hectares, un parcours de golf de 18 trous, un spa et des sources chaudes permettent une relaxation totale. Chaque chambre accueille son lot de mobilier artisanal pensé par Jaya Ibrahim, une belle hauteur sous plafond et une vue panoramique sur le parcours de golf, les montagnes ou la mer.

NED Het is het eerste internationale Golf & Spa-resort van Noord-Korea. Omringd door de schilderachtige bergketens van Kumgangsan, met uitzicht op de Japanse Zee, is het beslist het mooiste. 1.650.000 vierkante meter met een Championship-golfbaan met 18-holes. Een kuuroord en hete bronnen zorgen voor volmaakte ontspanning. Elke kamer is uitgerust met handgemaakte meubels, ontworpen door Jaya Ibrahim. Hoge plafonds, alle kamers met panoramisch uitzicht over golfbaan, bergen of de zee en een kuuroord met alles wat op z'n minst ultramodern kan worden genoemd.

THE CHEDI SPA

SULTANATE OF OMAN | MUSCAT | HEALTH & BEAUTY

ENG The CHEDI MUSCAT is an exclusive beach resort on a private stretch of Al Ghubra beach. It is a designer hotel & spa constructed in a purist fashion with clean lines and the traditional architecture of the Sultanate of Oman. Each room offers a spectacular view of water gardens or the Hajjar Mountains. Domes, characteristic of the Chedi Club suites, give a certain eastern charm to the property. There is also a spa in the modern Arabian style, equipped with everything that contemporary bath design has to offer.

DEU Das CHEDI MUSCAT ist ein exklusives Beach Resort am privaten Strand von Al Ghubbra. Es ist ein Designer-Hotel & Spa, puristisch, mit klaren Linien und in der traditionellen Architektur des Sultanats Oman erbaut. Jedes Zimmer verfügt über einen grandiosen Blick auf Wassergärten oder die Hajjar-Gebirgszüge. Kuppeln, die die Chedi Club Suiten kennzeichnen, verleihen dem Anwesen den orientalischen Charme. Dazu ein Spa in modernem arabischem Stil, ausgestattet mit dem, was die hochmoderne Badgestaltung heute zu bieten hat.

FR Le CHEDI MUSCAT est un complexe sélect situé sur une extension de la plage d'Al Ghubra. Cet hôtel & spa de designer est une construction puriste aux lignes nettes et à l'architecture traditionnelle du sultanat d'Oman. Chaque chambre offre une vue spectaculaire sur les jardins d'eau ou les monts Hajjar. Les dômes, caractéristiques des suites du Chedi Club, prodiguent un charme à l'orientale à cette propriété. Le spa d'inspiration arabe est moderne et équipé de tout ce que notre époque a su créer de mieux.

NED Het CHEDI MUSCAT is een exclusief strandresort aan het privéstrand van Al Ghubbra. Het is een designerhotel met kuuroord, puristisch, met heldere lijnen en in de traditionele architectuur van het Sultanaat Oman gebouwd. Elke kamer beschikt over een grandioos uitzicht op watertuinen of de Hajjar-bergketen. Koepels, die de Chedi Club suites kenmerken, verlenen het geheel zijn oosterse charme. Verder is het een kuuroord in moderne Arabische stijl, uitgerust met alles wat de uiterst moderne badvormgeving tegenwoordig te bieden heeft.

455

EVASON HIDEAWAY & SIX SENSES SPA AT ZIGHY BAY

SULTANATE OF OMAN | ZIGHY BAY | HEALTH & BEAUTY

ENG In the background are rugged mountain chains reaching up to 2100 meters (6890 feet) in elevation, in the foreground are fine sand beaches. The Musandam peninsula is an Omani enclave on the Strait of Hormuz, separated from the rest of the country by the United Arab Emirates. It has been called the Norway of the Middle East. The resort comprises 82 villas, all with generous rooms, decorated in traditional Omani style combined with the latest technology and baths that can be extended to form outdoor showers. Every villa has its own pool. You can dine at sea level on the sand, or up on the cliffs at 290 meters (950 feet), naturally with a gorgeous view.

DEU Im Hintergrund schroffe Gebirgszüge, die sich bis auf 2 100 Meter erheben, nach vorne feinsandige Strände. Die Musandam-Halbinsel ist eine Enklave von Oman an der Straße von Hormus, getrennt vom Rest des Landes durch die Vereinigten Arabischen Emirate. Genannt wird es auch das Norwegen des Mittleren Ostens. 82 Villen umfasst das Resort, alle mit großzügigen Räumen, eingerichtet in der Tradition des Oman, geknüpft an modernste Technik, und mit Bädern, die zu Outdoor-Duschen ausgeweitet werden können. Jede Villa hat einen eigenen Pool. Speisen kann man auf Meereshöhe im Sand oder in den Felsen in 290 Metern Höhe mit wunderschönem Ausblick.

FR En arrière-plan apparaît une chaîne de montagnes pouvant atteindre 2 100 mètres de hauteur et au premier plan s'étendent des plages de sable fin. La péninsule de Musandam est une enclave du sultanat d'Oman sur le détroit d'Hormuz, séparée du reste du pays par les Émirats Arabes unis, que l'on surnomme parfois la Norvège du Moyen-Orient. Le complexe compte 82 villas, toutes dotées de chambres spacieuses, décorées dans la plus pure tradition omani, proposant les dernières technologies et des salles de bains possédant une extension extérieure. Chaque villa a sa propre piscine et il est possible de dîner sur le sable ou au sommet d'une falaise de 290 mètres de haut, offrant naturellement une vue inoubliable.

NED Op de achtergrond steile bergketens 2100 meter en vooraan fijne zandstranden. Het Musandam-schiereiland is een enclave van Oman aan de Straat van Hormus, gescheiden van de rest van het land door de Verenigde Arabische Emiraten. Het wordt wel het Noorwegen van het Midden-Oosten genoemd. Het resort omvat 82 villa's, alle met royale kamers, ingericht in de traditie van Oman, gekoppeld aan de modernste techniek en baden, die tot buitendouches kunnen worden uitgebreid. Elke villa met eigen zwembad. Gegeten kan er worden op zeeniveau op het strand of op de rotsen op 290 meter hoogte met wondermooi uitzicht.

AMANGALLA SPA

SRI LANKA | DIAVARAM | HEALTH & BEAUTY

ENG THE BATHS is the name of the AMANGALLA's spa, located in Fort Galle, once a base for the former Dutch colonial rulers. Here old ayurveda traditions are harmonized with the luxury of the Aman resorts. And the setting? Antique furniture, sterling silver, precious chandeliers, four-poster beds, and freestanding bathtubs—colonial ambience combined with the amenities of modern life. The fort was built in 1663, the ensemble of colonial manors in 1684. These structures have housed the Oriental Hotel since 1863, the AMANGALLA since 2002. And it has been a Unesco World Heritage Site since 1988.

DEU THE BATHS heißt das Spa des AMANGALLA, das sich in Fort Galle, einem Stützpunkt der früheren holländischen Kolonial-herren, befindet. Hier werden alte Ayurveda-Traditionen mit dem Luxus der Amanresorts in Einklang gebracht. Und die Umgebung? Antike Möbel, edles Silber, kostbare Lüster, Himmelbetten und freistehende Badewannen – koloniales Ambiente kombiniert mit den Errungenschaften des modernen Lebens. 1663 wurde das Fort erbaut, 1684 das Ensemble kolonialer Herrenhäuser. Seit 1863 beherbergen die Häuser das Oriental Hotel. Seit 2002 das AMANGALLA. Und seit 1988 ist es Unesco-Weltkulturerbe.

FR THE BATHS est le nom donné au spa de l'AMANGALLA, situé à Fort Galle, ancien fief des colons néerlandais. Ici, les anciennes traditions ayurvédiques s'harmonisent à merveille avec le luxueux complexe d'Aman. Le cadre, le mobilier d'époque, l'argent massif, les chandeliers précieux, les lits à baldaquins et les baignoires sur pieds convoquent l'époque coloniale pour la combiner aux équipements de la vie moderne. Le fort a été construit en 1663 et l'ensemble des demeures coloniales en 1684. Ces structures accueillaient l'Hôtel Oriental depuis 1863 et l'AMANGALLA y a installé ses quartiers depuis 2002. Il est classé au patrimoine mondial par l'Unesco depuis 1988.

NED THE BATHS heet het kuuroord van het AMANGALLA, dat zich bevindt in fort Galle, een steunpunt van de vroegere Hollandse ko-loniale heersers. Hier worden oude ayurvedische tradities met de luxe van het Amanresort in overeenstemming gebracht. En de omgeving? Antieke meubels, edel zilver, kostbare lusters, hemelbedden en losstaande badkuipen – koloniale ambiance gecombi-neerd met de verworvenheden van het moderne leven. In 1663 werd het fort gebouwd, in 1684 het geheel van koloniale herenhui-zen. Sinds 1863 herbergen de huizen het Oriental Hotel. Sinds 2002 het AMANGALLA. En sinds 1988 is het Unesco-wereldcul-tuurerfgoed.

THE SPA – MILLENNIUM HILTON BANGKOK

THAILAND | BANGKOK | HEALTH & BEAUTY

ENG In the MILLENNIUM HILTON BANGKOK, guests can embrace the wellness experience without any eccentric bells or whistles. The spa is located at the foot of the hotel, directly on the shore of the Chao Phraya, the "River of Kings". In the middle are two very old, particularly beautiful banyan trees. They are the center of a modern structure with a sparse, no-frills appearance and complete devotion to its intended purpose.

DEU Ohne jeden esoterischen Schnörkel wird dem Gast im Spa des MILLENNIUM HILTON BANGKOK das Erlebnis Wellness nahe gebracht. Es liegt unmittelbar am Ufer des Chao Praya, des „Flusses der Könige" zu Füßen des Hotels. Zwei sehr alte, besonders schöne Banyan-Bäume bilden seine Mitte. Sie sind das Zentrum für einen modernen Ort, der sich schlicht und geradlinig gibt und einzig und allein seiner Aufgabe verschrieben hat.

FR Au MILLENNIUM HILTON BANGKOK, les hôtes font l'expérience du bien-être sans aucun cérémonial ésotérique. Le spa se trouve au pied de l'hôtel, directement sur la côte du Chao Phraya, le « Fleuve des rois ». Dans sa cour intérieure trônent deux magnifiques figuiers des banians centenaires. Ils sont aujourd'hui le centre de cette structure moderne à l'apparence épurée et sans fioritures, totalement dévouée à sa fonction.

NED Zonder enige esoterische franje wordt de gast in het kuuroord van het MILLENNIUM HILTON BANGKOK met de wellness-belevenis vertrouwd gemaakt. Het ligt direct aan de oever van de Chao Praya, de 'Rivier der Koningen' aan de voet van het hotel. Twee zeer oude, bijzonder mooie banyanbomen staan in het midden. Ze vormen het centrum van een modern oord, dat er eenvoudig en strak uitziet en enkel en alleen aan zijn taak is gewijd.

THE CHEDI CHIANG MAI SPA

THAILAND | CHIANG MAI | HEALTH & BEAUTY

[ENG] The hotel lobby is situated on the shores of Mae Ping, in the main building of the former British Consulate in Chiang Mai, nestled in a courtyard with reflecting pools. The other buildings are arranged around it and together create inner patios, each with its own character. Teak trellises, large roof overhangs, dark wood floors, the characteristic red tiles, furniture made from rattan and fine woods, local materials, and a traditional design are given a modern interpretation here. And then there are lanterns and natural light, baths that can be opened if you wish, everything with a view of the garden and surrounding river scenery. And the spa, with its steam showers and bathtubs on the terrace, is luxurious, contemporary, and characteristically Asian all at the same time.

[DEU] Am Ufer des Mae Ping, im Hauptgebäude des früheren Britischen Konsulats von Chiang Mai, befindet sich die Hotellobby, eingebettet in einen Hof mit reflektierendem Wasserbecken. Die anderen Gebäude sind rundum angeordnet und bilden im Zusammenspiel innen gelegene Patios, jeder mit eigenem Charakter. Teakholz-Spaliere, große überhängende Dächer, dunkle Holzböden, die typischen roten Kacheln, Möbel aus Rattan und edle Hölzer, lokale Materialien und traditionelles Design werden hier modern interpretiert. Dazu Lampions und natürliches Licht, Bäder, nach Belieben zu öffnen, alles mit Blick auf Garten und Flusslandschaft. Und das Spa mit Dampfduschen und Badewannen auf der Terrasse ist luxuriös, zeitgenössisch und typisch asiatisch zugleich.

[FR] L'entrée de l'hôtel se trouve sur les rives du Mae Ping, dans le bâtiment principal de l'ancien consulat britannique de Chiang Mai, lové dans une cour aux bassins miroitants. Les autres bâtiments s'articulent autour de lui en créant des patios, à l'identité unique. Des treilles en teck, de larges auvents, des sols de bois sombre, des céramiques rouges, du mobilier en rotin et en bois précieux, des matériaux locaux et un design traditionnel réinterprètent la modernité à leur manière. Sans parler des lampions et de la lumière naturelle, des bains que l'on peut ouvrir sur l'extérieur, des innombrables vues sur le jardin et sur la rivière… Le spa, avec ses douches de vapeur et ses baignoires à l'air libre, est à la fois luxueux, contemporain et typiquement asiatique.

[NED] Aan de oever van de Mae Ping, in het hoofdgebouw van het vroegere Britse consulaat van Chiang Mai, bevindt zich de hotellobby, verscholen op een binnenplaats met reflecterende waterbekkens. De andere gebouwen staan er omheen en vormen in samenspel ermee binnen gelegen patio's, elk met zijn eigen karakter. Teakhouten spalieren, grote overhangende daken, donkere houten vloeren, de typische rode tegels, meubels van rotan en kostbare houtsoorten, plaatselijke materialen en traditioneel ontwerp zijn hier modern geïnterpreteerd. Daarbij nog lampions en natuurlijk licht, baden, alles met blik op tuin en rivierlandschap. Het kuuroord met stoomdouches en badkuipen op het terras is luxueus, eigentijds en typisch Aziatisch tegelijk.

ASSAWAN SPA & HEALTH CLUB AT BURJ AL ARAB

UNITED ARAB EMIRATES | DUBAI | HEALTH & BEAUTY

ENG This luxury spa is located on the 18th floor of what might well be the world's most famous hotel, the BURJ AL ARAB. The "Tower of Arabs" is a unique hotel structure, built in the shape of a sail. A helipad on top, a waterfall in the atrium, all on an artificial island just off Dubai. To get to the ASSAWAN SPA you take a gilt panorama elevator up from the lobby. The ASSAWAN, done in the style of Eastern baths, is opulent, golden, decorated with mosaics, and equipped with high-tech equipment and the whole conceivable range of modern treatments and therapies. The spa is named after the "stone of purity", said to have special healing powers.

DEU Im 18. Stock des wohl berühmtesten Hotels der Welt, dem BURJ AL ARAB, befindet sich das Luxus-Spa. Der „Turm der Araber" ist ein Hotelbau der besonderen Art, in der Form eines Segels. Ein Hubschrauberlandeplatz in der Spitze, der Wasserfall im Atrium, alles auf einer künstlichen, Dubai vorgelagerten Insel. Der Weg zum ASSAWAN SPA führt über einen vergoldeten Panoramalift von der Lobby aus. Das ASSAWAN im Stil orientalischer Bäder ist prachtvoll, golden, verziert mit Mosaiken und ausgestattet mit Hightech-Geräten und dem gesamten vorstellbaren Spektrum an modernen Behandlungen und Therapien. Seinen Namen gibt ihm der „Stein der Reinheit". Man sagt, er verfüge über besondere Heilkraft.

FR Ce spa de luxe se trouve au 18ème étage de ce que l'on peut qualifier d'hôtel le plus célèbre au monde, le BURJ AL ARAB. La « Tour des Arabes » est une structure hôtelière unique, en forme de voile. Un héliport en son sommet et une cascade dans l'atrium caractérisent cette île artificielle sur les rives de Dubaï. Pour atteindre l'ASSAWAN SPA il faut emprunter un ascenseur panoramique doré. Opulent, doré, décoré de mosaïques et équipé des dernières nouveautés techniques, l'ASSAWAN rappelle les bains d'Orient et propose toutes les thérapies et traitements modernes. Le spa porte le nom d'une « pierre de pureté », réputée pour ses qualités thérapeutiques.

NED Op de 18e verdieping van het beroemdste hotel ter wereld, het BURJ AL ARAB, bevindt zich het luxekuuroord. De 'Toren der Arabieren' is een bijzonder hotelgebouw, in de vorm van een zeil. Een helikopterlandingsplaats op de top, de waterval in het atrium, alles op een kunstmatig, voor Dubai gelegen eiland. De route naar de ASSAWAN SPA loopt via een vergulde panoramalift vanuit de lobby. Het ASSAWAN in de stijl van oosterse baden is prachtig, goudglanzend, versierd met mozaïeken en uitgerust met hightechapparaten en het hele denkbare spectrum aan moderne behandelingen en therapieën. Het is vernoemd naar de Assawan-steen, de 'steen der reinheid'. Deze zou over speciale geneeskracht beschikken.

LIME SPA AT DESERT PALM

UNITED ARAB EMIRATES | DUBAI | HEALTH & BEAUTY

ENG An Arabian spa with color therapy, 24 karat gold lip balm, and live polo matches. Golden elements, but understated. Natural colors and materials meet rich chocolate tones. There are splashes of color in the form of retro patterns and contemporary art. Altogether a well-coordinated design concept that stretches through the entire structure, including the spa. A design that creates a relaxed atmosphere in a resort both close to the city and secluded at the same time.

DEU Ein arabisches Spa mit Farbtherapie, 24-Karat-Gold-Lippenbalsam und Live-Polo-Matches. Goldene Elemente, aber Understatement. Natürliche Farben und Materialien treffen auf satte Schokoladentöne. Retro-Muster und zeitgenössische Kunst sind die Farbtupfer. Im Ganzen ein stimmiges Designkonzept, das sich durch das ganze Anwesen hindurch zieht, das Spa inbegriffen. Ein Design, das eine entspannte Atmosphäre schafft in einem Resort, das nah der Stadt ist und abgeschieden zugleich.

FR La chromothérapie d'un spa arabe, un baume d'or 24 carats pour les lèvres et des matches de polo : voilà ce que l'on peut trouver au LIME SPA. Les couleurs et matériaux naturels croisent des tonalités chocolat, tandis que des taches de couleur forment des motifs rétro faisant écho aux œuvres d'art contemporain. Tout cela conduit à créer un concept unique, présent sur l'ensemble de la structure, y compris dans le spa. Celui-ci crée une atmosphère relaxante dans le complexe à la fois si proche et à l'abri du tumulte de la ville.

NED Een Arabisch kuuroord met kleurentherapie, 24 karaats gouden lippenbalsem en live polowedstrijden. Gouden elementen, maar met mate. Natuurlijke kleuren en materialen stuiten op diepe chocoladekleuren. Retro-patronen en eigentijdse kunst vormen de kleurstippen. In het geheel een kloppend ontwerpconcept, door het hele gebouw heen, inclusief het kuuroord. Een ontwerp dat een ontspannen sfeer schept in een resort dat tegelijk dicht bij de stad en ervan afgescheiden ligt.

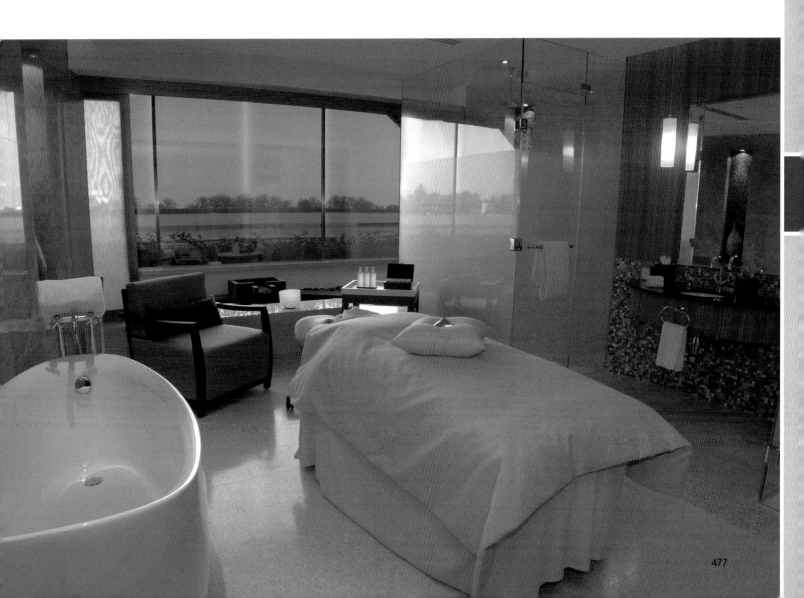

TALISE SPA AT MADINAT JUMEIRAH AL QASR

UNITED ARAB EMIRATES | DUBAI | HEALTH & BEAUTY

ENG The Arabic name of the MADINAT JUMEIRAH AL QASR means "Harbor of Peace". All the areas in this impressive hotel complex are connected by waterways that can be navigated with Arabian boats called abras. The 28 unique rooms of the TALISE SPA are as diverse as the hotel complex itself. They are connected, yet separate. Indoor and outdoor treatments are offered in island clusters, little private oases in gardens arranged around tropical landscapes and treatment areas in tents, all in harmonious convergence with nature.

DEU Der arabische Name des MADINAT JUMEIRAH AL QASR bedeutet soviel wie „Hafen der Ruhe und des Friedens". Alle Bereiche dieses beeindruckenden Hotelkomplexes sind durch ein System von Wasserwegen verbunden, die mit arabischen Booten, den Abras, befahren werden können. So mannigfaltig wie die Hotelanlage sind die 28 einzigartigen Räume des TALISE SPA. Sie sind miteinander verbunden und doch getrennt. Es gibt Indoor- und Outdoor-Behandlungen in Insel-Clustern, kleine private Oasen in Gärten, inmitten tropischer Landschaften, und Behandlungsplätze in Zelten, alles im Einklang und Zusammenspiel mit der Natur.

FR En arabe, MADINAT JUMEIRAH AL QASR signifie « port de paix ». Chaque lieu de ce complexe hôtelier impressionnant est relié aux autres par des canaux navigables où se déplacent des abras, les bateaux arabes. Les 28 pièces uniques du TALISE SPA sont aussi diverses que le complexe hôtelier lui-même. Elles sont connectées, tout en étant distinctes. Des soins en intérieur et en extérieur sont prodigués sur des îlots, de petites oasis privées entourées de jardins et de paysages tropicaux ou sous des tentes : la convergence avec la nature est on ne peut plus harmonieuse.

NED De Arabische naam van het MADINAT JUMEIRAH AL QASR betekent zoveel als 'Haven van Rust en Vrede'. Alle gedeelten van dit indrukwekkende hotelcomplex zijn met elkaar verbonden via een systeem van waterwegen, die met Arabische boten, de Abra's, kunnen worden bevaren. Net zo vol afwisseling als het hotelcomplex zijn ook de 28 unieke ruimten van de TALISE SPA. Ze zijn met elkaar verbonden en toch apart. Er zijn indoor- en outdoorbehandelingen op eilandclusters, kleine besloten oases in tuinen, te midden van tropische landschappen en behandelplaatsen in tenten, alles in harmonie en samenspel met de natuur.

ZEN SPA

ENG The ZEN SPA consists of four thatched huts arranged around a gorgeous garden of bamboo and lemongrass. It nestles against the West Lake, this peaceful refuge where the beauty of nature and the spa blend together. You won't find any modern amenities here. The Vietnamese believe that bathing in nature strengthens and purifies the soul. Soaking in a wooden bathtub filled with herbs and daisies, you can easily believe it.

DEU Das ZEN SPA ist ein Ort aus vier strohbedeckten Hütten, umgeben von einem wunderschönen Garten aus Bambus und Zitronengras. Er schmiegt sich an den West Lake, diesen Hort der Ruhe, an dem die Schönheit der Natur und das Spa miteinander verschmelzen. Moderne Errungenschaften kommen hier nicht vor. Vietnamesen glauben, dass das Baden in der Natur die Seele reiner und stärker macht. Im hölzernen Badezuber, voll mit Kräutern und Gänseblümchen, entsteht der Eindruck, es könnte stimmen.

FR Le ZEN SPA est composé de quatre huttes au toit végétal, entourées de somptueux jardins de bambous et de citronnelle. Lové au creux du lac West, ce refuge paisible permet de mêler la beauté de la nature aux principes bienfaiteurs du spa. Vous n'y trouverez aucun équipement moderne, car selon les Vietnamiens, se baigner en pleine nature renforce et purifie l'âme. Se relaxer dans une baignoire de bois remplie d'herbes et de marguerites est un plaisir à ne pas manquer.

NED De ZEN SPA bestaat uit vier strogedekte hutten, omringd door een wondermooie tuin van bamboe en citroengras. Het ligt tegen het Westelijke Meer aan, dit toevluchtsoord van rust, waar de schoonheid van de natuur en het kuuroord met elkaar versmelten. Moderne verworvenheden komen hier niet voor. De Vietnamezen geloven dat van baden in de natuur de ziel zuiverder en sterker wordt. In houten badkuipen, vol met kruiden en madeliefjes, krijgt men de indruk dat dit wel eens zou kunnen kloppen.

THE NAM HAI SPA

VIETNAM | HOI AN | HEALTH & BEAUTY

ENG 32 hectares (79 acres) of land on Ha My Beach, a breathtaking stretch of Chinese Beach, contain the resort with its 60 villas and 40 pool villas, each with its own garden and views of the South China Sea and Cham Island. The high ceilings, platforms, and various levels are characteristic. Sparse elegance and purist design meet Asian stylistic elements. The generously proportioned spa is set in the middle of an artificial lagoon and offers eight treatment rooms, each with its own sauna and steam bath. The result: traditional Vietnamese architecture, modern design, and the surrounding natural area—all three in perfect balance.

DEU 32 Hektar Land an der Ha My Beach, einem atemberaubenden Teilstück der Chinese Beach, darin das Resort mit 60 Villen und 40 Pool Villen, jede mit eigenem Garten und Blicken auf das Südchinesische Meer und die Cham Islands. Kennzeichnend sind die hohen Decken, Podeste und verschiedene Ebenen. Schlichte Eleganz und puristisches Design treffen auf asiatische Stilelemente. Das großzügig gestaltete Spa liegt inmitten einer künstlich angelegten Lagune und verfügt über acht Behandlungsräume mit jeweils eigener Sauna und Dampfbad. Das Resultat: traditionelle vietnamesische Architektur, modernes Design und die umgebende Natur – und alle drei in Balance.

FR Sur 32 hectares de terre situés à Ha My Beach, portion spectaculaire de Chinese Beach, s'élève un complexe de 100 villas, dont 40 avec piscine privée, chacune possédant son propre jardin et une vue sur la mer de Chine méridionale et l'île de Cham. Les hauts plafonds, les plateformes et les différents niveaux en font un endroit hors du commun où élégance et design épuré rencontrent le style asiatique. Le spa, généreusement proportionné se trouve au milieu d'un lagon artificiel et compte huit salons de soins, chacun proposant un sauna et un hammam. Le résultat tend vers une architecture traditionnelle vietnamienne, un design moderne et un cadre naturel en équilibre parfait.

NED 32 hectaren land aan het Ha My strand, een adembenemend gedeelte van het Chinese strand, met 60 villa's en 40 pool-villa's met zwembad, elk met eigen tuin en uitzichten op de Zuid-Chinese Zee en de Cham-eilanden. Kenmerkend zijn de hoge plafonds, platforms en verschillende niveaus. Eenvoudige elegantie en puristisch ontwerp ontmoeten Aziatische stijlelementen. Het royaal gevormde kuuroord ligt midden in een kunstmatig aangelegde baai en beschikt over acht behandelruimten, elke met een eigen sauna en stoombad. Het resultaat: traditionele Vietnamese architectuur, modern design en de omringende natuur – en alle drie in balans.

EVASON ANA MANDARA & SIX SENSES SPA - NHA TRANG

VIETNAM | NHA TRANG | HEALTH & BEAUTY

ENG "Ana Mandara" means "beautiful home for the guests". It refers to the interaction between architecture and nature in the resort, with its low cottages made of rattan and fine local woods, as well as the inner "home" of body, mind, and soul. This philosophy was the impulse behind the approach at SIX SENSES SPA. Next to the beach, in the middle of a coconut plantation, surrounded by lotus ponds and pools, open treatment rooms called "salas" offer an optimal environment for holistic treatments—even for those who might not really believe in it.

DEU „Ana Mandara" bedeutet „Schönes Zuhause für den Gast". Es meint das Zusammenspiel von Architektur und Natur im Resort, mit seinen niedrigen Häuschen aus einheimischen Edelhölzern und Rattan, aber auch das innere „Zuhause" aus Körper, Geist und Seele. Diese Philosophie war der äußere Anlass für den SIX SENSES SPA. Neben dem Strand, inmitten einer Kokosplantage, umgeben von Lotusblütenteichen und Pools, bieten offene Behandlungsräume, die „Salas", ein optimales Umfeld für ganzheitliche Anwendungen – auch dann, wenn man nicht so recht daran glauben mag.

FR « Ana Mandara » signifie « jolie maison d'hôtes ». Elle rappelle l'interaction entre l'architecture et la nature présente dans le resort, avec ses petits cottages faits de rotin et de bois précieux locaux, tout comme celle de la « maison » intérieure du corps, de l'âme et de l'esprit. C'est cette philosophie qui a inspiré l'approche du SIX SENSES SPA. En bordure de plage, au cœur d'une plantation de cocotiers, entourée de bassins et d'étangs parsemés de lotus, les soins en plein air dans les « salas » offrent un environnement optimal pour les traitements holistiques ; y compris pour ceux doutent de leur efficacité.

NED 'Ana Mandara' betekent 'Mooi Thuis voor de Gast'. Dit slaat op het samenspel van architectuur en natuur in het resort, met zijn lage huisjes van kostbaar inheems hout en rotan, maar ook het innerlijke 'thuis' van lichaam, geest en ziel. Deze filosofie was de uiterlijke reden voor de SIX SENSES SPA. Naast het strand, te midden van een kokosplantage, omringd door vijvers met lotusbloemen en zwembaden, bieden open behandelruimten, de 'sala's', een optimale omgeving voor holistische behandelingen – ook als men er niet zo erg in gelooft.

CULTURE
ART CENTERS AND CONCERT VENUES

THE PEARL MONUMENT
KINGDOM OF BAHRAIN | BAHRAIN CITY | CULTURE

ENG THE PEARL MONUMENT is undoubtedly Bahrain's most famous icon. Both delicate and monumental at the same time, it is constructed from pure white concrete. The structure consists of six stylized sails inspired by the sails of a dau, the traditional Arabian sailboat. They symbolize the six Gulf states. Together they grasp a pearl at the top of the monument, which stands as a symbol of a proud common cultural and economic heritage.

DEU THE PEARL MONUMENT ist das wohl bekannteste Wahrzeichen von Bahrain. Zart und monumental zugleich, aus reinem weißen Beton. Die Konstruktion besteht aus sechs stilisierten Dau-Segeln, den Segeln des typischen arabischen Segelschiffs. Sie stehen für die sechs Golfstaaten. Zusammen fassen sie eine Perle in der Spitze des Monuments, die als Symbol für ein stolzes gemeinsames kulturelles und wirtschaftliches Erbe steht.

FR THE PEARL MONUMENT est sans doute le symbole le plus célèbre du Bahreïn. À la fois délicat et monumental, il n'est composé que de béton d'un blanc immaculé. La structure est constituée de six voiles stylisées, inspirées du dau, le voilier arabe traditionnel. Elles symbolisent les six états du golfe et retiennent en leur sommet, une perle, symbole d'un héritage culturel et économique commun.

NED Het PEARL MONUMENT is beslist het bekendste herkenningsteken van Bahrein. Fragiel en monumentaal tegelijk, van zuiver wit beton. De constructie bestaat uit zes gestileerde dhow-zeilen, de zeilen van het typische Arabische zeilschip. Ze staan voor de zes Golfstaten. Samen vatten ze een parel in de punt van het monument, die als symbool voor een trots gemeenschappelijk cultureel en economisch erfgoed staat.

499

BEIJING NATIONAL STADIUM BIRD'S NEST

CHINA | BEIJING | CULTURE

ENG A shimmering silver network, bright lines that run in every direction—the biggest "bird's nest" in the world. It was built under the direction of Swiss architects Herzog & de Meuron. The exterior boasts the largest steel construction in the world, the interior a red "concrete seating bowl". No walls or towers, a network of steel beams without hierarchy because each and every branch, no matter how small, acts to stabilize the whole. The BIRD'S NEST is situated on an extended line connecting the symbolic landmarks of ancient China: the Forbidden City, Tiananmen Square, the Bell Tower, and Drum Tower. That makes it more than just a stadium.

DEU Ein silbern glänzendes Geflecht, strahlende Linien, die in alle Richtungen laufen – das größte „Vogelnest" der Welt. Gebaut unter der Federführung der Schweizer Architekten Herzog & de Meuron. Außen die größte Stahlkonstruktion der Welt, innen eine rote „Beton-Sitzschüssel". Keine Türen, keine Mauern, ein Geflecht aus Stahl ohne Hierarchie, denn jeder noch so kleine Zweig hat eine statische Funktion für die Stabilität des Ganzen. BIRD'S NEST liegt auf einer verlängerten Linie mit den Symbolbauten des alten China: Verbotene Stadt, Tian'anmen-Platz, Glocken- und Trommelturm. Damit ist es mehr als nur ein Stadion.

FR Le plus grand « nid d'oiseau » au monde est une toile d'argent scintillante dont les lignes épurées courent en tous sens. Construit sous la direction des architectes suisses Herzog & de Meuron, l'extérieur peut s'enorgueillir d'être la structure d'acier la plus importante au monde, tandis que l'intérieur est une « arène de béton rouge ». Sans murs ni piliers, le filet d'acier rayonne comme bon lui semble, car chaque infime branche participe à la stabilisation de l'ensemble. Le BIRD'S NEST se trouve sur une ligne reliant les grands monuments de la Chine millénaire : la Cité interdite, la place Tiananmen, les Bell et Drum towers : ce détail tend à en faire plus qu'un simple stade.

NED Een zilverglanzend vlechtwerk, stralende lijnen die alle kanten uit lopen – het grootste 'vogelnest' ter wereld. Gebouwd onder verantwoordelijkheid van de Zwitserse architecten Herzog & Meuron. Van buiten de grootste staalconstructie ter wereld, van binnen een rode 'betonnen zitkom'. Geen deuren, geen muren, een vlechtwerk van staal zonder hiërarchie, want elke tak heeft, hoe klein ook, een statische functie voor de stabiliteit van het geheel. Het BIRD'S NEST ligt in het verlengde van de symbolische bouwwerken van het oude China: Verboden Stad, Tian'anmen Plein, klokken- en trommeltoren. Daarmee is het meer dan alleen een stadion.

CAFA ART MUSEUM

CHINA | BEIJING | CULTURE

ENG The CAFA ART MUSEUM, built by Arata Isozaki for the Central Academy of Fine Arts, is a slate sculpture of impressive dimensions: 24 meters (79 feet) high, with two lower and three upper levels, spread out over 3546 square meters (38,169 square feet). The organic shape is reminiscent of a mussel. Natural light is provided by massive glazing on two sides and a glass roof that conforms to the shape of the building. The span that this achieves creates surfaces free of supporting walls or posts. Gray tiles, grayish green slates attached to the structure's organic shape, are the work of complex 3D computer simulations. Levels with various ceiling heights offer room for 13,000 very individual exhibits, skillfully presented in a modern architectural sculpture.

DEU Das CAFA ART MUSEUM, erbaut von Arata Isozaki für die Central Academy of Fine Arts, ist eine Schieferskulptur mit beeindruckenden Ausmaßen: 24 Meter hoch, mit zwei Unter- und drei Obergeschossen, auf 3546 Quadratmetern. Die organische Form erinnert an eine Muschel. Die großflächige Verglasung an zwei Schmalseiten, dazu ein der Gebäudeform angepasstes Glasdach sorgen für natürliches Licht. Das Tragwerk ist aus Stahlbeton, die Dachschale aus Stahl. Die erzielte Spannweite schafft Flächen fast ohne Stützen und Mauern. Grauer Ziegel, graugrüne Schieferplatten aufgebracht auf die organische Form, sind das Werk komplexer 3D-Computersimulationen. Stockwerke mit unterschiedlichen Raumhöhen bieten Raum für 13 000 sehr individuelle Exponate, sorgsam präsentiert in dieser Skulptur der modernen Architektur.

FR Le CAFA ART MUSEUM, édifié par Arata Isozaki pour la Central Academy of Fine Arts, est une sculpture en ardoise imposante : 24 mètres de haut, pour deux niveaux souterrains et trois étages, étendues sur 3 546 mètres carrés. L'envergure obtenue crée des surfaces pratiquement dépourvues de murs ou de piliers. Sa forme organique rappelle un coquillage et la lumière naturelle pénètre par d'imposants vitrages et un toit de verre suivant les courbes du bâtiment. La structure principale est faite de béton armé et le toit d'acier. La disposition des carreaux gris et ardoises vertes est le fruit de complexes simulations en 3D. Les hauteurs de plafond varient d'un étage à l'autre et permettent à cette sculpture architecturale moderne d'accueillir jusqu'à 13 000 visiteurs.

NED Het CAFA ART MUSEUM, gebouwd door Arata Isozaki voor de Central Academy of Fine Arts, is een leisteen sculptuur met indrukwekkende afmetingen: 24 meter hoog, met twee onder- en drie bovenverdiepingen, op 3546 vierkante meter. De organische vorm doet denken aan een schelp. De beglazing met haar grote oppervlak aan twee smalle zijden, en verder een aan de vorm van het gebouw aangepast glazen dak zorgen voor natuurlijk licht. De verkregen spanwijdte brengt vlakken bijna zonder steunen en muren tot stand. Grijze bakstenen, grijsgroene leisteenplaten aangebracht op de organische vorm, is het werk van ingewikkelde 3D-computersimulaties. Verdiepingen met verschillende hoogtes bieden plaats aan 13.000 zeer individuele tentoonstellingsstukken, met zorg gepresenteerd in een sculptuur van de moderne architectuur.

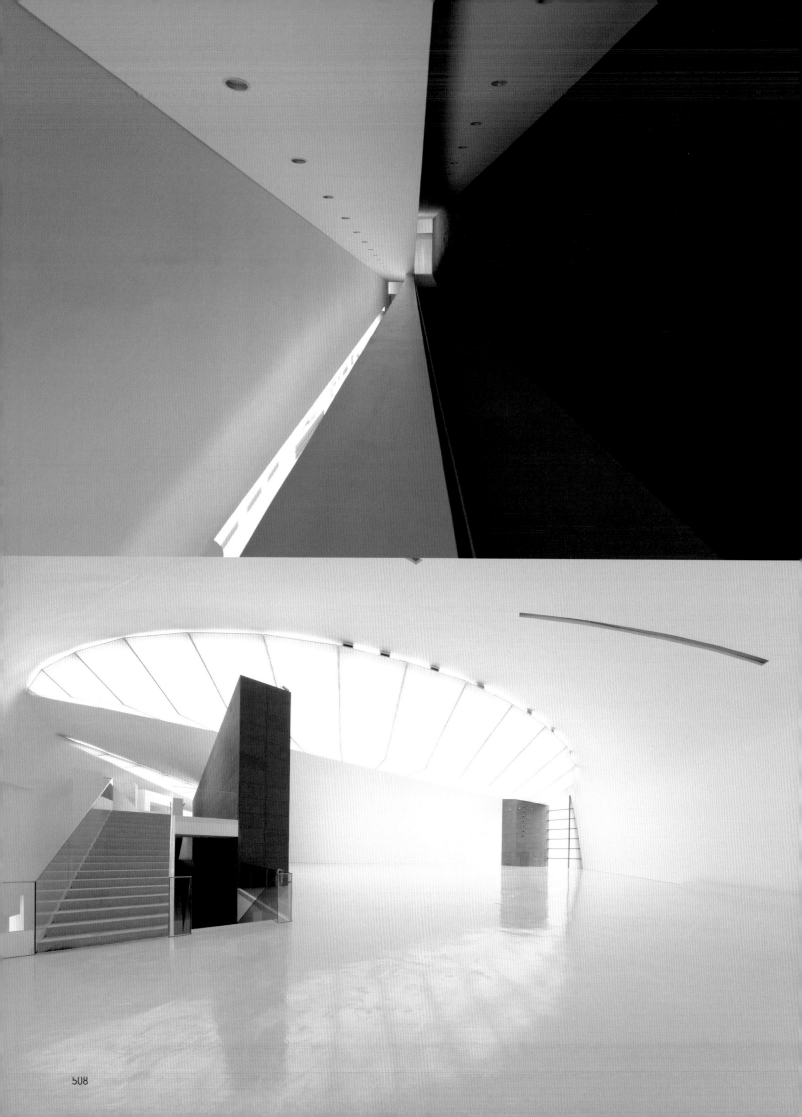

CR LAND GUANGANMEN GREEN TECHNOLOGY SHOWROOM

CHINA | BEIJING | CULTURE

ENG It's all about sustainable residential construction. There's a lot to this: energy efficiency, as low an impact on the surrounding area as possible, environmentally friendly materials and production techniques, recyclable building components, etc.—all in combination with design and aesthetics. Vector Architects are the creators behind this, the client is CR Land Limited. The CR LAND GUANGAN-MEN SHOWROOM is located in Beijing. A modern cube, a steel structure on feet, the walls clad in grass panels, and the top covered in a grass roof. Energy-efficient, functional, no-frills, completely recyclable. No earthmoving or any other major impact on the existing site, plus the option of dismantling the whole thing after three years, likewise with no impact on the surrounding area.

DEU Es geht um nachhaltigen Wohnungsbau. Das meint vieles: Energieeffizienz, so wenig Eingriffe in die Umgebung wie möglich, umweltfreundliche Materialien und Fertigungstechnologien, recycelbare Baustoffe, etc. – alles in Kombination mit Design und Ästhetik. Die Architekten sind Vector Architects, der Auftraggeber ist die CR Land Limited. Entstanden ist der CR LAND GUANGANMEN SHOWROOM in Peking. Ein moderner Kubus, eine Stahlkonstruktion auf Füßen, die Wände verkleidet mit Paneelen aus Gras und ein Grasdach. Energieeffizient, funktional, schnörkellos, komplett recycelbar. Ohne Gebäudeaushub oder sonstige gravierende Eingriffe in den bestehenden Ort mit der Option, nach Ablauf von drei Jahren gleichermaßen ohne Auswirkungen auf die Umgebung wieder abgebaut zu werden.

FR Tout n'est ici question que de construction durable et il y a beaucoup à dire : efficacité énergétique (pour diminuer au maximum son impact sur l'environnement), matériaux écologiques et techniques de production ou encore matériaux de construction recyclables, n'empêchent pas d'apporter une touche design et esthétique. Vector Architects en sont les créateurs, pour leur client CR Land Limited. Le CR LAND GUANGANMEN SHOWROOM se trouve à Pékin. C'est un cube moderne, une structure d'acier sur pieds, dont les murs sont recouverts de plantes et les toits sont végétalisés. Efficace en termes d'énergie, fonctionnel et sans fioritures, il est complètement recyclable. Aucune modification du terrain ou autre impact majeur sur le site n'ont été nécessaires et l'ensemble pourra être démonté après trois ans : les environs n'auront alors subi aucun changement.

NED Het gaat om duurzame woningbouw. Dat betekent: energie-efficiëntie, zo min mogelijk ingrepen in de omgeving, milieuvriendelijke materialen en fabricagetechnieken, enz. – alles in combinatie met ontwerp en esthetiek. De architecten zijn Vector Architects, de opdrachtgever is CR Land Limited. Tot stand gekomen is de CR LAND GUANGANMEN SHOWROOM in Peking. Een moderne kubus, een staalconstructie op voeten, de wanden bekleed met panelen van gras en een grasdak. Energie-efficiënt, functioneel, strak, geheel recyclebaar. Zonder grondwerk of andere ernstige ingrepen in de bestaande plaats met als optie na afloop van drie jaar eveneens zonder gevolgen voor de omgeving weer te worden opgebouwd.

513

NATIONAL GRAND THEATRE

CHINA | BEIJING | CULTURE

ᴱᴺᴳ The NATIONAL GRAND THEATRE, aka "the Egg", is Beijing's opera house. A massive elliptical cathedral made of titanium and glass, arranged around a man-made lake, with room for 5,452 people and divided into three areas, all designed by Paul Andreu. The titanium casing, which protects and covers the structure as well as provides shade, is divided by a sort of glass curtain. Andreu's design, with large open areas, water, and trees, is a counterpoint to the red walls of ancient Chinese monuments—conspicuously and intentionally so.

ᴰᴱᵁ Das NATIONAL GRAND THEATRE, auch „the Egg" genannt, ist das Opernhaus von Peking. Ein gewaltiger ellipsenförmiger Dom aus Titan und Glas, umschlossen von einem künstlichen See, für 5 452 Personen, aufgeteilt auf drei Hallen, designt von Paul Andreu. Die Titanhülle, die nicht nur schützt und bedeckt, sondern auch Schatten spendet, ist unterbrochen von einer Art gläsernem Vorhang. Andreus Design mit großen offenen Flächen, Wasser und Bäumen, ist ein Kontrapunkt zu den roten Mauern der Prachtbauten des alten China – offensichtlich und ganz bewusst.

ᶠᴿ Le NATIONAL GRAND THEATRE, surnommé « l'Œuf », est l'opéra de Pékin. Cette cathédrale elliptique massive faite de titane et de verre et entourée d'un lac artificiel, peut accueillir 5 452 personnes. Elle comprend trois zones, toutes pensées par Paul Andreu. L'enveloppe de titane, qui recouvre et protège la structure de la lumière, entre autres, se transforme en une sorte de rideau de verre. L'idée d'Andreu, avec ses larges espaces ouverts, la présence d'eau et d'arbres, s'oppose intentionnellement au style communiste des anciens monuments chinois.

ᴺᴱᴰ Het NATIONAL GRAND THEATRE, ook wel 'het ei' genoemd, is het operagebouw van Peking. Een enorme ellipsvormige koepel van titanium en glas, omsloten door een kunstmatig meer, voor 5452 personen, verdeeld in drie zalen, ontworpen door Paul Andreu. Het titanium omhulsel, dat niet alleen beschermt en bedekt, maar ook schaduw levert, wordt onderbroken door een soort glazen gordijn. Het ontwerp van Andreu met grote open vlakken, water en boompjes, vormt een contrapunt met de rode muren van de prachtige bouwwerken van het oude China – openlijk en heel bewust.

NINGBO HISTORIC MUSEUM

CHINA | NINGBO | CULTURE

ENG The massive, 24-meter-high (79-foot-high) walls of the NINGBO HISTORIC MUSEUM are splayed, some protruding at a surprising angle. Its appearance is determined by material collages, a patchwork, such as the windows and window slits, arranged across the walls seemingly at random, with 20 various local tiles in shades of gray and red, apparently without any formal logic. The buildings, designed by Wang Shu of Amateur Architecture Studio, all look as if they originated from a time long past, if not another world. Like relics of a high culture with a close connection to nature. Something not from this time, both old-fashioned and yet ultra-modern.

DEU 24 Meter hoch sind die gespreizten, teilweise nach vorne abgeknickten mächtigen Mauern des NINGBO HISTORIC MUSEUM. Sein Aussehen bestimmen Materialcollagen, ein Patchwork, wie über die Mauern wie zufällig verteilte Fenster, Schlitze, mit allein 20 verschiedenen lokalen Ziegeln in den Nuancen grau und rot, scheinbar ohne formale Logik. Die Gebäude von Wang Shu von Amateur Architecture Studio sehen alle so aus, als entstammten sie einer lange vergangenen Zeit, wenn nicht gar einer anderen Welt. Wie Relikte einer Hochkultur mit enger Verbundenheit zur Natur. Nicht aus dieser Zeit, archaisch und trotzdem ultramodern.

FR Les murs massifs hauts de 24 mètres du NINGBO HISTORIC MUSEUM sont obliques et parfois étonnamment penchés. L'apparence du bâtiment est le fruit d'une association de matériaux, une sorte de patchwork : les fenêtres et leurs ouvrants semblent disposés au hasard le long des murs, tout comme 20 différentes sortes de tuiles dans les tons gris et rouges. Les bâtiments, pensés par Wang Shu de l'Amateur Architecture Studio, semblent sortis d'une autre époque, si ce n'est d'un autre monde. Tel un vestige d'une civilisation étroitement liée à la nature, ce bâtiment a quelque chose d'intemporel archaïque et ultramoderne.

NED 24 meter hoog zijn de bombastische, deels naar voren geknikte ontzagwekkende muren van het NINGBO HISTORIC MUSEUM. Het uiterlijk wordt bepaald door materiaalcollages, een patchwork, zoals over de muren verdeelde vensters, spleten, met alleen al twintig verschillende plaatselijke baksteensoorten in de schakeringen grijs en rood, schijnbaar zonder formele logica. De gebouwen van Wang Shu van Amateur Architect Studio zien er allemaal uit alsof ze afkomstig zijn uit een lang vervlogen tijd, zo niet van een heel andere wereld. Als overblijfselen van een hoogstaande cultuur met een nauwe verbondenheid met de natuur. Niet van deze tijd, archaïsch en toch ultramodern.

BAHÁ'Í HOUSE OF WORSHIP LOTUS TEMPLE

INDIA | NEW DELHI | CULTURE

ENG This dazzling white Bahá'í temple has the appearance of a lotus flower opening. The lotus is a symbol of purity and peace, and here it is associated with the number nine. The choice of these two things, by architect Fariborz Sahba, is far from random. The number nine symbolizes immutable truth in both the Bahá'í teachings and Judaism. Nine entrances, one for each world religion. There are nine of everything—every circle, arch and pond. The interior houses a white-domed hall with simple seats and holy scriptures, without ornamentation, consciously neutral. The LOTUS TEMPLE is a place where all are welcome, regardless of creed, ethnicity, or status.

DEU Er sieht aus wie eine sich öffnende Lotusblüte, dieser blendend weiße Tempel der Bahá'í. Lotus gilt als Symbol für Reinheit und Frieden, gekoppelt ist er hier an die Ziffer Neun. Beides ist vom Architekten Fariborz Sahba nicht zufällig gewählt. Die Neun symbolisiert in Bahá'íscher Lehre und Judentum gleichermaßen die unveränderliche Wahrheit. Neun Eingänge, einer für jede Weltreligion. Jeder Kreis, Bogen, Teich, alles ist neunmal vorhanden. Innen eine weite überkuppelte Halle, mit schlichter Bestuhlung und heiligen Schriften, ohne schmückende Elemente, bewusst neutral. Der LOTUS TEMPLE ist ein Ort der Einkehr für jeden Menschen, unabhängig von Glauben, Herkunft oder Status.

FR Cet éblouissant temple bahaï ressemble à un lotus en pleine éclosion, symbole de pureté et de paix ; la fleur est ici associée au chiffre neuf. Le choix de ces deux éléments par l'architecte Fariborz Sahba n'a rien d'un hasard, car le chiffre neuf symbolise la vérité immuable de l'enseignement bahaï et du judaïsme. Ici tout existe par neuf : les cercles, les arches, les étangs ou les neuf entrées au lotus, rappelant chacune des religions du monde. À l'intérieur, tout est volontairement neutre et dépourvu d'ornements : dans le grand hall surmonté d'un dôme blanc, de simples sièges et des écritures sacrées accueillent les fidèles. Le LOTUS TEMPLE ouvre ses portes à tout un chacun, indépendamment de ses croyances, de son origine ou de son statut.

NED Hij ziet eruit als een opengaande lotusbloem, deze verbindend witte tempel van de Bahá'í. De lotus wordt beschouwd als het symbool voor zuiverheid en vrede, en hier is hij gekoppeld aan het cijfer negen. Beide zijn door architect Fariborz Sahba niet toevallig gekozen. De negen symboliseert in de leer van de Bahá'í en het jodendom de onveranderlijke waarheid. Negen ingangen, een voor elke wereldgodsdienst. Elke cirkel, boog, vijver, alles is in negenvoud aanwezig. Binnen een brede overkoepelde hal, met eenvoudige zitplaatsen en heilige geschriften, zonder versieringen, bewust neutraal. De LOTUS TEMPEL is een plaats van inkeer voor ieder mens, onafhankelijk van geloof, herkomst of status.

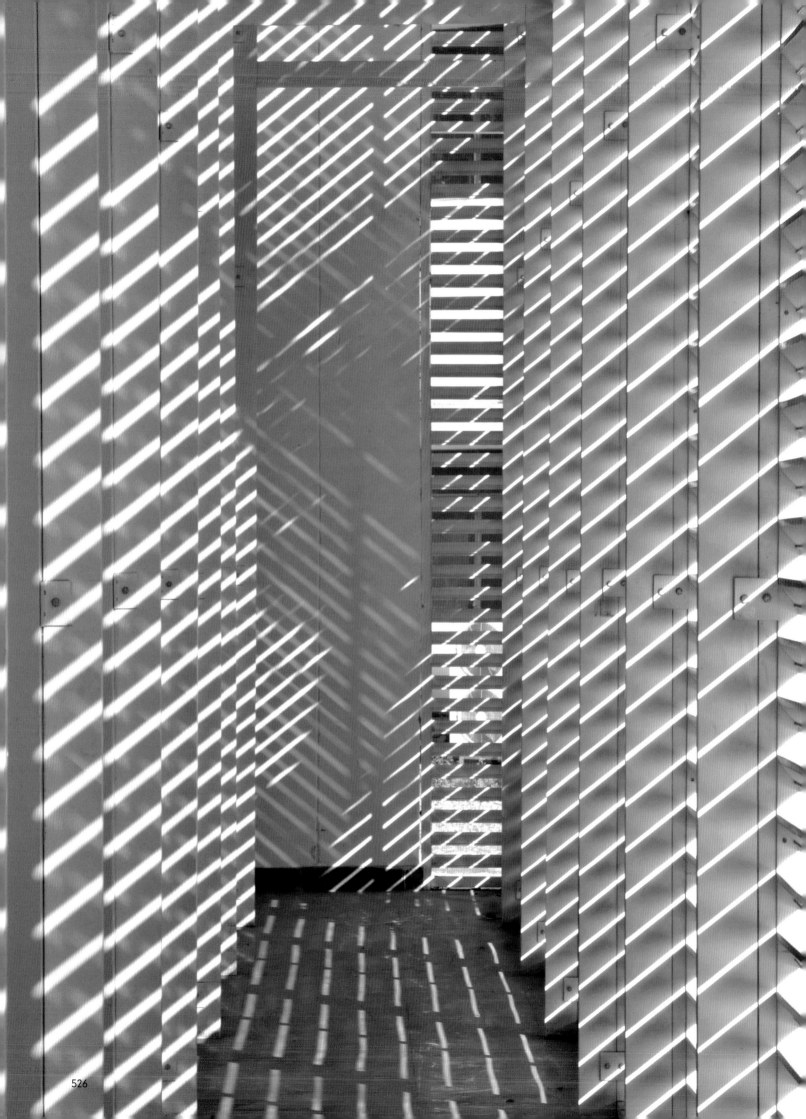

CASTRO CAFÉ AND M.F. HUSSAIN CULTURAL CENTER

INDIA | NEW DELHI | CULTURE

ENG The architects at Romi Khosla Design Studios were commissioned with designing an unconventional location where students could converse and share their ideas; they have responded with a semi-open-air café and a fully climate-controlled contemporary art gallery, named after Indian painter M.F. Hussain, arranged around a courtyard. The cafeteria is constructed of steel and stone, the gallery of concrete and glass. White marble in the cafeteria, white metal louvers in the gallery. The walls don't touch the floor, the ceiling doesn't touch the walls. All the building's elements are independent of each other. The lines between interior and exterior are intentionally blurred, acting as intermediaries between climate and people.

DEU Um dem Wunsch nach einem ungewöhnlichen Ort des kommunikativen Austausches für die Studenten zu entsprechen, entwarfen die Architekten von Romi Khosla Design Studios ein Semi-Open-Air-Café und eine vollklimatisierte Galerie für zeitgenössische Kunst, benannt nach dem indischen Maler M.F. Hussain, angeordnet um einen gestalteten Hof. Die Cafeteria ist aus Stahl und Stein, die Galerie aus Beton und Glas. Weißer Marmor in der Cafeteria, weiße Metall-Jalousien in der Galerie. Die Wände berühren nicht den Boden, das Dach nicht die Wände. Alle Elemente des Gebäudes sind unabhängig voneinander. Die Grenzen zwischen Innen und Außen sind bewusst verwischt, sie dienen als Vermittler zwischen Mensch und Klima.

FR Les architectes de chez Romi Khosla Design Studios avaient pour mission de créer un lieu non-conventionnel où les étudiants puissent échanger leurs idées ; ils ont ainsi proposé un café à demi-ouvert sur l'extérieur et une galerie d'art contemporain, portant le nom du peintre indien M.F. Hussain. La cafeteria est faite de pierre, d'acier et de marbre blanc, tandis que béton, verre et claires-voies de métal blanc habillent la galerie. Le sol est indépendant des murs, eux-mêmes ne touchant pas le plafond. Chaque élément du bâtiment reste indépendant des autres et les limites entre intérieur et extérieur sont volontairement brouillées, pour jouer les intermédiaires entre le climat et les hommes.

NED Om het verlangen naar een ongewone plek voor communicatieve uitwisseling voor de studenten te vervullen, ontwierpen de architecten van Romi Khosla Design Studios een semi-openluchtcafé en een galerie met klimaatregeling voor eigentijdse kunst, vernoemd naar de Indiase schilder M.F. Hussain, geplaatst rond een ingerichte binnenplaats. De cafetaria is van staal en steen, de galerie van beton en glas. Wit marmer in de cafetaria, witte metalen jaloezieën in de galerie. De muren raken de vloer niet, het dak niet de muren. Alle elementen van het gebouw zijn onafhankelijk van elkaar. De grenzen tussen binnen en buiten zijn bewust weggewist, ze dienen als bemiddelaars tussen mens en klimaat.

BIASA ARTSPACE
INDONESIA | BALI | CULTURE

ENG The BIASA ARTSPACE is not merely a space for exhibiting contemporary Asian art. It is also an initiative that strives to promote the development of young, aspiring Asian artists in a responsible and supportive way. Its goal is to help modern artists achieve international recognition. The creators have developed a master plan from a modern, subdued, and unadorned building that, rather than hogging the spotlight for itself, provides space for, and attention to, the actual art, which enables a deep engagement with the work.

DEU Das BIASA ARTSPACE ist nicht nur ein Raum für die Präsentation zeitgenössischer asiatischer Kunst. Es ist eine Initiative, die sich verantwortungsvoll und unterstützend in die Entwicklung von jungen aufstrebenden asiatischen Künstlern einbringen möchte. All das mit dem Ziel, modernen Künstlern zu internationaler Anerkennung zu verhelfen. Geschaffen haben die Macher ein Gesamtkonzept aus einem modernen, schnörkellosen, sich zurücknehmenden Gebäude, das der Kunst Raum und Aufmerksamkeit verschafft, diese somit nicht für sich beansprucht, und einem tiefen Engagement in der Sache.

FR Le BIASA ARTSPACE n'est pas qu'un lieu d'exposition pour l'art contemporain en Asie. C'est également une initiative tendant à promouvoir l'envol d'artistes asiatiques, de manière responsable et solidaire. L'objectif est d'aider de jeunes artistes à être reconnus sur le marché international. Ses créateurs ont élaboré une structure moderne, feutrée et peu décorée, qui au lieu de se mettre en avant, propose un espace de visibilité à l'art lui-même et permet ainsi de s'y engager pleinement.

NED De BIASA ARTSPACE is niet alleen een ruimte voor het presenteren van eigentijdse Aziatische kunst. Het is een initiatief dat een verantwoordelijke en ondersteunende bijdrage wil leveren aan de ontwikkeling van jonge opkomende Aziatische kunstenaars. Dit alles met het doel moderne kunstenaars te helpen internationale erkenning te verwerven. De makers hebben een totaalconcept gecreëerd van een modern, strak, ingetogen gebouw, dat de kunst ruimte en aandacht verschaft en deze niet voor zichzelf opeist, met een sterke betrokkenheid bij de zaak.

AOMORI MUSEUM OF ART

JAPAN | AOMORI | CULTURE

ENG A museum for everyone, a place of art and culture in harmony with the adjacent archeological digs of the Sannai Maruyama Historical Site, and a way to display the unique local art and culture of the Aomori Prefecture to the world—these are the tasks set for the AOMORI MUSEUM OF ART. The adjacent archeological site was the main inspiration for architect Jun Aoki. The result: white-walled rooms, white cubes, and rooms made of earthen walls and trenches. Two contrasting characteristics that, when combined, create a perfect whole.

DEU Ein Museum für alle, ein Platz für Kunst und Kultur in Harmonie mit dem benachbarten Ausgrabungsgelände Sannai Maruyama Historical Site und eine Präsentation der einmaligen lokalen Kunst und Kultur der Präfektur Aomori gegenüber der Welt – all das soll das AOMORI MUSEUM OF ART erfüllen. Für den Architekten Jun Aoki war das benachbarte Ausgrabungsgelände die wichtigste Quelle der Inspiration. Das Ergebnis: Räume aus weißen Wänden, weiße Kuben und Räume aus irdenen Wänden und Gräben. Zwei gegensätzliche Merkmale, aber in Kombination ergeben sie ein perfektes Ganzes.

FR C'est un musée pour tous, un lieu d'art et de culture en parfaite harmonie avec les fouilles entamées sur le site historique de Sannai Maruyama. C'est aussi un moyen de montrer au monde entier l'art local et la culture uniques de la préfecture d'Aomori : voilà l'objectif de l'AOMORI MUSEUM OF ART. C'est le site archéologique voisin qui a principalement inspiré l'architecte Jun Aoki. Le résultat est un ensemble de salles totalement blanches, formées par des cubes, des tranchées ou des murs de terre. Une fois combinés, ces deux traits de caractère forment un tout absolument parfait.

NED Een museum voor iedereen, een plek voor kunst en cultuur in harmonie met het naburige opgravingsterrein Sannai Maruyama Historical Site en een presentatie van de lokale kunst en cultuur van weleer van de prefectuur Aomori ten overstaan van de wereld – aan dit alles moet het AOMORI MUSEUM OF ART voldoen. Voor architect Jun Aoki was het naburige opgravingsterrein de belangrijkste inspiratiebron. Het resultaat: ruimten van witte wanden, witte kubussen en ruimten van aarden wanden en greppels. Twee tegenovergestelde kenmerken, maar in combinatie vormen ze een volmaakt geheel.

NAOSHIMA CONTEMPORARY ART MUSEUM

JAPAN | GOTANI NAOSHIMA-CHO | CULTURE

ENG Naoshima, the little island in Japan's Inland Sea, is home not only to Japanese fishermen, but to art as well. The investor Soichiro Fukutake commissioned a private gallery to be built here to house his family's collection of contemporary American art. Both the client and the architect, Tadao Ando, wanted to have as low an impact as possible on the island's pristine landscape. This is the reason why more than half of the building is below ground, built into the cliffs. As always, Ando's architecture is characterized by its minimalism—concrete, wood, and light interact with the raw beauty of untouched nature.

DEU Naoshima, die kleine Insel in Japans Inland Sea, ist Heimat japanischer Fischer, aber auch der Kunst. Der Verleger Soichiro Fukutake ließ dort eine private Galerie für die Familiensammlung zeitgenössischer amerikanischer Kunst erbauen. Auftraggeber und der Architekt Tadao Ando wollten die unberührte Landschaft so wenig wie möglich tangieren. Das erklärt, dass mehr als 50 Prozent des Gebäudes unterirdisch in die Klippen gebaut sind. Und wie immer steht Andos Architektur für Minimalismus – Beton, Holz und Licht im Zusammenspiel mit der unberührten rauen Natur.

FR Naoshima, la petite île de la mer intérieure de Seto, n'abrite pas que des pêcheurs japonais. Ce lieu artistique est l'idée de Soichiro Fukutake, qui a financé la construction d'une galerie privée afin d'exposer sa collection personnelle d'art contemporain américain. Le client et l'architecte, Tadao Ando, désiraient diminuer au maximum son impact sur le paysage encore vierge de l'île. C'est la raison pour laquelle la moitié du bâtiment se trouve sous terre, à même les falaises. Comme toujours, l'architecture d'Ando respire le minimalisme : béton, bois et lumière interagissent avec la beauté brute d'une nature préservée.

NED Naoshima, het kleine eiland in de Japanse Binnenzee, is de geboortegrond van Japanse vissers, maar ook van de kunst. Uitgever Soichiro Fukutake liet er een particuliere galerie voor de familieverzameling van eigentijdse Amerikaanse kunst bouwen. Opdrachtgever en architect Tadao Ando wilden het ongerepte landschap zo min mogelijk beïnvloeden. Dit verklaart dat meer dan 50 procent van het gebouw ondergronds in de klippen is gebouwd. En als altijd staat de architectuur van Ando voor minimalisme – beton, hout en licht in samenspel met de ongerepte ruige natuur.

INUJIMA ART PROJECT

JAPAN | INUJIMA ISLAND | CULTURE

ENG On Naoshima's neighboring Inujima Island, the ramshackle beauty of a dilapidated copper factory inspired arts patron Soichiro Fukutake to launch a museum project. His goal: a structure with minimal impact on the surrounding area. He has realized the first phase of the project, entitled "Seirensho" or "Refinery", along with architect Hirachi Sambushi and conceptual artist Yukinori Yanagi. The largest of six smokestacks became the conceptual heart of the T-shaped, partially subterranean building. This chimney was in a good enough condition to create an artificial stack effect. This all remains true to Fukutake's mantra: utilize and preserve existing elements instead of creating new elements.

DEU Auf Inujima, einer Nachbarinsel von Naoshima Island, inspirierte die marode Schönheit einer verfallenen Kupferfabrik Kunstmäzen Soichiro Fukutake zu einem Museumsprojekt. Sein Ziel: ein Bau, der nur minimal in die Umgebung eingreifen durfte. Mit dem Architekten Hirachi Sambushi und dem Konzeptkünstler Yukinori Yanagi realisierte er die erste Phase des Projekts, „Seirensho" oder „Raffinerie" genannt. Der größte von sechs Schornsteinen wurde das konzeptionelle Herzstück des T-förmigen, in Teilen unterirdischen Gebäudes. Der Schornstein war intakt genug, um in ihm einen künstlichen Schlot-Effekt zu erzielen. Getreu Fukutakes Mantra, das besagt, man solle Bestehendes nehmen und erhalten und Dinge schaffen, die noch nicht existieren.

FR Sur Inujima, une île voisine de Naoshima, la beauté délabrée d'une ancienne usine de cuivre a incité le mécène Soichiro Fukutake à lancer un projet de musée. Son objectif : créer une structure dont l'impact visuel sur le cadre naturel serait minime. Il a réalisé la première phase de son projet, appelé « Seirensho » ou « raffinerie », avec l'architecte Hirachi Sambushi et l'artiste Yukinori Yanagi. La plus imposante des six cheminées est devenue le centre conceptuel de ce bâtiment en forme de T, partiellement souterrain. Cette cheminée était assez bien conservée pour créer un effet d'aspiration artificiel. Tout est fidèle à l'idée initiale de Fukutake : utiliser et préserver les éléments préexistants pour en créer de nouveaux.

NED Op Inujima, een buureiland van Naoshima, inspireerde de geruïneerde schoonheid van een vervallen koperfabriek mecenas Soichiro Fukutake tot een museumproject. Zijn doel: een bouwwerk dat slechts minimaal in de omgeving mocht ingrijpen. Met architect Hirachi Sambushi en conceptkunstenaar Yukinori Yanagi realiseerde hij de eerste fase van het project, 'Seirensho' of 'Raffinaderij' genoemd. De grootste van zes schoorstenen werd het conceptuele hoofdbestanddeel van het T-vormige, deels ondergrondse gebouw. De schoorsteen was voldoende intact om er een kunstmatig fabrieksschoorsteeneffect mee te bereiken. Overeenkomstig de mantra van Fukutake, die stelt dat het bestaande moet worden genomen en behouden, en dingen moeten worden gemaakt die nog niet bestaan.

CHAPELLE DES ANGES NAGOYA

JAPAN | NAGOYA | CULTURE

[ENG] A chapel of the angels, white as snow. Outside you will find a column-lined courtyard and marble mosaics, while the chapel itself is a white cube, decorated with arabesques, and ultra-modern. The nave is seven meters (23 feet) tall, and airy. There are copper pipes like precious curtains on the sides. Sparkling chandeliers give an opulent shimmer. The defining element is a massive mystical cross, over three meters (ten feet) tall, constructed by Takahiro Kondo out of porcelain. The inlays in the white center aisle are made from marble and promise a happy life.

[DEU] Eine Kapelle der Engel, schneeweiß. Außen ein mit Säulen gesäumter Hof und Mosaiken aus Marmor. Die Kapelle selbst ist ein weißer Kubus, verziert mit Arabesken, ultramodern. Das Kirchenschiff sieben Meter hoch, luftig. Kupferrohre wie edle Vorhänge an den Seiten. Glitzernde Lüster mit prachtvollem Glanz. Bestimmendes Element ist ein gewaltiges mystisches Kreuz, mehr als drei Meter hoch, gemacht aus Porzellan, von Takahiro Kondo. Aus Marmor sind die Intarsien im weißen Mittelgang. Sie verheißen ein glückliches Leben.

[FR] Une chapelle des anges, blanche comme neige. On trouve à l'extérieur une cour entourée de colonnes et des mosaïques de marbre, tandis que le cube blanc de la chapelle elle-même, décoré d'arabesques, est ultramoderne. La spacieuse nef mesure sept mètres de haut. De chaque côté, des tuyaux de cuivre imitent des tentures précieuses. Des lustres scintillants apportent une touche miroitante, mais l'élément le plus représentatif est une croix massive en porcelaine de plus de trois mètres, créée par Takahiro Kondo. Elle fait face aux incrustations de marbre dans l'allée centrale qui promettent la félicité.

[NED] Een kapel van de engelen, sneeuwwit. Van buiten een met pilaren omzoomde binnenplaats en mozaïeken van marmer. De kapel zelf is een witte kubus, versierd met arabesken, ultramodern. Het kerkschip zeven meter hoog, luchtig. Koperen buizen als kostbare gordijnen aan de zijkanten. Glinsterende lusters met een prachtige glans. Bepalend element is een enorm, mystiek kruis, meer dan drie meter hoog, gemaakt van porselein, door Takahiro Kondo. Van marmer is het inlegwerk in de witte middengang. Ze beloven een gelukkig leven.

CHICHU ART MUSEUM

JAPAN | NAOSHIMA ISLAND | CULTURE

ENG "Chichu" means "in the earth". And that's exactly where you will find the CHICHU ART MUSEUM, likely the most important contemporary art museum in Japan. Incorporated into a mountain ridge with a breathtaking view of the Seto Inland Sea, it embodies the dream of investor and art collector Soichiro Fukutake. The museum was built to provide a suitable framework for the works of Claude Monet, Walter de Maria, and James Turell. A masterpiece by architect Tadao Ando.

DEU "Chichu" bedeutet "in der Erde". Und eben dort befindet sich das CHICHU ART MUSEUM, das wahrscheinlich wichtigste Museum für zeitgenössische Kunst in Japan. Eingelassen in einen Bergrücken mit einem atemberaubenden Blick über Seto Inland Sea ist es Wirklichkeit gewordener Traum des Kunstsammlers und Verlegers Soichiro Fukutake. Erbaut, um den Werken Claude Monets, Walter de Marias und James Turrells einen angemessenen Rahmen zu bieten. Ein Meisterstück des Architekten Tadao Ando.

FR « Chichu » signifie « dans la terre », et c'est bien dans la terre que se trouve le CHICHU ART MUSEUM : sans doute le musée d'art contemporain le plus important au Japon. Ce chef-d'œuvre de Tadao Ando devait accueillir de la meilleure manière les travaux de Claude Monet, Walter de Maria et James Turell. Intégré à un flan montagneux, il offre une vue spectaculaire sur la mer intérieure de Seto et concrétise le rêve de l'investisseur et collectionneur d'art Soichiro Fukutake.

NED 'Chichu' betekent 'in de aarde'. En precies daar bevindt zich het CHICHU ART MUSEUM, waarschijnlijk het belangrijkste museum voor eigentijdse kunst in Japan. Aangebracht in een bergrug met een adembenemend uitzicht over de Japanse Binnenzee is de werkelijkheid geworden droom van kunstverzamelaar en uitgever Soichiro Fukutake. Gebouwd om de werken van Claude Monets, Walter de Marias en James Turrells een passende omlijsting te bieden. Een meesterstuk van architect Tadao Ando.

SUNTORY MUSEUM OF ART

ENG The SUNTORY MUSEUM OF ART was designed by Kengo Kuma based on one of the concepts of Japanese modernism. It combines traditional and contemporary Japanese elements. The exterior, which is constructed of porcelain-colored slats modeled after traditional Japanese "musogoushi" windows, lends the building transparency. The interior's warm color scheme is derived from wood and Japanese paper, which gives a soft light resembling that in traditional Japanese houses. Kengo Kuma's design goal was to turn the museum into the city's "parlor". The creation is an artistic space: inviting, inspiring, and relaxing all at the same time.

DEU Das SUNTORY MUSEUM OF ART ist ein Entwurf von Kengo Kuma basierend auf einem Konzept des Japanischen Modernismus. Er kombiniert traditionelle und zeitgenössische japanische Elemente. Das Äußere aus porzellanfarbenen Lamellen, dem traditionellen japanischen Fenster „Musogoushi" nachempfunden, verleiht dem Gebäude Transparenz. Holz und Japanisches Papier sorgen im Inneren für eine warme Farbgebung, mit einem sanften Licht, den klassischen japanischen Häusern ähnlich. Das Design-Ziel von Kengo Kuma war es, aus dem Museum „die gute Stube" der Stadt zu machen. Entstanden ist ein Raum der Kunst: einladend, inspirierend und entspannend zugleich.

FR Le SUNTORY MUSEUM OF ART est une œuvre de Kengo Kuma, inspirée par le modernisme japonais qui combine ainsi des éléments traditionnels et contemporains. L'extérieur, composé de lattes d'un blanc de porcelaine, imite les fenêtres traditionnelles japonaises appelées « musogoushi » et confère au bâtiment une jolie transparence. Les teintes chaudes employées à l'intérieur s'inspirent du bois et du papier japonais et laissent pénétrer une lumière douce, semblable à celle des maisons traditionnelles du pays. L'objectif de Kengo Kuma était de transformer le musée en un « salon » de la ville ; il a ainsi créé un espace artistique accueillant, évocateur et relaxant à la fois.

NED Het SUNTORY MUSEUM OF ART is een ontwerp van Kengo Kuma, gebaseerd op een concept van het Japanse modernisme. Hij combineert traditionele en eigentijdse Japanse elementen. Het buitenwerk van porseleinkleurige lamellen, naar de traditionele Japanse vensters, 'musogoushi', verleent het gebouw transparantie. Hout en Japans papier zorgen binnen voor een warme kleurstelling, met zacht licht, als in de klassieke Japanse huizen. Het ontwerpdoel van Kengo Kuma was van het museum 'de pronkkamer' van de stad te maken. Ontstaan is een ruimte van de kunst: uitnodigend, inspirerend en ontspannend tegelijk.

TAMA ART UNIVERSITY LIBRARY

JAPAN | TOKYO | CULTURE

ENG Arches, curves, columns, these are the classical elements of this not-so-classic building. Toyo Ito designed the impressive library in Tokyo's TAMA ART UNIVERSITY. He created a two-story building exclusively from glass and concrete. The result is both elegant and sparse, spacious and bathed in light, almost without walls or doors. A place sure to inspire diligent studying.

DEU Bögen, Kurven, Säulen, das sind die klassischen Elemente dieses so gar nicht klassischen Gebäudes. Der Entwurf dieser beeindruckenden Bibliothek der TAMA ART UNIVERSITY in Tokio ist von Toyo Ito. Er schuf ein Gebäude mit zwei Stockwerken ausschließlich aus Glas und Beton. Das Ergebnis ist elegant und schlicht zugleich, lichtdurchflutet und großzügig, nahezu ohne Wände und Türen. Ein Ort, an dem sich sicher trefflich studieren lässt.

FR Arches, courbes et colonnes sont les seuls éléments classiques de ce bâtiment peu conventionnel et Toyo Ito en est le créateur. Pour l'impressionnante bibliothèque de la TAMA ART UNIVERSITY de Tokyo, il a créé un bâtiment de deux étages entièrement composé de béton et de verre. Le résultat, qui ne comporte quasiment ni portes ni murs, est à la fois élégant, épuré, spacieux et baigné de lumière. C'est l'endroit rêvé pour des études d'exception.

NED Bogen, rondingen, zuilen, dat zijn de klassieke elementen van dit totaal niet klassieke gebouw. Het ontwerp van deze indrukwekkende bibliotheek van de TAMA ART UNIVERSITY in Tokyo is van Toyo Ito. Hij schiep een gebouw met twee verdiepingen van uitsluitend glas en beton. Het resultaat is elegant en eenvoudig tegelijk, doorstroomd met licht en royaal, bijna zonder wanden en deuren. Een plek waar beslist uitstekend kan worden gestudeerd.

TOWADA ART CENTER
JAPAN | TOKYO | CULTURE

ENG The arrangement of 16 snow-white pavilions seems almost arbitrary, without any apparent order. The large alternate with the small like tossed dice, without symmetry, completely at random. Rye Nishizawa of SANAA was given free rein, free from all convention. The difference from other art centers does not lie in the permanent or special exhibitions or in the row of public spaces. It lies in the way that all these are presented. The interior and exterior blend together, the art determines the architecture and vice versa. The art and its setting expand upon each other and exist as separate entities. Both simultaneously. The TOWADA ART CENTER is a work composed of architecture, of tailor-made art, of the viewer and the urban surroundings.

DEU Wie zufällig, ohne jede Ordnung wirkt dieses Arrangement aus 16 schneeweißen Pavillons. Große und kleine wechseln sich ab, wie hingewürfelt, ohne Geometrie, einfach so. Bar jeglicher Konventionen durfte sich Rye Nishizawa von SANAA ausleben. Der Unterschied zu anderen Kunsthäusern besteht nicht in den Permanent- und Sonderausstellungen und einer Reihe öffentlicher Räume. Er besteht in der Präsentation all dessen. Innen und außen verschmelzen, die Kunst bedingt die Architektur und umgekehrt. Kunst und Umgebung ergänzen sich oder ergänzen sich nicht. Beides existiert. Das TOWADA ART CENTER ist eine Komposition aus Architektur, in Teilen maßgeschneiderter Kunst, dem Betrachter und dem urbanen Umfeld.

FR La disposition de ces 16 pavillons blancs comme neige semble aléatoire. Les cubes de tailles différentes se côtoient tels des dés lancés. Rye Nishizawa, de chez SANAA, a reçu carte blanche pour ce projet qui ne se différencie des autres centres artistiques ni par l'espace public qu'il offre à la ville, ni par les expositions permanentes ou temporaires qu'il accueille. Ce qui le rend unique, c'est sa manière de les présenter. L'intérieur et l'extérieur n'ont pas de frontières, car ici c'est l'art qui détermine l'architecture, et inversement. L'art et le lieu s'interpénètrent mais existent aussi simultanément en tant qu'entités séparées. Le TOWADA ART CENTER est une œuvre patchwork réunissant l'architecture du lieu, les œuvres d'art, les visiteurs et l'environnement urbain.

NED Dit arrangement van zestien sneeuwwitte paviljoens doet als terloops, zonder enige ordening aan. Grote en kleine wisselen elkaar af, alsof ze erheen zijn gerold, zonder geometrie, zomaar. Zonder enige conventies mocht Rye Nishizawa van SANAA zich uitleven. Het verschil met andere kunsthuizen zit hem niet in de permanente of speciale tentoonstellingen en een reeks openbare ruimtes. Het zit hem in de presentaties van dit alles. Binnen en buiten versmelten, de kunst bepaalt de architectuur en omgekeerd. Kunst en omgeving vullen elkaar aan of vullen elkaar niet aan. Allebei komt dit voor. Het TOWADA ART CENTER is een compositie van architectuur, deels op maat gemaakte kunst, de toeschouwer en de stedelijke omgeving.

ZA-KOENJI PUBLIC THEATRE

JAPAN | TOKYO | CULTURE

ENG Toyo Ito's ZA-KOENJI PUBLIC THEATRE, designed for the non-commercial "Creative Theatre Network", is a small contemporary theater for performing arts in Suginami, a district of Tokyo. The building resembles a top-heavy black iceberg, a meteor, or monolith. The multifunctional theater encompasses six floors, three below ground and three above. There are three main areas, one with a flexible stage and viewing area, the largest, the traditional theater space with a fixed stage and viewing area, plus a studio for rehearsals and workshops. The building leaves a lasting impression with its complex geometry and dark steel casing.

DEU Das ZA-KOENJI PUBLIC THEATRE, von Toyo Ito für das nicht-kommerzielle „Creative Theatre Network" geschaffen, ist ein kleines, kontemporäres Theater der darstellenden Künste in Suginami, einem Stadtteil von Tokio. Wie ein kopflastiger schwarzer Eisberg, ein Meteor oder Monolith mutet dieses Gebäude an. Sechs Stockwerke, drei unter und drei über der Erde, umfasst das multifunktionale Theater. Innen drei Haupträume, einer mit flexiblen Bühnen- und Zuschauerrängen, der größte, der traditionelle Theatersaal mit fixer Bühne und ebensolchen Rängen, dazu ein Studio für Proben und Workshops. Mit seiner komplexen Geometrie und der dunklen Haut aus Stahl hinterlässt dieses Gebäude einen bleibenden Eindruck.

FR Le ZA-KOENJI PUBLIC THEATRE de Toyo Ito, créé pour le théâtre public du « Creative Theatre Network », est une petite structure contemporaine dédiée aux arts du spectacle, dans le quartier de Suginami, à Tokyo. Le bâtiment ressemble au sommet d'un iceberg noir, à un météore ou à un monolithe. Ce théâtre multifonction comprend six niveaux, dont trois sont en sous-sol. Les trois zones principales comptent une importante salle de représentation dotée d'une scène mobile, un espace théâtral traditionnel dont la scène est fixe, ainsi qu'un studio de répétitions et de cours. L'intérieur de cette grande boîte de métal sombre laisse comme un goût persistant de géométrie complexe.

NED Het ZA-KOENJI PUBLIC THEATRE, van Toyo Ito voor het niet-commerciële 'Creative Theatre Network', is een klein, eigentijds theater voor de toneelkunst in Suginami, een wijk in Tokyo. Dit gebouw doet aan als een topzware zwarte ijsberg, een meteoor of een monoliet. Zes verdiepingen, drie onder en drie boven de grond, omvat het multifunctionele theater. Binnen drie hoofdruimten, een met flexibel toneel en toeschouwerrangen, de grootste, de traditionele theaterzaal met vast toneel en dito rangen, en verder een studio voor repetities en workshops. Met zijn complexe geometrie en de donkere bekleding van staal laat dit gebouw een blijvende indruk achter.

THE ESPLANADE
REPUBLIC OF SINGAPORE | SINGAPORE | CULTURE

ENG Singaporeans affectionately refer to THE ESPLANADE as "the Durian", referring to the prickly fruit so beloved in Asia. THE ES-PLANADE is a multifunctional art and cultural center of immense proportions. The conspicuous focal point is a building complex consisting of two vaulted halls, gigantic "bubbles" for holding performances and concerts, encased in a structured envelope, more precisely a steel-frame latticework of glass and protruding aluminum sunshades. The design by DP Architects Pte. Ltd. and Michael Wilfort & Partners is a successful combination of Asian architectural tradition and the latest technology—all with the appearance of a prickly durian fruit.

DEU „Durian" nennen die Singapurer THE ESPLANADE liebevoll, nach der in Asien beliebten stacheligen Frucht. THE ESPLANADE ist ein multifunktionales Kunst- und Kulturzentrum von immensem Ausmaß. Auffälliger Mittelpunkt ist ein Gebäudekomplex mit zwei Hallengewölben, zwei gigantischen „Blasen" für Theater und Konzerte mit einer strukturierten Hülle, genauer einer Stahlrahmen-Gitter-Konstruktion, Teilflächen aus Glas und vorgesetzten Aluminium-Sonnensegeln. Der Entwurf von DP Architects Pte. Ltd. und Michael Wilfort & Partners ist eine gelungene Kombination aus asiatischer Bautradition und modernster Technik – all das mit der Optik einer stacheligen Durian.

FR Les Singapouriens appellent gentiment THE ESPLANADE « le durian », en référence à ce fruit piquant si apprécié en Asie. THE ESPLANADE est un centre artistique et culturel multifonctions aux proportions démesurées. Le complexe est principalement composé de deux halles voûtées, semblables à de gigantesques « bulles » accueillant performances artistiques et concerts. Elles sont recouvertes d'une enveloppe, plus précisément un treillis de verre et d'acier, protégé par des panneaux d'aluminium. Le projet de DP Architects Pte. Ltd. et Michael Wilfort & Partners allie à merveille la tradition architecturale asiatique aux dernières technologies, tout en gardant l'apparence de ce fruit piquant.

NED De Singaporezen noemen THE ESPLANADE liefdevol 'Doerian', naar de in Azië geliefde stekelige vrucht. THE ESPLANADE is een multifunctioneel kunst- en cultuurcentrum van immense afmetingen. Opvallend middelpunt is een gebouwencomplex met twee zalengewelven, twee gigantische 'blazen' voor theater en concerten met een gestructureerd omhulsel, om precies te zijn een constructie van stalen raamwerken en roosters, deelvlakken van glas en ervoor geplaatste aluminium zonneschermen. Het ontwerp van DP Architects Pte. Ltd. en Michael Wilfort & Partners is een geslaagde combinatie van Aziatische bouwtraditie en de modernste techniek – dit alles met het uiterlijk van een stekelige doerian.

MUSEUM OF ISLAMIC ART

QATAR | DOHA | CULTURE

ᴱᴺᴳ I.M. Pei has traced the diverse footsteps of Islamic art to create the MUSEUM OF ISLAMIC ART, inspired by the Ahmad Ibn Tulun mosque in Cairo and influenced by what he saw on his travels. The result is an ultra-modern, minimalist building, with cubist shapes and fine detail work from Islamic art and culture, nestled in a large park, 35,000 square meters (376,737 square feet) in size. The building's clarity and sparseness reflect the interior and lighting design by Jean-Michel Wilmotte. He has created an atmosphere that he theatrically calls a play on light and darkness.

ᴰᴱᵁ I.M. Pei begab sich auf die Spuren der so vielfältigen islamischen Kunst und baute dann das MUSEUM OF ISLAMIC ART, inspiriert von der Moschee von Ahmad Ibn Tulun in Kairo, und beeinflusst von dem, was er auf seiner Reise erfuhr. Das Ergebnis ist ein ultramodernes Gebäude, minimalistisch, mit kubistischen Formen und feinen Details der muslimischen Kunst und Kultur, eingebettet in einen großen Park, mit einer Fläche von 35 000 Quadratmetern. Der Klarheit und Schlichtheit des Gebäudes entsprechen die Innenarchitektur und das Lichtdesign von Jean-Michel Wilmotte. Er schuf eine Atmosphäre, die er theatralisch nennt: Ein Spiel aus Licht und Dunkel.

ᶠᴿ Inspiré par la mosquée Ahmad Ibn Tulun du Caire et influencé par ses nombreux voyages, I.M. Pei a su marier les différents aspects de l'art islamique pour créer son MUSEUM OF ISLAMIC ART. Ce bâtiment ultramoderne et minimaliste, aux formes géométriques et aux décorations fidèles à la culture et à l'art islamique est le fruit de son travail. Lové dans un gigantesque parc de 3,5 hectares, clarté et épure sont les maîtres-mots de ce bâtiment créé par Jean-Michel Wilmotte. Ce dernier a réussi à produire une atmosphère qu'il qualifie théâtralement de « jeu des ombres et de la lumière ».

ᴺᴱᴰ I.M. Pei volgde de sporen van de zo veelsoortige islamitische kunst en bouwde toen het MUSEUM OF ISLAMIC ART, geïnspireerd door de moskee van Ahmad Ibn Tulun in Cairo, en beïnvloed door wat hij op zijn reis beleefde. Het resultaat is een ultramodern gebouw, minimalistisch, met kubistische vormen en fijne details uit de islamitische kunst en cultuur, verscholen in een groot park, met een oppervlak van 35.000 vierkante meter. De helderheid en eenvoud van het gebouw stemmen overeen met de binnenhuisarchitectuur en het lichtontwerp van Jean-Michelle Wilmotte. Hij creëerde een sfeer die hij theatraal noemt: een spel van licht en donker.

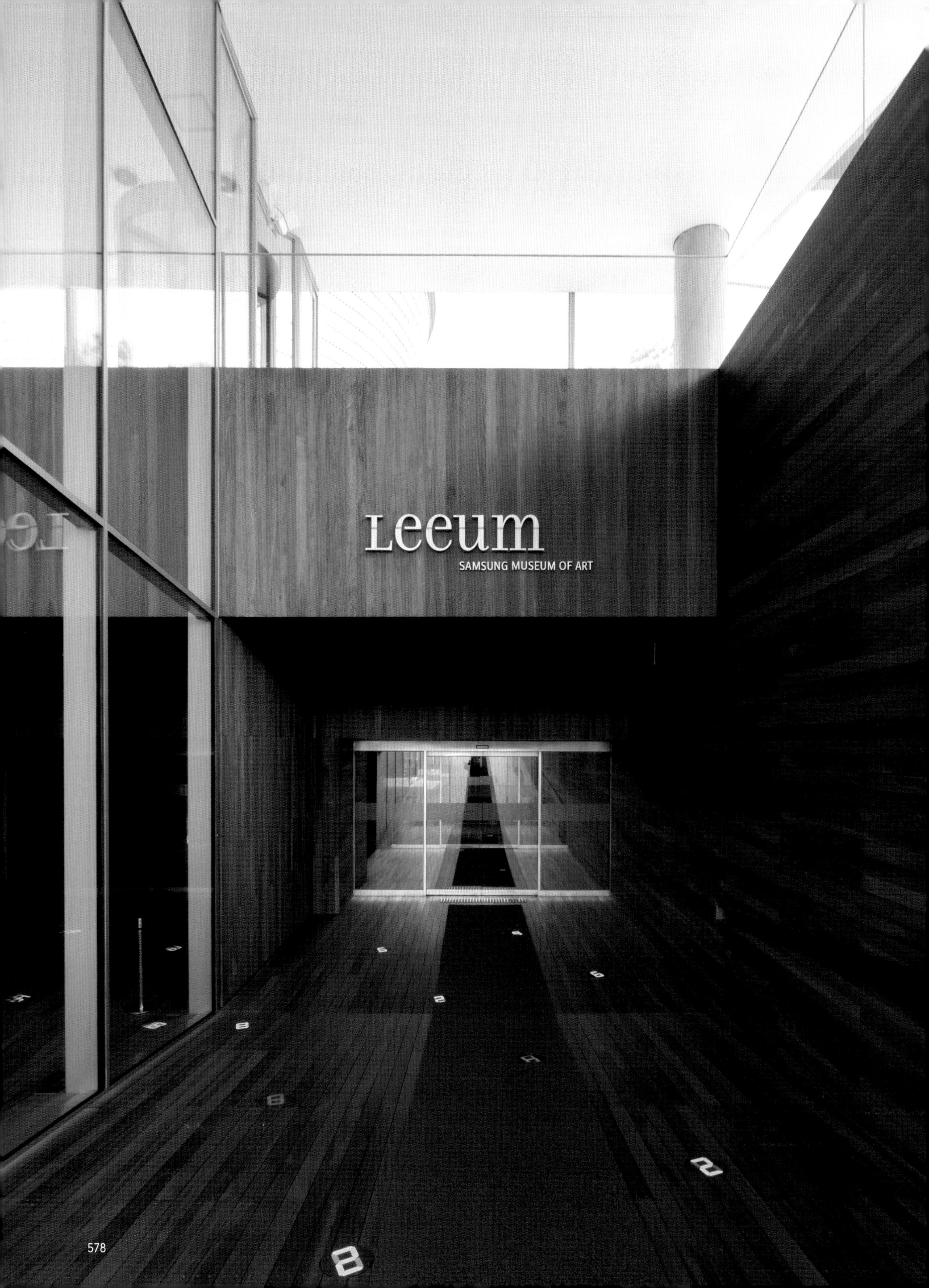
Leeum
SAMSUNG MUSEUM OF ART

LEEUM, SAMSUNG MUSEUM OF ART

SOUTH KOREA | SEOUL | CULTURE

ᴱᴺᴳ The task must have sounded like a challenge even for three of the world's most renowned architects: "Construct a museum building for each type of art, one that will express its individuality—but which together create a place that visually unifies everything and thereby bridges traditional Korean art, international contemporary art, and that of the future." From this assignment, Mario Botta, Jean Nouvel, and Rem Koolhaas have created a must for every art enthusiast in the world.

ᴰᴱᵁ Die Aufgabe muss selbst für drei der weltweit namhaftesten Architekten herausfordernd geklungen haben: „Bauen Sie jeweils einen Museumsbau für jede Kunstrichtung, der deren Individualität zum Ausdruck bringt – aber zugleich im Zusammenwirken einen Ort schafft, der alles optisch eint und damit eine Brücke schlägt zwischen traditioneller koreanischer Kunst, internationaler zeitgenössischer Kunst und dem Zukünftigen." Was Mario Botta, Jean Nouvel und Rem Koolhaas aus dieser Aufgabenstellung gemacht haben, ist ein Muss für jeden Kunstinteressierten weltweit.

ᶠᴿ Le projet devait davantage s'apparenter à un défi, même pour les trois plus célèbres architectes au monde : « Construire un musée dédié aux différentes formes d'art, afin que chacune puisse y exprimer son individualité ; l'unité créée pour ce lieu permettra de découvrir l'art traditionnel coréen puis l'art contemporain international ou les expressions artistiques en devenir. » C'est en travaillant sur ces conditions que Mario Botta, Jean Nouvel et Rem Koolhaas ont créé le lieu parfait pour les amoureux de l'art du monde entier.

ᴺᴱᴰ De opdracht moet zelfs voor de drie meest gerenommeerde architecten ter wereld als een uitdaging hebben geklonken: 'Bouw voor alle kunstrichtingen een museumgebouw, dat de individualiteit van elke ervan tot uiting laat komen – maar tegelijk een samenhangende plek doet ontstaan die alles optisch één maakt en daarmee een brug slaat tussen traditionele Koreaanse kunst, internationale eigentijdse kunst en kunst van de toekomst.' Wat Mario Botta, Jean Nouvel en Rem Koolhaas van deze taakstelling hebben gemaakt, is een must voor alle kunstliefhebbers ter wereld.

PLATOON KUNSTHALLE
SOUTH KOREA | SEOUL | CULTURE

ENG 28 cargo containers stand on a city square in Cheongdam-dong, a district of Seoul, surrounded by skyscrapers and upscale buildings. No matter whether you belong to a subculture, counter-culture, or the in-crowd—the PLATOON KUNSTHALLE is a remarkable meeting place for artists of various genres, including street art, graphic design, fashion, music, programming, and more. The containers form a 700 square meter (7535 square foot) area for events, exhibitions, and workshops. A multifunctional site with a chill zone, the result of a collaboration between the Platoon art communication network and Graft Architects, with interior design by Baik Jiwon.

DEU Zwischen Wolkenkratzern und Luxusbauten auf einem Platz in Cheongdam-dong, einem Stadtviertel von Seoul, stehen 28 Frachtcontainer. Ganz unabhängig für wen, Vertreter der Sub-, Gegenkultur oder Szene – die PLATOON KUNSTHALLE ist ein bemerkenswerter Treffpunkt für Künstler verschiedener Stilrichtungen wie Street Art, Grafikdesign, Mode, Musik, Programmierung und mehr. Die Container formen ein 700 Quadratmeter großes Areal für Veranstaltungen, Ausstellungen, Workshops. Ein multifunktionaler Ort mit Chill-Zone, entstanden aus einer Kooperation des Kunstkommunikations-Netzwerks Platoon mit Graft Architects und Baik Jiwon für das Interior Design.

FR Dans le quartier Cheongdam-dong de Séoul, entouré de gratte-ciels et de bâtiments luxueux, 28 containers semblent avoir été déposés par erreur sur une place. Que l'on appartienne à une sous-culture, à une contre-culture ou à la foule anonyme, le PLATOON KUNSTHALLE est un lieu de rencontre remarquable pour les artistes en tout genre, représentants du street art, du design graphique, de la mode, de la musique, de la programmation ou d'autres mouvements. Les containers forment une zone de 700 mètres carrés, un site multifonctions doté d'une salle de repos et dédié à des évènements, des expositions et des ateliers. Cet ensemble, dont l'architecture d'intérieur est signée Baik Jiwon, est le fruit d'une collaboration unique entre le réseau artistique the Platoon et Graft Architects.

NED Tussen wolkenkrabbers en luxe gebouwen op een plein in Cheongdam-dong, een wijk in Seoul, staan 28 vrachtcontainers. Geheel onafhankelijk voor wie, vertegenwoordigers van de sub-, tegencultuur of het circuit – is de PLATOON KUNSTZAAL een opmerkelijk trefpunt voor kunstenaars van verschillende stijlrichtingen als straatkunst, grafisch ontwerp, mode, muziek, programmering en meer. De containers vormen een 700 vierkante meter groot terrein voor manifestaties, tentoonstellingen en workshops. Een multifunctionele plaats met chill zone, ontstaan uit een samenwerkingsverband van het kunstcommunicatienetwerk Platoon met Graft Architects en Baik Jiwon voor het interieurontwerp.

LANDMARKS
PUBLIC BUILDINGS AND PLACES OF INTEREST

WORLD TRADE CENTER

KINGDOM OF BAHRAIN | MANAMA | LANDMARKS

ENG It consists of two towers, rising more than 240 meters (787 feet), and is one of the tallest buildings in Bahrain, 50 floors, 34 of them for offices. Plus stores, a five-star hotel, restaurants, and more. But the WORLD TRADE CENTER is more than just a building embodying of financial success. It is the modern interpretation of the traditional Arabian wind-catcher, the world's first building with an integrated wind energy plant. The building is unique due to its wind turbines, which are secured to 30 meter wide (98 foot wide) skybridges linking the buildings. Each with a diameter of 29 meters (95 feet), they are expected to generate between 11 and 15 percent of the building's electrical energy needs.

DEU Es besteht aus zwei Türmen, mehr als 240 Meter hoch, und es ist eines der höchsten Gebäude Bahrains, 50 Stockwerke, 34 davon für Büros. Dazu Ladengeschäfte, Fünf-Sterne-Hotel, Restaurants und mehr. Aber das WORLD TRADE CENTER ist mehr als ein Bauwerk, das von wirtschaftlichem Erfolg erzählt. Es ist die moderne Interpretation des traditionellen arabischen Windfängers, das erste Gebäude mit einer integrierten Windturbinen-Energieanlage weltweit. Die Besonderheit sind drei auf 30 Meter breiten Querstreben zwischen den Gebäuden angebrachte Windturbinen. Mit einem Durchmesser von 29 Metern sollen sie zwischen elf und 15 Prozent des Gebäude-Energiebedarfs decken.

FR Ce complexe, constitué de deux tours de plus de 240 mètres, est l'un des plus hauts immeubles du Bahreïn : il compte 50 étages, dont 34 de bureaux. Quelques magasins s'y sont aussi installés, ainsi qu'un hôtel cinq étoiles et des restaurants. Mais le WORLD TRADE CENTER exprime plus que la réussite financière... Cette interprétation moderne des « badgirs », ces tours traditionnelles servant à piéger le vent, est le premier bâtiment au monde à intégrer une structure énergétique éolienne. Les turbines placées à 30 mètres au-dessus du sol sur des ponts reliant les deux tours, sont le point fort de ce bâtiment unique. Mesurant chacune 29 mètres de diamètre, elles sont supposées générer entre 11 et 15 pourcents des besoins en énergie électrique des deux tours.

NED Het bestaat uit twee torens, ruim 240 meter hoog, en is een van de hoogste gebouwen van Bahrain, 50 verdiepingen, waarvan 34 voor kantoren. Verder winkels, een vijfsterrenhotel, restaurants en nog meer. Maar het WORLD TRADE CENTER is meer dan een bouwwerk dat getuigt van economisch succes. Het is de moderne interpretatie van de traditionele Arabische windvanger, het eerste gebouw met een geïntegreerde windturbine energie-installatie ter wereld. Het bijzondere zijn drie op 30 meter brede dwarsbalken tussen de gebouwen aangebrachte windturbines. Met een doorsnee van 29 meter moeten ze voorzien in tussen 11 en 15 procent van de energiebehoefte van het gebouw.

CCTV TOWER

CHINA | BEIJING | LANDMARKS

ENG The CCTV TOWER has left an impression on the world from the very start. It is one of the boldest and most controversial projects of our time. Rem Koolhaas of OMA designed the tower for China Central Television. It is unmistakable with its two angled towers connected above and below like a Moebius strip. An audacious and costly project that sends a message to the world: that of a self-confident China that has entered the modern age. A demonstration of power and strength not through size, but through a form of cultural creative power.

DEU Der CCTV TOWER hat die Welt von Beginn an nicht unbeeindruckt gelassen. Er ist eines der umstrittensten und kühnsten Projekte unserer Zeit. Entworfen hat ihn Rem Koolhaas von OMA für das Staatliche Chinesische Fernsehen. Zwei schiefe Türme, die oben und unten miteinander verbunden sind, die Form eines Möbiusbandes, machen ihn unverwechselbar. Ein kühnes und kostspieliges Projekt mit einer Botschaft an die Welt: Es berichtet von einem in der Jetztzeit angekommenen selbstbewussten China. Eine Demonstration von Macht und Stärke nicht durch Größe, sondern durch eine Form von kulturel-ler Schaffenskraft.

FR La CCTV TOWER étonne le monde entier depuis sa construction. C'est l'un des projets les plus osés et les plus controversés de notre époque. Rem Koolhaas de chez OMA a créé cette structure pour la chaîne chinoise CCT. Ses deux tours inclinées et reliées entre elles comme un ruban de Möbius en font un monument inimitable. Ce projet audacieux et onéreux envoie un message au monde entier : la Chine a confiance en elle et entre dans l'ère moderne. Elle effectue ici une démonstration de puissance, non par la force, mais à travers cette forme de pouvoir qu'est la création.

NED De CCTV TOWER heeft van meet af aan indruk op de wereld gemaakt. Het is een van de meest omstreden en vermetelste pro-jecten van onze tijd. Hij is ontworpen door Rem Koolhaas van OMA voor de Chinese staatstelevisie. Twee scheve torens, die van bo-ven en onderen met elkaar zijn verbonden, de vorm van een möbiusring, maken hem op-en-top karakteristiek. Een vermetel en duur project met een boodschap aan de wereld: het beschrijft het in de huidige tijd ontstane zelfbewustzijn van China. Een vertoon van macht en sterkte, niet door de grootte, maar door een vorm van culturele scheppingskracht.

DIGITAL BEIJING

CHINA | BEIJING | LANDMARKS

ENG The north and south sides are reminiscent of a bar code, the east and west of a circuit board. DIGITAL BEIJING is part of the "Digital Beijing Plan". It was the data and control center during the 2008 Olympics, and is now used as a virtual museum and presentation space for manufacturers of digital products. The four sections look like circuit boards lined up on end, seemingly unconnected. These massive blocks of reinforced concrete are eleven stories high, with two additional levels below ground. The exterior walls are made of glass and prefabricated gray concrete components, plus metal latticework covering the spaces between the blocks. With this building, architect Pei Zhu has created an architectural symbol of China's significant role in the digital world.

DEU Nord- und Südseite erinnern an einen Barcode, Ost- und Westseite an Leiterplatten. Das DIGITAL BEIJING ist ein Gebäude im digitalen Look mit einer digitalen Funktion als Teil des „Digital Beijing Plan". Während der Olympischen Spiele 2008 war es Daten- und Kontrollzentrum, jetzt wird es als virtuelles Museum und Präsentationsfläche für Hersteller digitaler Produkte genutzt. Die vier Gebäudeteile wirken wie hintereinander gesteckte Platinen, scheinbar unverbunden. Mächtig sind diese Blöcke aus Stahlbeton, elf Stockwerke hoch, mit zwei weiteren unter der Erde. Die vorgehängten Fassaden sind aus grauen Betonfertigteilen und Glas, dazu Metallgitter, die die Schächte zwischen den Blöcken verkleiden. Architekt Pei Zhu schuf ein architektonisches Symbol für Chinas eindrucksvolle Rolle in der digitalen Welt.

FR Les faces nord et sud font penser à des codes barres géants, tandis que les faces est et ouest se rapprochent davantage du circuit imprimé. Le DIGITAL BEIJING fait partie du « Digital Beijing Plan ». Centre de données et de contrôle durant les jeux olympiques de 2008, il est aujourd'hui devenu musée virtuel et espace de présentation pour les fabricants de produits numériques. Les quatre bâtiments à priori indépendants forment un alignement de circuits intégrés. Ces blocks imposants de béton armé comptent onze étages et deux niveaux en sous-sol. Les murs-rideaux sont faits de verre, d'éléments en béton gris et d'un treillis métallique recouvrant les espaces situés entre les quatre bâtiments. Avec ce projet, l'architecte Pei Zhu a voulu symboliser de manière architecturale le rôle important tenu par la Chine dans le monde numérique.

NED De noord- en zuidkant doen denken aan een streepjescode, de oost- en westkant aan printkaarten. Het DIGITAL BEIJING is een onderdeel van het 'Digital Beijing Plan'. Tijdens de Olympische Spelen in 2008 was het een gegevens- en controlecentrum, nu wordt het als virtueel museum en presentatieoppervlak gebruikt. De vier gebouwdelen hebben het effect van achter elkaar gestoken printplaten. Imposant zijn ze, deze blokken van staalbeton, elf verdiepingen hoog, met nog eens twee onder de grond. De ervoor gehangen gevels zijn van grijze geprefabriceerde betonelementen en glas, verder metalen roosters, die de schachten tussen de blokken bekleden. Architect Pei Zhu schiep een architectonisch symbool voor China's indrukwekkende rol in de digitale wereld.

ᴱᴺᴳ The Beijing Economic Technological Development Area was a wasteland before Keiichiro Sako began "revitalizing" it. A multifunctional building complex housing stores and office space, with a building freeze at the fourth floor. It lacked life, business atmosphere, and business. Sako was commissioned with renovating, transforming, reinventing it. Offices were converted to single-bedroom apartments, the shops rented out. Lighted ads on the first four floors bear witness to the inhabitants. Sako's goal was to create a presence. His visual stylistic device: a mosaic, everywhere. Intricate reflective surfaces divide, enlarge, and distort movement. The mosaic runs through everything, including the signs, the interior, and the landscape.

ᴰᴱᵁ Die Beijing Economic Technological Development Area war eine Brache, bevor Keiichiro Sako mit der „Belebung" begann. Ein multifunktionaler Gebäudekomplex aus Ladengeschäften und Geschäftsräumen, mit Baustopp im vierten Stock. Es fehlte Leben, Businessatmosphäre, Geschäftigkeit. Sako sollte renovieren, umwandeln, neu starten. Aus Büros wurden Ein-Zimmer-Apartments, die Geschäfte vermietet. Beleuchtete Reklamen in den ersten vier Stockwerken zeugen von den Bewohnern. Sakos Ziel war es, Präsenz zu erzeugen. Sein optisches Stilmittel: ein Mosaik, überall. Komplizierte reflektierende Flächen trennen, vergrößern, verzerren Bewegung. Das Mosaik zieht sich durch alles, auch durch die Beschilderung, das Interieur und die Landschaft.

ᶠᴿ L'Economic Technological Development Area de Pékin était en friche avant que Keiichiro Sako ne commence sa « revitalisation ». Ce complexe multifonctions accueillait magasins et bureaux sur quatre étages, mais ne semblait attirer aucun flux commercial. Sako fut nommé pour sa transformation : les bureaux devinrent des studios, et les magasins furent loués, dont l'activité retrouvée est visible depuis la rue grâce aux enseignes lumineuses des quatre premiers étages. Sako souhaitait créer une présence, rendue visible par un outil visuel et stylistique : la mosaïque. Omniprésente, sur les enseignes, dans la décoration du bâtiment et jusque dans le paysage urbain, ces surfaces réfléchissantes et finement ouvragées divisent, agrandissent ou modifient l'environnement.

ᴺᴱᴰ Het Beijing Economic Technological Development Area was een barak voordat Keiichiro Sako met de 'verlevendiging' begon. Een multifunctioneel gebouwencomplex met winkels en kantoren, met bouwstop op de vierde etage. Het ontbrak aan levendigheid, zakensfeer, bedrijvigheid. Sako moest renoveren, veranderen, opnieuw beginnen. Kantoren werden eenkamerappartementen, de winkels werden verhuurd. Verlichte reclames op de eerste vier etages tonen dat er bewoners zijn. Sako's doel was aanwezigheid te bewerkstelligen. Zijn optische stijlmiddel: een mozaïek, overal. Gecompliceerde reflecterende vlakken scheiden, vergroten, vertekenen beweging. Het mozaïek loopt door alles heen, ook door de beschildering, het interieur en het landschap.

ENG With their lush vegetation, the SIEEB's many terraces can seem to be competing for sunlight. Italian architect Mario Cucinella was responsible for the construction of this 40 meter high (131 foot high), 20,000 square meter (215,278 square foot) building. Like a leaf, the building is meant to transform sunlight into energy. For this purpose, over 1000 square meters (10,764 square feet) of photoelectric collectors have been installed on the building's terraces. These collectors are intended to provide the bulk of the building's electrical energy needs. In addition, the structure's horseshoe shape is designed to optimize the available sunlight in wintertime, provide protection from intense summer sun, curb energy needs, and ensure constant natural lighting.

DEU Es sieht so aus, als befänden sich die vielen üppig bepflanzten Terrassen des SIEEB im Wettstreit um die Gunst des Sonnenlichts. Gebaut hat dieses 40 Meter hohe und 20 000 Quadratmeter große Gebäude der italienische Architekt Mario Cucinella. Wie ein Blatt soll das Gebäude das Sonnenlicht nutzen und in Energie umwandeln. Dazu sind auf den Terrassen mehr als 1 000 Quadratmeter fotoelektrischer Kollektoren installiert. Sie haben die Aufgabe, den Großteil des internen elektrischen Energiebedarfs zu decken. Darüber hinaus soll der hufeisenförmige Entwurf den Bedarf an Sonnenlicht im Winter optimieren, im Sommer Schutz vor den Sonnenstrahlen bieten, den Energiebedarf drosseln und eine kontinuierliche natürliche Beleuchtung gewährleisten.

FR Avec leur végétation luxuriante, les nombreuses terrasses du SIEEB semblent prises dans une course vers le soleil. L'architecte italien Mario Cucinella s'est vu chargé de construire ce bâtiment de 40 mètres de haut, sur 20 000 mètres carrés. Tel une feuille, il transforme la lumière du soleil en énergie et compte plus de 1 000 mètres carrés de panneaux photoélectriques, installés sur ces terrasses et sensés fournir l'énergie nécessaire au bâtiment. La structure en fer à cheval du bâtiment optimise l'exposition au soleil en hiver, protège des rayons trop puissants en été, limite les besoins en énergie et assure un éclairage naturel constant.

NED Het lijkt wel alsof de vele weelderig beplante terrassen van het SIEEB strijden om de gunst van het zonlicht. Dit 40 meter hoge en 20.000 vierkante meter grote gebouw is gebouwd door de Italiaanse architect Mario Cucinella. Als een blad moet het gebouw het zonlicht benutten en in energie omzetten. Daarvoor is op de terrassen meer dan 1000 vierkante meter aan fotovoltaïsche panelen geïnstalleerd. Ze hebben tot taak te voorzien in het grootste deel van de interne energiebehoefte. Bovendien moet het hoefijzervormige ontwerp de behoefte aan zonlicht in de winter optimaliseren, in de zomer bescherming tegen de zonnestralen bieden, de energiebehoefte afremmen en een continue natuurlijke verlichting waarborgen.

HANGZHOU WATERFRONT

CHINA | HANGZHOU | LANDMARKS

ENG The problem: Hubin Road, a freeway that cuts the shore of West Lake off from the rest of the city. The solution: redirecting traffic through a tunnel that runs under the lake. The freeway was transformed into a pedestrian-friendly boulevard. The tree-lined park that connects the lakeshore with the newly created boulevard is 650 meters (2133 feet) long and 40 meters (131 feet) wide. "Little canals" that once flowed through Hangzhou were reconstructed. As in the past, they now lead pedestrians directly to the lake. A 54,000-square-meter (581,251-square-foot) site has been created there, both public and private. The creators: SWA Group of Houston and Zhejiang South Architecture Design Company.

DEU Das Problem: die Hubin Road, ein Freeway, der das Ufer des Westlake vom Rest der Stadt abschnitt. Die Lösung: Umleitung des Verkehrs in einen Tunnel unter dem See. Der Freeway wurde zum fußgängerfreundlichen Boulevard. 650 Meter lang und 40 Meter breit ist der mit Bäumen gesäumte Park, der zwischen dem Uferstreifen und dem neu geschaffenen Boulevard vermittelt. „Kleine Kanäle", die schon früher einmal durch Hangzhou flossen, wurden rekonstruiert. Damals wie heute leiten sie den Fußgänger direkt zum See. Dort entstand auf rund 54 000 Quadratmetern ein Ort, privat und öffentlich. Die Macher: SWA Group of Houston and Zhejiang South Architecture Design Company.

FR Un problème : Hubin Road, une autoroute coupant la côte du lac West du reste de la ville. Une solution : rediriger la circulation vers un tunnel sous le lac. L'autoroute s'est alors transformée en un boulevard piétonnier. Le parc arboré reliant les rives du lac à ce nouveau boulevard mesure 650 mètres de long et 40 mètres de large. Les « petits canaux » qui coulaient autrefois à travers Hangzhou ont été recréés et conduisent maintenant les piétons directement au lac. Un site de 54 000 mètres carrés mêlant espaces publics et privés a ainsi été créé par le SWA Group de Houston et la Zhejiang South Architecture Design Company.

NED Het probleem: de Hubin Road, een autoweg, die de oever van het Westelijke Meer van de rest van de stad afsneed. De oplossing: omleiding van het verkeer door een tunnel onder het meer. De autoweg is een voetgangervriendelijke boulevard geworden. 650 meter lang en 40 meter breed is het met bomen omzoomde park, dat tussen de oeverstrook en de nieuwe boulevard bemiddelt. 'Kleine kanalen', die vroeger ooit al door Hangzhou stroomden, zijn gereconstrueerd. Net als toen leiden ze voetgangers direct naar het meer. Daar is op zo'n 54.000 vierkante meter een plaats ontstaan die tegelijk besloten en openbaar is. De makers: SWA Group uit Houston en Zhejiang South Architecture Design Company.

JINHUA ARCHITECTURE PARK
CHINA | JINHUA | LANDMARKS

ENG There are 17 pavilions, created by 17 national and international architects and spread across a narrow shoreline of Yiwu, in memory of the poet Ai Qing, the father of artist and curator Ai Weiwei. 17 pavilions with a defined function that ranges from reception to reading room, from a museum for traditional Chinese ceramics to the toilets. The architecture was inspired by Chinese culture: Chinese gardens, the traditional tea ceremony, the food culture, the special relationship between books and architecture in Chinese history, dragons, trees, etc. A modern architectural interpretation that combines an internal and external perspective.

DEU Es sind 17 Pavillons, gestaltet von 17 nationalen und internationalen Architekten, die verteilt sind auf einen schmalen Uferstreifen entlang des Yiwu, in Erinnerung an den Poeten Ai Qing, Vater des Künstlers und Kurators Ai Weiwei. 17 Pavillons mit einer definierten Funktion vom Empfang, über den Leseraum, ein Museum für traditionelle chinesische Keramik, bis hin zu den Toiletten. Die Architektur ist inspiriert von der chinesischen Kultur: den chinesischen Gärten, der Tee-Zeremonie, der Speisekultur, dem besonderen Verhältnis zwischen Buch und Architektur in der chinesischen Geschichte, den Drachen, Bäumen, etc. Eine moderne architektonische Interpretation aus einer inneren und einer äußeren Perspektive.

FR Les 17 pavillons, pensés par 17 architectes nationaux et internationaux, sont disséminés sur l'étroite rive d'un lac de Yiwu, en mémoire au poète Ai Qing, père de l'artiste Ai Weiwei. Chacun des 17 pavillons possède une fonction définie allant de la salle de réception à la salle de lecture, d'un musée des céramiques chinoises aux toilettes. L'architecture rend ici hommage à la culture chinoise : ses jardins, sa cérémonie du thé, sa gastronomie, sa relation historique liant le livre et l'architecture, ses dragons, ses arbres, etc. Cette interprétation culturelle et architecturale moderne allie à merveille les perspectives intérieure et extérieure.

NED Het zijn zeventien paviljoens, vormgegeven door zeventien nationale en internationale architecten, die verspreid zijn over een smalle oeverstrook langs de Yiwu, ter nagedachtenis aan de dichter Ai Qing, vader van de kunstenaar en curator Ai Weiwei. Zeventien paviljoens met vastgelegde functies van receptie, via de leesruimte, een museum voor traditionele Chinese keramiek, tot en met de toiletten. De architectuur is geïnspireerd door de Chinese cultuur: de Chinese tuin, de theeceremonie, de eetcultuur, de speciale verhouding tussen boek en architectuur in de Chinese geschiedenis, de draken, bomen, enzovoort. Een moderne architectonische interpretatie van een innerlijk en een uiterlijk perspectief.

MACAU TOWER

CHINA | MACAU | LANDMARKS

ENGWith its filigreed appearance, the MACAU TOWER, designed by Gordon Möller and his architectural firm CCM, is among Macau's most iconic buildings. 248 meters (814 feet) high, not counting the antenna, it is a television tower, observation tower with restaurant, and, not for the faint of heart, a bungee-jump tower, from which jumpers can enjoy a protected fall without the yo-yo effect. Five observation platforms, including the walkable main platform, without railings, not even two paces wide, for the Skywalk X, the precursor to the Sky Jump. And when you're not jumping from heights, you can gaze into the distance.

DEU Eines der sinnbildlichen Gebäude Macaus ist der filigran wirkende MACAU TOWER von Gordon Möller und seinem Architektenbüro CCM. 248 Meter Höhe misst er, ohne Antenne. Er ist Fernsehturm, Aussichtsturm mit Restaurant und für alle Unerschrockenen, Sprungturm – von 233 Metern, gesichert versteht sich, und ohne Jo-Jo-Effekt. Fünf Aussichtsplattformen, davon die begehbare Hauptaussichtsplattform, ohne Geländer, nicht mal zwei Schritte breit, für den Skywalk X, die Vorstufe vom Sky Jump. Und wenn man nicht in die Tiefe springt, dann blickt man in die Ferne.

FRFrêle et élancée, la MACAU TOWER est l'œuvre de Gordon Möller et de son cabinet d'architecture CCM. Du haut de ses 248 mètres sans compter l'antenne, elle figure parmi les bâtiments les plus symboliques de Macao. Cette tour d'observation et de télévision accueille un restaurant mais aussi, pour les plus téméraires, une plateforme de saut à l'élastique très protégée. Celle-ci ne possède pas de balustrade et est large de seulement quelques pas car elle permet à l'équipe de Skywalk X, précurseur du saut à l'élastique, de faire sauter ses clients dans le vide. Si vous n'êtes pas encore venu, vous pouvez toujours vous émerveiller de cette hauteur depuis l'une des quatre autres plateformes.

NEDEen van de meest symbolische gebouwen van Macau is de als filigraan ogende MACAU TOWER van Gordon Müller en zijn architectenbureau CCM. 248 meter hoog meet hij, zonder antenne. Het is een televisietoren, uitzichttoren met restaurant en voor onverschrokken personen, springtoren – van 233 meter, uiteraard gezekerd, en zonder jojo-effect. Vijf uitzichtplateaus, met het begaanbare hoofduitzichtplateau, dat zonder balustrade nog geen twee stappen breed is, voor de Skywalk X, het voorstadium van de Sky Jump. En wie niet de diepte in springt, kijkt in de verte.

CENTRE OF SUSTAINABLE ENERGY

CHINA | NINGBO | LANDMARKS

ᴱᴺᴳ Nottingham University of Ningbo's CENTER OF SUSTAINABLE ENERGY sets the bar in two respects. First of all, it serves as a model building for the latest technologies in the realm of responsible, environmentally friendly utilization of energy sources and building materials. It is also an architectural artwork by Italian architect Mario Cucinella. His design was inspired by the famous Chinese lanterns and traditional wooden screens. It combines aesthetics with sustainability—in an impressive way.

ᴰᴱᵁ Das CENTER OF SUSTAINABLE ENERGY der Nottingham University of Ningbo setzt in zweierlei Hinsicht Maßstäbe. Zum einen dient es als Beispielgebäude für die neuesten Techniken rund um den verantwortungsvollen und umweltgerechten Umgang mit Energien und Baustoffen. Zum anderen ist es ein bauliches Kunstwerk des italienischen Architekten Mario Cucinella. Sein Design ist inspiriert durch die typischen chinesischen Laternen und die traditionellen hölzernen Wandschirme. Er verbindet Ästhetik mit Nachhaltigkeit – und das auf beeindruckende Art und Weise.

ᶠᴿ Le CENTER OF SUSTAINABLE ENERGY (Centre énergétique durable) de la Nottingham University de Ningbo place la barre assez haut pour deux raisons. La première est qu'il est précurseur dans son mode de consommation (responsable et écologique) des ressources énergétiques et matériaux de construction. Le bâtiment est également une œuvre d'art architecturale de l'Italien Mario Cucinella. Il tire son idée des célèbres lampions chinois et des panneaux de bois traditionnels grâce auxquels il conjugue ainsi de manière impressionnante esthétique et développement durable.

ᴺᴱᴰ Het CENTER OF SUSTAINABLE ENERGY van de University of Nottingham Ningbo heeft in twee opzichten de bakens verzet. Ten eerste dient het als voorbeeldgebouw voor de nieuwste technieken rond verantwoordelijk en in overeenstemming met de milieuwetten omgaan met energie en bouwmaterialen. Ten tweede is het een architectonisch kunstwerk van de Italiaanse architect Mario Cucinella. Zijn ontwerp is geïnspireerd door de typische Chinese lantaarns en de traditionele houten kamerschermen. Hij verbindt esthetiek met duurzaamheid – en wel op indrukwekkende wijze.

RED RIBBON PARK

CHINA | QINHUANGDAO | LANDMARKS

ᴱᴺᴳ The RED RIBBON is a city planning project to connect newly developed areas via a corridor of more than 20 hectares (49 acres) along the Tanghe River. This 500-meter-long (1640-foot-long) red band, 60 centimeters (two feet) high and 30 to 150 centimeters (one to five feet) wide, is constructed of steel fiber and illuminated from within. It integrates a boardwalk, lighting, and seating, interprets the surrounding environment, and acts as orientation. Four cloud-shaped pavilions are spread out along the Red Ribbon, places to rest and relax, four flower gardens in white, yellow, blue, and violet, all turn the previously neglected area into an urbanized and modernized recreational area without disturbing the natural balance.

ᴰᴱᵁ Das RED RIBBON ist ein städtebauliches Projekt, um neu entwickelte Stadtteile über einen mehr als 20 Hektar großen Korridor entlang des Tanghe-Flusses anzubinden. Auf einer Länge von 500 Metern erstreckt sich dieses rote, von innen leuchtende Band aus Stahlfasern, 60 Zentimeter hoch und 30 bis 150 Zentimeter breit. Es integriert einen Weg aus Bohlen, Licht, Sitzgelegenheiten, interpretiert die Umgebung und gibt Orientierung. Vier wolkenförmige Pavillons sind auf dem roten Band verteilt, Orte der Rast und Ruhe, vier Blumengärten in Weiß, Gelb, Violett und Blau, all das macht aus dem vormals ungepflegten, unbeachteten Areal ein urbanisiertes und modernisiertes Erholungsgebiet, ohne das natürliche Gleichgewicht zu stören.

ᶠᴿ Le RED RIBBON est un projet de développement urbain visant à relier les zones récemment développées de la ville par un corridor de plus de 20 hectares, le long du fleuve Tanghe. Ce ruban rouge illuminé de l'intérieur et mesurant 500 mètres de long, 60 centimètres de haut et de 30 à 150 centimètres de large, est fait de fibre d'acier. Il offre une promenade, de l'éclairage et de quoi s'asseoir, il sert d'interprète à son environnement immédiat et aide à l'orientation. Quatre pavillons en forme de nuages disséminés le long de ce ruban rouge permettent un peu de repos, et quatre jardins floraux, aux tons de blanc, jaune, bleu et violet, transforment cet endroit auparavant laissé à l'abandon en une zone de divertissement urbaine et moderne. La ville retrouve une dynamique et l'équilibre naturel est respecté.

ᴺᴱᴰ Het RED RIBBON PARK is een stedenbouwkundig project, om pas ontwikkelde wijken via een ruim 20 hectare grote corridor langs de Tanghe-rivier bereikbaar te maken. Over een lengte van 500 meter loopt dit rode, van binnenuit verlichte lint van staalvezels, 60 centimeter hoog en 30 tot 150 centimeter breed. Het integreert een weg van planken, licht, zitgelegenheden, interpreteert de omgeving en geeft oriëntering. Vier wolkvormige paviljoens zijn over het rode lint verdeeld, plaatsen om te rusten en pauze te houden, vier bloementuinen, wit, geel, violet en blauw, dit alles maakt van het vroeger onverzorgde, onopgemerkte terrein een verstedelijkt en gemoderniseerd recreatiegebied, zonder het natuurlijke evenwicht te verstoren.

ORIENTAL PEARL TOWER

CHINA | SHANGHAI | LANDMARKS

ENG Situated on the shore of the Huangpu River, directly next to Shanghai's World Financial Center and the Jin Mao Tower in the Pudong financial and commercial district, the structure is affectionately known as the "Pearl of the East". At 468 meters (1535 feet), it is the tallest and most acclaimed television tower in Asia. The building's most distinctive features are eleven large spheres—pearls—supported by columns of various height. The hallmark of Shanghai's skyline, it is a symbiosis of fascinating architecture and pure functionality.

DEU Am Ufer des Huangpu steht er, in direkter Nachbarschaft zu Shanghais World Financial Center und dem Jin-Mao-Turm im Geschäfts- und Finanzviertel Pudong, liebevoll die „Perle des Ostens" genannt. 468 Meter beträgt seine Höhe. Er ist Asiens höchster und beliebtester Fernsehturm. Die besonders markanten Teile seiner Konstruktion bestehen aus elf verschieden großen Kugeln – Perlen – , getragen von Säulen auf verschiedenen Höhen. Das Erkennungszeichen in der Skyline von Shanghai, eine Symbiose aus faszinierender Architektur und reiner Funktionalität.

FR Situé sur les rives du fleuve Huangpu, juste à côté du World Financial Center de Shanghai et de la tour Jin, la structure porte le surnom de « Perle de l'orient ». À 468 mètres au dessus du quartier commercial et financier de Pudong, c'est la tour de télévision la plus haute et la plus appréciée des asiatiques. La principale caractéristique du bâtiment prend la forme de onze larges sphères (les perles) soutenues par des colonnes de différentes hauteurs. Construction emblématique de Shanghai, elle conjugue la fascination exercée par l'architecture à une fonctionnalité pure et simple.

NED Op de oever van de Huang staat hij, vlak naast Shanghai's World Financial Center en de Jin Mao toren in de financiële en zakenwijk Pudong, liefdevol de 'Parel van het Oosten' genoemd. 468 meter hoog is hij, de hoogste en meest geliefde televisietoren van Azië. De buitengewoon markante elementen van de constructie bestaan uit elf verschillende kogels – parels -, gedragen door zuilen op verschillende hoogten. Het herkenningsteken in de skyline van Shanghai, een symbiose van fascinerende architectuur en pure functionaliteit.

SHENZHEN CIVIC CENTER

CHINA | SHENZHEN | LANDMARKS

ᴱᴺᴳ The unique appearance of this government building is not due merely to its enormous size of approximately 91,000 square meters (979,500 square feet). Its undulating roof looks like the outstretched wings of an enormous bird, specifically the "roc", symbol of the city of Shenzhen. At the same time, it is reminiscent of the elegant architecture of the Tang Dynasty. A gigantic pagoda designed by Li Mingyi takes on a special appearance at night, when brightly illuminated by countless solarpowered lights.

ᴰᴱᵁ Ein Regierungsgebäude mit einer besonderen Ausstrahlung, und das macht nicht allein seine gewaltige Größe von rund 91 000 Quadratmetern. Sein wellenförmiges Dach wirkt wie die ausgebreiteten Schwingen eines gewaltigen Vogels, des „Roc", dem Symbol der Stadt Shenzhen. Zugleich erinnert es an die elegante Architektur der Tang-Dynastie. Eine riesenhafte Pagode von Li Mingyi, die ihren besonderen Auftritt bei Dunkelheit hat, wenn unzählige Solarlichter sie hell erleuchten.

ᶠᴿ L'apparence unique de ce bâtiment administratif, le « rocher », n'est pas uniquement due à ses proportions gigantesques d'environ 9 hectares. Symbole de la ville de Shenzhen, il rappelle l'architecture élégante de la dynastie Tang, grâce à son toit ondulant semblable aux ailes déployées d'un énorme oiseau. Une imposante pagode réalisée par Li Mingyi se transforme à la tombée de la nuit, lorsque ses innombrables lampes solaires s'illuminent.

ᴺᴱᴰ Een regeringsgebouw met een speciale uitstraling, en dat komt niet alleen door zijn enorme grootte van zo'n 91.000 vierkante meter. Het golfvormige dak heeft het effect van de uitgespreide vleugels van een reusachtige vogel, de 'Rok', het symbool van de stad Shengzhen. Tegelijk herinnert het aan de elegante architectuur van de Tang-dynastie. Een kolossale pagode van Li Mingyi, die haar speciale optreden heeft als het donker is en ontelbare zonnelichten haar helder verlichten.

TAIPEH FINANCIAL CENTER 101

CHINA | TAIPEH | LANDMARKS

ENG This building is nicknamed "Taipei 101," after the number of floors. For a long time it was the highest in the world, a proud 509 meters (1670 feet). In addition to the "ordinary" visual and static challenges that come with a building of this height, chief architect Chang Yong Lee also had to take account of special climatic and tectonic factors—typhoons and earthquakes. The result is the world's largest, and publicly accessible, pendulum mass damper. TAIPEI 101 was built according to the laws of Feng Shui. Not just the pagoda-like shape, but also the recurrence of the lucky number eight, are derived from Chinese tradition and intended to guard against negative influences.

DEU „Taipei 101" ist sein Spitzname. 101, weil er 101 Stockwerke hat. Er war lange die Nummer 1 in der Welt, mit stolzen 509 Metern Höhe. Chefarchitekt Chang Yong Lee musste neben den ganz „normalen" optischen und statischen Herausforderungen eines Gebäudes dieser Höhe noch die besonderen klimatischen und tektonischen Gegebenheiten berücksichtigen – Zyklone und Erdbeben. Heraus kam das größte und dazu öffentlich zugängliche Tilgerpendel der Welt. Erbaut wurde TAIPEI 101 nach den Gesetzen des Feng Shui. Nicht nur die pagodenähnliche Gestalt, auch die immer wiederkehrende Präsenz der Glückszahl Acht entstammt der chinesischen Tradition und soll vor schlechten Einflüssen schützen.

FR On surnomme ce bâtiment «Taipei 101 », en raison du nombre de ses étages. Il a longtemps été l'immeuble le plus haut du monde, arborant fièrement ses 509 mètres. En plus des « habituels » défis visuels et statiques liés à la construction d'un édifice de cette taille, l'architecte principal Chang Yong Lee a également dû prendre en compte les facteurs climatiques et tectoniques spécifiques à la région (cyclones et tremblements de terre). Il a ainsi créé le plus grand amortisseur de masse au monde, accessible au public. TAIPEI 101 obéit aux lois du feng shui, non seulement par sa forme de pagode, mais également par la récurrence du chiffre huit, considéré comme un porte-bonheur : l'objectif étant de se protéger contre les influences négatives.

NED 'Taipei 101' is zijn bijnaam. 101 omdat hij 101 verdiepingen heeft. Hij was lang de nummer één van de wereld, met zijn imposante 509 meter hoogte. Hoofdarchitect Chang Yong Lee moest naast de heel 'normale' optische en statische uitdagingen van een gebouw van deze hoogte ook nog rekening houden met de speciale klimatologische en tektonische feiten – cyclonen en aardbevingen. Hieruit ontstond de grootste en daarbij publiekelijk toegankelijke trillingsdemper ter wereld. TAIPEI 101 werd gebouwd volgens de wetten van Feng Shui. Niet alleen de pagodeachtige vorm, ook de steeds terugkerende aanwezigheid van het geluksgetal acht komen voort uit de Chinese traditie en moeten bescherming bieden tegen slechte invloeden.

THE KANAGAWA INSTITUTE OF TECHNOLOGY

JAPAN | KANAGAWA | LANDMARKS

ᴱᴺᴳ The task was to design a work space for students on the KANAGAWA INSTITUTE OF TECHNOLOGY campus. The architects at Junya Ishigama & Associates created a space bathed in light. There are no walls, instead there are countless filigree supports arranged in a computer-generated pattern. The space is separated from the outside by sheets of glass, creating flowing borders between interior and exterior. On the inside, individual areas can be separated by the users of the space. Nothing is prescribed, everything is possible.

ᴰᴱᵁ Die Aufgabe war, einen Arbeitsraum für Studenten auf dem Campus des KANAGAWA INSTITUTE OF TECHNOLOGY zu konzipieren. Die Architekten von Junya Ishigama & Associates schufen einen lichtdurchfluteten Raum. Wände gibt es nicht, dafür unzählige filigrane Stützen in einer computergenerierten Anordnung. Nach außen wird der Raum begrenzt durch Glasflächen. So sind die Grenzen zwischen innen und außen fließend. Innen erfolgt die Abgrenzung einzelner Bereiche durch die Nutzer. Nichts ist vorgegeben, alles ist möglich.

ᶠᴿ L'objectif était ici de créer un espace de travail pour les étudiants du campus du KANAGAWA INSTITUTE OF TECHNOLOGY. Les architectes de chez Junya Ishigama & Associates leur ont ainsi fourni un espace baigné de lumière où les utilisateurs peuvent créer des séparations à leur guise. Rien n'est interdit, tout est possible : il n'y a aucun mur, mais d'innombrables supports ciselés, disposés au hasard de l'informatique. L'espace est séparé de l'extérieur par des plaques de verre, brouillant ainsi la limite entre intérieur et extérieur.

ᴺᴱᴰ De opdracht was een werkruimte voor studenten te bedenken op de campus van het KANAGAWA INSTITUTE OF TECHNOLOGY. De architecten van Junya Ishigama & Associates schiepen een met licht doorstroomde ruimte. Wanden zijn er niet, in plaats daarvan ontelbare filigraansteunen in een door de computer gegenereerde ordening. Naar buiten toe wordt de ruimte begrensd door glasvlakken. Zo zijn de grenzen tussen binnen en buiten vloeiend. Vanbinnen vindt de afgrenzing plaats door de gebruikers. Niets is vastgelegd, alles is mogelijk.

KOBE PORT TOWER

JAPAN | KOBE | LANDMARKS

ENG The KOBE PORT TOWER is shaped like a hyperboloid. A lattice tower, 108 meters high (354 feet), constructed of red steel with a scaffolded top. This is the landmark of Kobe, a harbor city on Honshu with a major seaport, one of the ten largest cities in Japan. A tourist attraction with a rotating observation deck at a height of just over 90 meters (295 feet), completely bedecked with lights, it is truly a "lighthouse", especially at night.

DEU Der KOBE PORT TOWER, gebaut in der Form eines Hyperboloiden. Ein Stahlfachwerkturm, 108 Meter hoch, aus rotem Stahl mit einer eingerüsteten Spitze. Er ist das Wahrzeichen von Kobe, der Hafenstadt auf der Insel Honshu, einer der zehn größten japanischen Städte, mit einem bedeutenden Seehafen. Eine Touristenattraktion mit einem rotierenden Aussichtsdeck in rund 90 Metern Höhe, über und über dekoriert mit Lichtern. Ein „Leuchtturm", besonders bei Nacht.

FR La KOBE PORT TOWER, tour de forme hyperbolique à l'armature d'acier rouge, mesure 108 mètres de hauteur. C'est l'emblème de Kobe, une ville portuaire de Honshu comptant parmi les dix villes les plus importantes du Japon. Totalement illuminée, c'est un véritable phare, surtout de nuit. Elle figure ainsi au palmarès des attractions touristiques grâce à son point d'observation tournant, situé juste au-dessus des 90 mètres.

NED De KOBE PORT TOWER, gebouwd in de vorm van een hyperboloïde. Een stalen vakwerktoren, 108 meter hoog, van rood staal met een door een rasterwerk omgeven spits. Hij is het herkenningsteken van Kobe, de havenstad op het eiland Honshu, een van de tien grootste Japanse steden, met een belangrijke zeehaven. Een toeristische attractie met een draaiend uitzichtdek op ongeveer 90 meter hoogte, overvloedig versierd met lichten. Een 'vuurtoren', vooral 's nachts.

NOH THEATER
JAPAN | TOKAMACHI | LANDMARKS

ENG The architects responsible for designing the layout of this open air pavilion in Kaino River Park at the feet of Mount Tokamachi took the traditional architecture of the centuries-old Noh theater as their model. Their interpretation, on the other hand, is very modern: The stage is defined by four columns spaced six meters (20 feet) apart. A small bridge, symbolizing the transition from the world of yesterday to today, functions as a stage entrance for the actors. When the shiny metal roof, reminiscent of a butterfly, opens, it converges with the water of the sea and reflects the gorgeous landscape. Even when no performance is on, this is a wonderful place to spend a little time.

DEU Für den Aufbau des Freilicht-Pavillons im Kaino River Park am Fuße des Mount Tokamachi orientierten sich die Architekten an der traditionellen Architektur der jahrhundertealten NOH-THEATER. Ihre Interpretation hingegen ist sehr modern: Vier Säulen, jeweils sechs Meter auseinander, definieren die Bühne. Eine kleine Brücke, Symbol für den Übergang der Welt von gestern zu heute, dient den Schauspielern als Bühnenaufgang. Ist das glänzende Metalldach mit der Anmutung eines Schmetterlings geöffnet, geht es eine Verbindung mit dem Wasser des Sees ein und reflektiert die wunderschöne Landschaft. Mit oder ohne Aufführung, dies ist ein wunderbarer Ort zum Verweilen.

FR Les architectes responsables des plans de ce pavillon à ciel ouvert, dans le Kaino River Park, se sont inspirés de l'architecture traditionnelle du théâtre Nô. Leur interprétation, au pied du Mont Tokamachi, reste cependant très moderne : la scène est délimitée par quatre colonnes espacées de six mètres. Un petit pont, symbolisant la transition du monde d'hier à celui d'aujourd'hui, sert d'entrée de scène aux acteurs. Lorsque le toit de métal brillant s'ouvre tel un papillon, il se confond avec l'eau de la mer et reflète le cadre sublime qui l'entoure. Même en l'absence de représentation, l'endroit est parfait pour passer quelques heures au calme.

NED Voor de bouw van het openluchtpaviljoen in het Kaino River Park aan de voet van de berg Tokamachi richtten de architecten zich op de traditionele architectuur van het eeuwenoude noh-theater. Hun interpretatie is daarentegen modern: vier zuilen, telkens zes meter uit elkaar, bakenen het toneel af. Een kleine brug, symbool voor de overgang van de wereld van gisteren naar nu, dient voor de toneelspelers als toneelopgang. Staat het glanzende metalen dak dat aandoet als een vlinder open, dan gaat het een verbinding aan met het water van het meer en weerspiegelt het wondermooie landschap. Met of zonder uitvoering is dit een schitterende plek om te vertoeven.

SAMIR KASSIR SQUARE

LEBANON | BEIRUT | LANDMARKS

ENG The Central District of Beirut is increasingly becoming home to public spaces for people of all stripes. One of these spaces is the redesigned SAMIR KASSIR SQUARE, named in honor of the murdered columnist. Vladimir Djurovic's design frames two enormous ficus trees that, as a testament to the area's checkered past, dominate the new incarnation of this tranquil spot. A large reflecting pool separates the square from the bustling street. Its surface reflects the city's silhouette with its mosques and churches, a reminder of bygone days.

DEU Der Beiruter Central District wird mehr und mehr Heimat von öffentlichen Räumen für Menschen aller Couleur. Einer dieser Räume ist der neu gestaltete, nach dem ermordeten Kolumnisten benannte SAMIR KASSIR SQUARE. Vladimir Djurovics Entwurf umrahmt zwei gewaltige Ficus-Bäume, Zeugen der wechselhaften Geschichte, die wie natürliche Skulpturen die neue Gestalt dieses Ortes der Ruhe dominieren. Ein großes reflektierendes Wasserbecken trennt den Platz von der geschäftigen Straße. Seine Oberfläche spiegelt die Silhouette der Stadt mit ihren Moscheen und Kirchen, die Erinnerung an vergangene Tage.

FR Le quartier central de Beyrouth voit de plus en plus d'espaces publics s'ouvrir aux visiteurs de tous bords. L'un des ces espaces est le nouveau SAMIR KASSIR SQUARE, portant le nom d'un journaliste assassiné. La création de Vladimir Djurovic encadre deux énormes ficus qui, témoignant de l'histoire mouvementée du petit square, dominent la nouvelle incarnation de ce lieu tranquille. Un large bassin scintillant isole le jardin des bruits de la rue. Sa surface reflète les cimes de la ville, entre mosquées et églises, et rappelle ainsi son passé.

NED Het centrum van Beiroet wordt steeds meer een plaats van openbare ruimten voor mensen van allerlei kleur. Een van deze ruimten is het opnieuw vormgegeven, naar de vermoorde columnist vernoemde SAMIR KASSIR SQUARE. Vladimir Djurovics ontwerp omlijst twee kolossale ficusbomen, getuigen van de wisselvallige geschiedenis, die als natuurlijke sculpturen de nieuwe gedaante van dit oord van rust overheersen. Een groot reflecterend waterbekken scheidt het plein van de drukke straat. Het oppervlak weerspiegelt het silhouet van de stad met zijn moskeeën en kerken, de herinnering aan voorbije dagen.

PETRONAS TWIN TOWERS

MALAYSIA | KUALA LUMPUR | LANDMARKS

ENG As an icon of Kuala Lumpur, the PETRONAS TOWERS are both an expression of economic strength and of the high hopes for Malaysia's future development. The 452 meter high (1,482.9 foot high) towers are in the tradition of the erstwhile Twin Towers of the World Trade Center in New York. Architect César Antonio Pelli has created a modernist composition out of steel, aluminum, concrete, and glass in a polygonal layout, a design inspired by Islamic architecture. The ground plan of the towers, each consisting of two overlaid squares, is in the shape of an eight-pointed star, the Islamic "Rub el Hizb". The towers are connected to a skybridge at a height of 172 meters (558 feet); this two-story bridge is 58 meters (190 feet) long and totally unique.

DEU Die PETRONAS TOWERS sind als Wahrzeichen Kuala Lumpurs Ausdruck wirtschaftlicher Stärke und großer Hoffnungen in die zukünftige Entwicklung Malaysias zugleich. Die 452 Meter hohen Türme stehen in der Tradition der ehemaligen Zwillings-türme des World Trade Center in New York. Architekt César Antonio Pelli schuf eine modernistische Komposition aus Stahl, Aluminium, Beton und Glas mit einem aus der islamischen Architektur entlehnten polygonalen Aufbau. Die Grundrisse der Zwillinge, jeweils zwei übereinander gelegte Quadrate, entsprechen der Form eines achteckigen Sterns, dem islamischen „Rub al-hizb". Verbunden sind sie in 172 Metern Höhe durch die Skybridge: 58 Meter lang, doppelgeschossig und einzigartig.

FR Véritables icônes de Kuala Lumpur, les PETRONAS TOWERS expriment toutes deux la puissance économique et les espoirs de croissance que le futur réserve à la Malaisie. Ces tours de 452 mètres sont construites sur le modèle des Tours jumelles du World Trade Center de New York. L'architecte César Antonio Pelli a créé une composition moderne d'acier, d'aluminium, de béton et de verre sur une base polygonale, une idée inspirée de l'architecture islamique. Le plan des tours, formées par deux carrés super-posés, schématise une étoile à huit branches connue dans l'islam sous le nom de « Rub el Hizb ». Celles-ci sont reliées à un pont suspendu à double niveau d'une hauteur de 172 mètres : unique en son genre, il mesure 58 mètres de long.

NED De PETRONAS TOWERS zijn als herkenningspunt in Kuala Lumpur tegelijk uiting van economische kracht en van hoge ver-wachtingen van de toekomstige ontwikkeling van Maleisië. De 452 meter hoge torens staan in de traditie van de tweelingtorens van weleer van het World Trade Center in New York. Architect César Antonio Pelli schiep een modernistische compositie van staal, aluminium, beton en glas met een aan de islamitische architectuur ontleende polygonale bouw. De plattegronden van de tweelingen, twee over elkaar gelegde vierkanten, stemmen overeen met de vorm van een achthoekige ster, de islamitische 'rub al-hizb'. Op 172 hoogte zijn ze verbonden met de luchtbrug: 58 meter lang, met twee verdiepingen en uniek.

LANGKAWI SKY BRIDGE

MALAYSIA | LANGKAWI | LANDMARKS

ENG The LANGKAWI SKY BRIDGE is a crescent-shaped pedestrian bridge 700 meters (2297 feet) above sea level. This unique 1.8 meter wide (5.9 foot wide) bridge actually makes it possible to take a walk in the clouds. It spans 125 meters (410 feet) across a spectacular chasm and enables a 360º view of the Langkawi Islands and the Andaman Sea. There are two triangular niches where you can sit and enjoy both the beauty of nature and this marvelous feat of engineering. To enhance pedestrians' feeling of safety, there are double steel railings, wire mesh guards, and a timber parapet below.

DEU Die LANGKAWI SKY BRIDGE ist eine Fußgängerbrücke in Form eines Halbmondes, 700 Meter über dem Meer. Diese einzigartige 1,80 Meter breite Brücke ermöglicht einen Spaziergang in den Wolken. Auf 125 Metern umspannt sie eine spektakuläre Schlucht und ermöglicht einen Rundum-Blick auf Langkawi Islands und die Andamanen-See. In zwei dreieckigen Nischen sitzend kann man zweierlei genießen: die phantastische Natur und dieses Meisterstück der Ingenieurskunst. Und für das subjektive Sicherheitsempfinden gibt es ein zweifaches Stahlgeländer, ein Drahtnetz, dazu unten eine Verstärkung aus Holz.

FR Le LANGKAWI SKY BRIDGE est un pont piétonnier en forme de croissant s'élevant à 700 mètres au-dessus du niveau de la mer. Ce pont unique d'1,8 mètre de large permet une véritable ballade dans les nuages. Il s'étend sur 125 mètres à travers un gouffre spectaculaire et offre une vue à 360 degrés sur les îles Langkawi et la mer d'Andaman. Deux niches triangulaires permettent de s'asseoir pour profiter de la beauté de la nature et de cette merveille d'ingénierie. Une double rambarde d'acier, un grillage et un parapet de bois situé au-dessous de la passerelle permettent de renforcer le sentiment de sécurité.

NED De LANGKAWI SKY BRIDGE is een voetgangersbrug in de vorm van een halvemaan, 700 meter boven de zeespiegel. Deze unieke 1,8 meter brede brug maakt het mogelijk een wandeling in de wolken te maken. Op 125 meter overspant hij een spectaculaire kloof en biedt rondom uitzicht op de Langkawi-eilanden en de Andamanse Zee. Gezeten in twee driehoekige nissen kan men genieten van twee dingen: de fantastische natuur en dit meesterlijk stukje ingenieurskunst. En voor het subjectieve veiligheidsgevoel is er een dubbele stalen leuning, draadgaas, en verder een houten versterking.

SERI WASAWAN BRIDGE

MALAYSIA | PUTRAJAYA | LANDMARKS

ᴱᴺᴳ The SERI WASAWAN BRIDGE, "Jambatan Seri" in Malaysia, is reminiscent of an enormous sailboat. A concrete bridge with a combination of backstay and tensile steel cables. Like a gigantic sail, the 3-lane bridge is 37.2 meters (122 feet) wide and open to pedestrians as well as road traffic. It spans 240 meters (787 feet) across Putrajaya Lake, a manmade lake that provides a nearby recreational area and cooling for the sweltering metropolis. The architect behind it: Perbadanan Putrajaya.

ᴰᴱᵁ Sie erinnert an ein gewaltiges Segelschiff, die SERI WASAWAN BRIDGE, malaiisch „Jambatan Seri". Eine Betonbrücke mit einer Kombination aus Achterstag und gespannten Stahlseilen. Wie ein gigantisches Segel, 3-spurig, 37,20 Meter breit, für Fußgänger und alles, was sich auf Rädern bewegt. Auf einer Länge von 240 Metern überspannt sie den Putrajaya Lake, einen künstlich geschaffenen See, der Naherholungsgebiet ist und Kühlung für die in der Sonne schmachtende Großstadt. Ihr Baumeister: Perbadanan Putrajaya.

ᶠᴿ Le projet architectural du SERI WASAWAN BRIDGE est l'œuvre de Perbadanan Putrajaya. Le « Jambatan Seri » en malaisien, fait d'abord penser à un énorme voilier de 37,2 mètres de large. Ce pont de béton à trois voies combine pataras et câbles d'acier élastique pour offrir ses services aux piétons et à tous les véhicules sur roues. Il s'étend sur 240 mètres au-dessus du lac artificiel de Putrajaya, lieu de détente et de fraîcheur éloigné de la métropole étouffante.

ᴺᴱᴰ Hij doet denken aan een enorm zeilschip, de SERI WASAWAN BRIDGE, in het Maleisisch 'Jambatan Seri'. Een betonnen brug met een combinatie van achterstag en gespannen staaldraden. Als een reusachtig zeil, driebaans, 37,2 meter breed, voor voetgangers en alles wat zich op wielen voortbeweegt. Over een lengte van 240 meter overspant hij het kunstmatige Putrajaya-meer, een recreatiegebied dat de in de zon smachtende grote stad verkoeling biedt. De bouwmeester: Perbdanan Putrajaya.

665

BAMBOO GARDEN

SOUTH KOREA | DAEDUK | LANDMARKS

ENG Renowned landscape architect Mikyoung Kim has planted a "bamboo garden" in the middle of the LG Research & Development Centers, an unadorned modern office complex. Combinations of tall, lush vegetation and ground creepers act as screens around granite benches, fountains, and little inner courtyards. They filter and soften the light as it comes through. Like a little green oasis, it is the perfect place to pause and catch your breath.

DEU Die renommierte Landschaftsarchitektin Mikyoung Kim hat einen „Bambusgarten" inmitten des LG Research & Development Centers, einem modernen Bürokomplex ohne jeden Schnörkel, gepflanzt. Üppige hohe und nur den Boden bedeckende Pflanzen formen Schutzwände um Bänke aus Granit, Brunnen und die kleinen Plätze im Inneren. Sie filtern das Licht, machen es sanft. Wie eine kleine grüne Oase lädt dieser Ort ein zum Innehalten und Durchatmen.

FR Le célèbre architecte paysager Mikyoung Kim a planté son « jardin de bambous » au beau milieu du LG Research & Development Centers, un complexe d'activités plutôt moderne et austère. Combiner une végétation haute et luxuriante à des plantes rampantes permet de former comme un écran autour des bancs de granit, des fontaines et des petites cours intérieures. La lumière est ainsi filtrée et adoucie ; comme une petite oasis, c'est l'endroit parfait pour faire une pause et reprendre son souffle.

NED De gerenommeerde landschapsarchitecte Mikyoung Kim heeft een 'bamboetuin' aangeplant midden in het LG Research & Development Center, een modern kantorencomplex zonder enige franje. Weelderige hoge en slechts de bodem bedekkende planten vormen beschuttingen rond banken van graniet, putten en de pleintjes in het hart. Ze filteren het licht, maken het zacht. Als een kleine groene oase nodigt deze plek uit tot even stilhouden en diep adem halen.

EWHA CAMPUS CENTER

SOUTH KOREA | SEOUL | LANDMARKS

ENG The Campus Center at EHWA Womans University, a prestigious women's university with a current enrollment of 20,000 female students (and about seven men), is a six-story structure that Architect Dominique Perrault has literally buried in the surrounding parkland. A 200 meter long (656 foot long) gorge cut into the surface allows light through. The result is a meta-building that in many respects exceeds the limits of conventional architecture.

DEU Das sechsgeschossige Campus Center der EWHA Woman's University, einer Prestige-Universität für derzeit 20 000 Frauen – und etwa sieben Männer, hat Architekt Dominique Perrault in die umgebende Parklandschaft förmlich eingegraben. Licht fällt durch einen 200 Meter langen Einschnitt in die Oberfläche. Entstanden ist ein Meta-Gebäude, das die Grenzen herkömmlicher Bauwerke in vielerlei Hinsicht überschreitet.

FR Le Campus Center de l'EHWA Womans University, université féminine prestigieuse de femmes ne comptant pas moins de 20 000 étudiantes (et environ sept hommes), est une structure de six étages que l'architecte Dominique Perrault a littéralement enterrée au cœur d'un parc. Seule une tranchée de 200 mètres de long permet à la lumière de pénétrer. Elle a ainsi créé un méta-bâtiment qui dépasse en de nombreux points les limites de l'architecture conventionnelle.

NED Het zes verdiepingen tellende campuscentrum van de EHWA Woman's University, een prestigieuze universiteit voor thans 20.000 vrouwen – en ongeveer zeven mannen, heeft architect Dominique Perrault in het omringende parklandschap ingegraven. Het licht valt door een 200 meter lange insnijding in het oppervlak. Er is een metagebouw tot stand gekomen dat de grenzen van gewone gebouwen in veel opzichten overschrijdt.

CHONGGAE CANAL SOURCE POINT PARK

SOUTH KOREA | SEOUL | LANDMARKS

ENG A contaminated river has been transformed into a clean body of water, arranged around an impressive area that uses a pedestrian corridor to link two parts of Seoul previously separated by motor traffic. Yet this project is meant to express much more than this: it stands for the hoped-for future reunification of North and South Korea. Individual stone sculptures, regionally-sourced stone, and nine source points symbolize the nine provinces of North and South Korea. Once again, a stunning landscape project bears the signature of Mikyoung Kim and her design team, in this case in collaboration with SeoAhn Total Landscape.

DEU Aus einem kontaminierten wurde ein sauberer Fluss und dazu entstand ein eindrucksvolles Areal, das die straßenbedingte Trennung zweier Stadtteile Seouls aufhebt und sie wieder über einen Korridor für Fußgänger zusammenführt. Ausdrücken soll dieses Projekt allerdings viel mehr. Es steht für die erhoffte zukünftige Wiedervereinigung von Nord- und Südkorea. Individuelle Steinskulpturen, regionaler Stein und neun Quellpunkte verkörpern die neun Provinzen, aus denen Nord- und Südkorea bestehen. Einmal mehr trägt ein beeindruckendes Landschaftsprojekt die Handschrift von Mikyoung Kim und ihrem Design-Team, in diesem Fall in Zusammenarbeit mit SeoAhn Total Landscape.

FR Une rivière contaminée a été transformée en un lit d'eau claire, puis entourée par un corridor piétonnier servant à relier deux quartiers de Séoul, autrefois séparées par la circulation. Toutefois, ce projet audacieux a une autre dimension : il symbolise en réalité les espoirs d'une future réunification des Corée du Nord et du Sud. Les sculptures de pierre, la pierre régionale et les neuf petites sources représentent les neuf provinces des deux Corées. Une fois de plus, un projet paysager étonnant voit le jour grâce à Mikyoung Kim et son équipe, en collaboration, cette fois, avec SeoAhn Total Landscape.

NED Een vervuilde rivier werd een schone rivier en daarbij is een indrukwekkend terrein ontstaan, dat de door wegen gemaakte scheiding van twee wijken in Seoul opheft en ze weer via een corridor voor voetgangers bij elkaar brengt. Dit project wil echter nog veel meer tot uitdrukking brengen. Het staat voor de verhoopte hereniging van Noord- en Zuid-Korea. Afzonderlijke steensculpturen, regionaal steen en negen bronpunten belichamen de negen provincies waaruit Noord- en Zuid-Korea bestaan. En weer eens draagt een indrukwekkend landschapsproject de signatuur van Mikyoung Kim en haar ontwerpteam, in dit geval in samenwerking met SeoAhn Total Landscape.

THE EMIRATES PALACE

UNITED ARAB EMIRATES | ABU DHABI | LANDMARKS

ᴱᴺᴳ Here, all that glitters is indeed gold. Wimberley Allison Tang and Goo constructed this luxury palace, which looks like something from the Arabian Nights, only more impressive. Traditional Arabian elements and ultimate luxury are combined with the latest technology. The numbers speak for themselves: 302 rooms, 92 Suites, one large dome measuring 42 meters (138 feet) in diameter, 114 smaller ones, a total area of 243,000 square meters (2,615,630 square feet), a park, private beach, and its own yacht harbor. A monumental arch, 40 meters (131 feet) high and 36 meters (118 feet) wide—bigger than the triumphal arches in most major cities. And a personal butler for each guest.

ᴰᴱᵁ Hier ist tatsächlich alles Gold, was glänzt. Wimberley Allison Tang and Goo erbauten diesen Luxuspalast, der aussieht wie jene aus den arabischen Märchen, nur noch imposanter. Traditionelle arabische Elemente und ultimativer Luxus sind hier verknüpft mit modernster Technik. In Zahlen: 302 Räume, 92 Suiten, eine große Kuppel mit 42 Metern Durchmesser, 114 weitere kleine, Gesamtfläche 243 000 Quadratmeter, Park, Privatstrand und ein eigener Yachthafen. Ein Monumentalbogen, 40 Meter hoch und 36 Meter breit – größer als die meisten Triumphbögen der großen Metropolen. Und für jeden Gast der eigene Butler.

ᶠᴿ Ici, tout ce qui brille est effectivement de l'or. Wimberley Allison Tang et Goo ont construit ce luxueux palais tout droit sorti des Mille et une nuits où des éléments traditionnels arabes et le luxe dernier cri épousent une technologie de pointe. Les chiffres parlent d'eux-mêmes : 302 chambres, 92 suites, un large dôme mesurant 42 mètres de diamètre, 114 petits dômes, pour une surface totale d'environ 24 hectares, un parc, un maître d'hôtel attitré pour chaque hôte, une plage et une marina privées. L'arche monumentale, haute de 40 mètres et large de 36 mètres surpasse de loin bon nombre des arcs de triomphe des capitales occidentales.

ᴺᴱᴰ Hier is werkelijk alles goud wat er blinkt. Wimberly Allison Tong & Goo bouwden dit luxepaleis, dat zo uit een Arabisch sprookje lijkt te komen, alleen nog imposanter. Traditionele Arabische elementen en ultieme luxe zijn hier gekoppeld aan de modernste techniek. In getallen: 302 kamers, 92 suites, een grote koepel van 42 meter doorsnee, nog 114 kleinere, totaaloppervlak 243.000 vierkante meter, park, privéstrand en eigen jachthaven. Een monumentale boog, 40 meter hoog en 36 meter breed – groter dan de meeste triomfbogen in de grote metropolen. En voor elke gast een eigen butler.

THE PALM JUMEIRAH

UNITED ARAB EMIRATES | DUBAI | LANDMARKS

ENG Dubai needs beaches. The solution: a project of mind-blowing proportion—THE PALM JUMEIRAH, one of three artificial islands, collectively known as "The Palm Islands." The figures alone are impressive: 2000 villas; 40 luxury hotels, shopping centers, and yacht harbors; 100 kilometers (62 miles) of sandy beaches; a diameter of five kilometers (3.1 miles). Three sections: the trunk, four kilometers (2.5 miles) long; 16 palm fronds for residential areas; and a crescent moon eleven kilometers (6.5 miles) long with hotels and entertainment venues that acts as a breakwater for storm surges. A 300 meter long (984 foot long) bridge leads to the mainland. There are also around 1,200 palms, replicas of Japanese gardens, rainforest and Grand Canal, the Trump International Hotel Tower, and the Atlantis Palm Jumeirah.

DEU Dubai braucht Strände. Die Lösung: Ein Projekt von unvorstellbarem Ausmaß – THE PALM JUMEIRAH, eine von drei künstlichen Inseln, zusammen „The Palm Islands" genannt. In Zahlen: 2 000 Villen, 40 Luxushotels, Shoppingzentren und Yachthäfen, 100 Kilometer Sandstrand, Durchmesser fünf Kilometer. Drei Abschnitte: der Stamm, vier Kilometer lang, 16 Palmwedel zum Wohnen und ein sichelförmiger Mond von elf Kilometern Länge mit Hotels und Entertainment, Schutz gegen Sturmfluten. Zum Festland führt eine 300 Meter lange Brücke. Dazu rund 1 200 Palmen, Nachbildungen von japanischen Gärten, Regenwald und Canale Grande, der Trump International Hotel Tower und das Atlantis Palm Jumeirah.

FR Dubaï n'a pas de plages et il lui en faut. La solution au problème est un projet aux proportions démentes : THE PALM JUMEIRAH, l'une des trois îles artificielles, connues collectivement sous le nom de « The Palm Islands ». Les chiffres parlent d'eux-mêmes : 2 000 villas, 40 hôtels de luxe, des centres commerciaux et des marinas, 100 kilomètres de plages de sable pour cinq kilomètres de diamètre. Trois parties : le tronc du palmier, mesurant quatre kilomètres de long, les 16 feuilles destinées aux zones résidentielles et un croissant de lune de onze kilomètres de long accueillant hôtels et lieux de divertissement. Le projet comprend aussi une digue, protégeant la structure des tempêtes, un pont de 300 mètres de long conduisant sur la terre ferme. Il compte également 1 200 palmiers, des répliques de jardins japonais, une forêt tropicale et un grand canal, la Trump International Hotel Tower ainsi que l'Atlantis Palm Jumeirah.

NED Dubai heeft stranden nodig. De oplossing: een project van onverstelbare omvang: THE PALM JUMEIRAH, een van drie kunstmatige eilanden, samen de 'Palmeilanden' genoemd. In getallen: 2000 villa's, 40 luxehotels, winkelcentra en jachthavens, 100 kilometer zandstrand, doorsnede vijf kilometer. Drie gedeelten: de stam, vier kilometer lang, zestien palmbladeren om te wonen en een sikkelvormige maan van 11 kilometer lang met hotels en amusement, bescherming tegen stormvloeden. Naar het vasteland loopt een 300 meter lange brug.

BURJ DUBAI

UNITED ARAB EMIRATES | DUBAI | LANDMARKS

ENG The "Dubai Tower" is currently the tallest building in the world, with the largest number of stories and the highest usable floor level—as well as the highest residential level. It is intended to become the center of downtown Dubai, a new commercial, residential, shopping, entertainment, and leisure district. It measures 818 meters (2684 feet) high, comprising of 162 floors, 37 of which are hotel space, 70 for apartments, plus 43 offices and several suites. The lobby is located on the 123rd floor, while the 124th houses an observation platform and terrace. Designed by architect Adrian Smith of Skidmore, Owings, & Merrill, the structure is made of reinforced concrete and steel, the facade of aluminum and glass.

DEU Der „Turm von Dubai" ist derzeit das höchste Gebäude der Welt, mit den meisten Stockwerken, dem höchstgelegenen nutzbaren Stockwerk – und dem höchsten zu Wohnzwecken genutzten. Er soll zum Zentrum von Downtown Dubai werden, einem neuen Stadtquartier für Handel, Wohnen, Einkaufen, Unterhaltung und Freizeit. 818 Meter misst er verteilt auf 162 Stockwerke, 37 Etagen Hotel, 70 für Apartments, darüber 43 Büros und einige Suiten. In der 123. Etage befindet sich die Lobby, in der 124. ein Aussichtsplateau mit Terrasse. Die Konstruktion besteht aus Stahlbeton und Stahl, die Fassade aus Aluminium und Glas und der Architekt ist Adrian Smith von Skidmore, Owings & Merrill.

FR La « Dubaï Tower » est actuellement le plus haut bâtiment au monde, ainsi que celui comptant le plus grand nombre d'étages, le niveau accessible et le niveau résidentiel les plus élevés. Il est supposé devenir le cœur du centre ville de Dubaï, un nouveau quartier, à la fois quartier résidentiel, commerçant, d'affaires et de loisirs. Il mesure 818 mètres de haut et compte 162 étages, dont 37 appartiennent à l'hôtel, 70 abritent des appartements et 43 sont réservés aux bureaux et à quelques suites. L'accueil se trouve au 123ème étage, tandis que le 124ème offre une plate-forme avec terrasse. Créée par l'architecte Adrian Smith de chez Skidmore, Owings & Merrill, la structure est faite de béton armé et d'acier tandis que la façade est en aluminium et en verre.

NEO De 'Toren van Dubai' is thans het hoogste gebouw ter wereld, met de meeste verdiepingen, de hoogstgelegen bruikbare verdieping – en de hoogste voor woondoeleinden gebruikte verdiepingen. Hij moet het centrum van Downtown Dubai worden, een nieuwe stadswijk voor handel, wonen, winkelen, amusement en vrije tijd. 818 meter meet hij, verdeeld over 162 verdiepingen, 37 etages hotel, 70 voor appartementen, en verder 43 kantoren en enkele suites. Op de 123e etage bevindt zich de lobby, op de 124e een uitzichtplateau met terras. De constructie bestaat uit staalbeton en staal, de voorgevel uit aluminium en glas en de architect is Adrian Smith van Skidmore, Owings & Merrill.

DUBAI INTERNATIONAL AIRPORT TERMINAL 3

UNITED ARABIAN EMIRATES | DUBAI | LANDMARKS

ENG TERMINAL 3 of the Dubai International Airport is a concrete, steel, and glass colossus—yet another superlative construction for Dubai, especially in terms of dimension. The design: conceived by Aéroports de Paris International in the shape of an airplane wing. You could easily get lost in this building. Six levels, most of them below ground, 157 elevators, 97 escalators, 82 moving walkways, and eight sky trains. Two Zen gardens of considerable size give the terminal a tropical appearance. Bright and airy with glass facades, natural light, and wide open spaces, it is the largest airport terminal in the world.

DEU TERMINAL 3 des Dubai International Airport ist ein Koloss aus Beton, Stahl und Glas. Ein weiterer Bau der Superlative made in Dubai. Vor allem in Sachen Dimension. Das Design: die Form einer Flugzeugtragfläche konstruiert von Aéroports de Paris International. Man könnte verloren gehen in diesem Gebäude. Sechs Stockwerke, die meisten unterirdisch, 157 Aufzüge, 97 Rolltreppen, 82 Fahrsteige und acht Sky-Trains. Zwei Zen-Gärten von beachtlicher Größe verleihen dem Terminal sein tropisches Aussehen. Hell, luftig und mit Fassaden aus Glas. Natürliches Licht und offene Räume. Das größte Airport-Terminal der Welt.

FR Le TERMINAL 3 de l'aéroport international de Dubaï est un colosse de béton, d'acier et de verre. Encore une construction incroyable à ajouter au palmarès de Dubaï, principalement pour ses dimensions. Le projet a été réalisé par Aéroports de Paris International et prend la forme d'une aile d'avion. Il est facile de se perdre dans ce bâtiment comptant six niveaux, la plupart souterrains, 157 ascenseurs, 97 escalators, 82 tapis roulants et huit navettes. Deux jardins zen de taille considérable confèrent au terminal une apparence tropicale. Clair et aéré grâce à des façades de verre, la lumière naturelle et de larges espaces, c'est le plus grand terminal d'aéroport au monde.

NED TERMINAL 3 van het Dubai International Airport is een kolos van beton, staal en glas. Weer een gebouw van superlatieven made in Dubai, vooral wat betreft omvang. Het ontwerp: de vorm van een vliegtuigdraagvlak geconstrueerd door Aéroports de Paris International. In dit gebouw kun je verdwaald raken. Zes verdiepingen, de meeste ondergronds, 157 liften, 97 roltrappen, 82 loopbanden en acht sky-trains. Twee zen-tuinen van aanzienlijke grootte verlenen de terminal zijn tropische voorkomen. Licht, luchtig en met gevels van glas. Natuurlijk licht en open ruimtes. De grootste luchthaventerminal ter wereld.

694

HEALTH & WELLNESS